Dimensions of
Pāṇini Grammar
— The Indian Grammatical System —

by

Kapil Kapoor

DK PRINTWORLD
Publishers of Indian Traditions

Cataloging in Publication Data — DK
[Courtesy: D.K. Agencies (P) Ltd. <docinfo@dkagencies.com>]
Kapoor, Kapil, author.
Dimensions of Pāṇini grammar : the Indian grammatical system / by Kapil Kapoor. – Third impression.
pages cm
"First published in India in 2005" – Title page verso.
ISBN 9788124603314

1. Pāṇini. Aṣṭādhyāyī. 2. Sanskrit language – Grammar. I. Title. II. Title: Pāṇini grammar.

LCC PK519.K26 2020 | DDC 491.25 23

ISBN 978-81-246-0331-4
First Published in India in 2005
Second Impression in 2010
Third Impression in 2020

Printed and published by :
D.K. Printworld (P) Ltd.
Regd. office : H-12, Bali Nagar
Ramesh Nagar Metro Station, New Delhi - 110 015
Phones : (011) 2545 3975, 2546 6019
e-mail : indology@dkprintworld.com
Web : www.dkprintworld.com

Preface

PĀṆINI's grammar, *Aṣṭādhyāyī*, is the only complete, explicit and rule-bound grammar of any human language and as such has been appreciated as "the greatest monument of human intelligence" (Bloomfield in his *Language*). It is also acknowledged by modern linguists as a linguistic grammar *par excellence*. A study of this grammar is a serious exercise in understanding how the human mind works and in sharpening our own mental faculty.

Over almost at least fifteen years, a course in *Aṣṭādhyāyī* had been given to post-graduate students at Jawaharlal Nehru University, New Delhi. It had always drawn a large number of students who said that this book (*grantha*) alters their mode of thinking and also gives them an insight into how they think.

These essays originated as lectures in the classroom and were subsequently presented in conferences or as invited lectures. I hope they are found useful as introductions to some highly complex dimensions of *Aṣṭādhyāyī*.

As always, I am grateful to the students of JNU who make you think and organize your ideas. Besides, I am particularly grateful to my former student and now a distinguished colleague, Dr. Rajnish Kumar Mishra, who at many stages of this composition, discussed the subject with me and gave extremely valuable opinions and suggestions. He read the manuscript and also the final proof of the book.

I am also very thankful to my Ph.D student Ms Joavani Lourdes, who with her characteristic efficiency and accuracy prepared the index to this book.

I am also thankful to my other Ph.D student Mr. Tulsidas Majhi, who helped in proof-reading the text completed the index and generally helped me in preparing this book.

I am deeply grateful, finally, to Shri Susheel Mittal ji of D.K. Printworld who agreed to publish this volume and has brought it out so beautifully and with so much care.

Contents

1

Introduction

Study of Language in India

THE origin of 'linguistics' as an independent discipline may be traced in India to a number of thinkers belonging to different schools of thought. What is important to observe in this context is that the same conceptual frame in one form or another served as the argumentative platform for the philosophical disputation between different schools of thought — for instance, between Nyāya realism and Buddhist phenomenalism.

It is true that the dispute between the Naiyāyikas (logicians), the Buddhists, and the Jains over many crucial themes concerning diverse epistemological and ontological questions lasted for over twelve centuries, in which each group structured its arguments around postulates related to the nature of reality — the accredited means of knowing this reality (such as perception and inference), the relationship between language, reality, and logic, and other vital issues of ontology, semantics, and pragmatics. Indian thinkers were not hesitant in drawing information from all sectors of knowledge to build models characterizing the "knowables" (cognizable entities) which basically constitute the world. Had there not been a recognition of some trans-disciplinary principles behind their conceptual frames, their theories would never have moved toward epistemological harmonization of information drawn from diversified fields of knowledge and the possibility of such exhaustive debate between different schools of thought over issues concerning the object, the means, and the criteria of valid knowledge would never have existed. It is the tacit acceptance of and adherence to these principles and their analytical potential that allowed the emergence and development of competing schools with divergent ontologies whose disputations brought into being the science of the sources of knowledge.

It is important to stress in this context that though certain important semiotic themes — the nature of generic sign (*nimitta*) and of verbal sign (*śabda*), the process of signification, the pragmatic parameters and the structural principle of reducing multifarious and multiple reality into layers of increasing generality — came into focus in this prolonged disputation, semiotic principles remained implicit throughout the period. More recently, attempts have been made to throw light on the nature and significance of classical Indian theories of knowledge (Matilal 1971), but so far virtually nothing has been done to explicate the semiotic principles embedded in these theories that offered a conceptually integrated frame of mind for argumentation and for a multi-disciplinary endeavour to make sense of the reality.

What is true of the classical Indian theories of knowledge and their exponents is true of Indian grammatical tradition and its practitioners as well. Indian grammarians, considered by the tradition as the first among philosophers, worked out a general epistemology that kept the axis of language at the centre, and were therefore more directly concerned with both semiosis and communication. It is important to observe that the philological hermeneutic tradition devoted to the study and preservation of the sacred Vedic hymns motivated the Indian scholars to develop six components of Vedic study (the Vedāṅgas) — *Śikṣā* (phonetics), *Kalpa* (ritual), *Vyākaraṇa* (grammar), *Nirukta* (etymology), *Chandas* (metrics), and *Jyotiṣa* (astronomy).

While it is true that grammar is one of the six of the Vedāṅgas, which literally means "disciplines auxiliary to the Vedas," grammar did not remain restricted to Vedic exegesis — it in fact developed into a science, an independent and complete discipline for the study of language. As pointed out by Indian grammarians themselves, grammar is a meta-discipline, and as such belongs to all the disciplines: just as all universals of things depend upon the form of their words for their communication, so is this science the basis of all other sciences. "All kinds of meanings depend upon the power of words . . . all this (world/universe) is the transformation (resultant) of the word. . . . All knowledge is, as it were, brought into being by the word. . . ." (Bhartṛhari, in Iyer 1971: 22). This point of view is echoed by Sebeok's contention (1985: 365) that language — or, more precisely, grammar — is a "proto primary modelling system lodged in the brain." Pāṇini's grammar, in fact, articulates an abstract system that underlies the diversity and the multiplicity of apparently unrelated forms of Sanskrit language. Thus Indian grammarians not only developed the science of language, but also showed how language may serve as "a primary modelling system" of knowledge. The fact has always been recognized that any reflection on signs that leads to any aspect of knowledge is inseparable from reflection on grammar. That is why a whole range of concepts of philosophy and logic in ancient India are closely intertwined with Sanskrit grammatical theories.

It was a common concern for illuminating, within the conspectus of a model of knowledge, the idea of "reality" in relation to the empirical reality that motivated philosophers and grammarians to posit parallel constructs such as substance (*dravya*) quality (*guṇa*) and *padārtha* (object/word-meaning), in both philosophy and grammar. In the study of language, an important line of thinkers often belonging to such contending schools of thought as the Buddhists, the Naiyāyikas (logicians), and the Vaiyākaraṇas (grammarians) explicated, in their investigation of word and meaning, the nature of relationship between language and reality on the one hand, and between language and thought on the other. Among grammarians, reference may be made here to the grammarian-philosopher Bhartṛhari (fifth century AD) who is best known for considering language as the primary epistemology, for arguing the inseparability of human consciousness from language, and for emphasizing the theoretical indivisibility of the sentence as a reflection of the indivisibility of thought and reality (Brough 1952, 1953; B. Bhattacharya 1962; Matilal 1985).

Thus we see that some of the major problems of modern linguistics have been at the centre of the philosophical and linguistic speculations in the Indian tradition although an independent term was never used for this discipline and its principles were never explicitly formulated. It was essentially an interdisciplinary scholarship which either postulated common explanatory categories or developed parallel constructs with the same significance to make the models functionally optional and efficient. In modern times, however, we find an almost total disjunction between the study of classical Indian philosophical and linguistic tradition and modern theories of knowledge and linguistics; only recently have we seen a revival of interest in the heritage of our traditional knowledge.

Since in Indian philosophy (*darśana* — literally "that which enables one to see") the basic assumption has been that "meaning" — *tattvārtha* — lies beyond the multiplicity and diversity of miraculously ever-changing objects, philosophical enquiry has led to the postulation and employment of various constructs of transcendence. And since "transcendence" as a process of determining or comprehending meaning necessarily involves relating a series of "signs" in a chain of signification, it is not surprising that the concerns, constructs, and methods of traditional Indian philosophy have a deep affinity with modern semiotics. In one of the major streams of thought in the field of the theory of knowledge, it has been argued by linguistic philosophers (Vaiyākaraṇas) such as Bhartṛhari and Śabarasvāmin that language is the chief epistemology, the sole determinant, of knowledge of this "meaning of reality," and that therefore language (i.e., grammar) itself is a universal system of cognition, a massive shaping construct. As the well-known Ṛgvedic hymn says, "The principle of *vāk* (speech) creates or fashions out the manifold forms out of the waters of the infinite ocean of ultimate Reality" (*Ṛgveda* 1.164.41; see Griffith 1963). It is language that creates an impression of segmented, discrete, ordered reality out of what is essentially non-discrete and non-sequential. Grammar is thus, in the Indian mode of expression, "the Veda of Veda," the knowledge of knowledge, and provides in all fields of inquiry what one may call an overarching model. It is to be expected, therefore, that all the major schools of philosophy would debate the problem of word-meaning relationship, build systematic theories to explain and account for the phenomenon of signification, and also investigate the possibilities of a formal language — logic — that would ensure the validity of knowledge thus gained. In the Indian philosophical tradition, in all systems and disputations, the *tattvārtha* or "essential meaning" is studied in conjunction with *śabdārtha*, "signifier-signified," and this in turn necessarily involves an investigation of the properties of *śabda* as a sign.

Though the roots of semiotic thinking in India are to be found in Indian medicine (*āyurveda*), rhetoric (*alaṅkāra*), dialectics (*tarka*), logic (*nyāya*), philosophy (*darśana*) and grammar (*vyākaraṇa*), the set of essays here focuses only on grammar and incidentally on philosophy. In the following essays devoted to various themes, we see how the discussion of signs was involved in the highest levels of grammatical and philosophical speculation. We also see that the discussion of linguistic issues in classical India, as for example in Pāṇini and in Bhartṛhari, always took place with reference to or was identified with the more general, basic sphere of the problem of knowledge.

We may conclude this introduction with two obsevations. We have referred to Pāṇini as a seventh century BC grammarian and Yāska as ninth century BC grammarian. These are all postulates. Indians have not been a biographical people and details of an individual's life have not really mattered. What matters is the relative chronology of ideas. So, Pāṇini while employing the word *nirvāṇa,* does not do so in the Buddhist sense. And then he makes no reference to Gautama Buddha which is surprising in view of the almost encyclopedic information he provides about extra-linguistic matters. Now there is a meta-rule in Indian thought — "Not to mention Buddha is not to know Buddha and not to know Buddha is to have been born before Buddha." Hence, Pāṇini is placed in seventh century BC. And as he evidently employs the categories of Yāska and his work explicates the derivations implicit in Yāska's principles of etymology, Yāska is randomly placed around two centuries before him — he could be even much earlier. This the first issue.

Secondly, some subjects appear in more than one discussion in the essays. Thus for example the question of goal of grammar occurs in essays 5, 13 and 14. But as the discussions show, the contexts are different and the subject links up the questions. There is always an added insight. So these have been left as they are.

2

Linguistic Thought in India

LINGUISTIC thinking has a long history in India, having originated in the need to maintain and interpret the vast, oral Vedic literature of great antiquity. Pāṇini marks a great divide in this history. Before Pāṇini, linguistics was predominantly descriptive, concerned with an empirical analysis of language usage (speech, including recitation) and language structure and it culminated in Pāṇini's *Aṣṭādhyāyī*, an explicit, rule-bound, comprehensive description of both the spoken language (*bhāṣā*) and the compositional language (*vaidikī*). After Pāṇini, there is an elaboration of linguistic thought into areas beyond description — for example, theory of grammar (Patañjali) and the philosophy of grammar and of language in relation to thought and reality (Bhartṛhari). The post-Pāṇini period is divisible into four phases:

1. From Pāṇini (seventh century BC) to Patañjali (second century BC) — the age of critical examination and evaluation of the rules of *Aṣṭādhyāyī*.

2. From/after Patañjali to Bhojarāja (eleventh century AD) — a rich period which saw the extension of linguistic thinking into philosophy and literary theory besides considerable exegetical work in grammar centered on *Aṣṭādhyāyī* and *Mahābhāṣya*.

3. From Rāmacandra (twelfth century AD) to Nāgeśa Bhaṭṭa (nineteenth century) — the age of simplification or re-ordered texts; and

4. The modern period which began with the work of William Jones (1794), the thirty-third 'Vyāsa' — this period saw the renewal of texts through reconstruction from the dispersed, and, often, damaged and fragmented manuscripts.

It is obvious that the need to maintain the pre-eminent Vedic texts provided the initial impulse for linguistic studies. Maintenance of texts in the oral tradition depended on a complete understanding of (i) the phonetics of speech, (ii) the morphology of continuous utterances, which in turn depended on, and (iii) an understanding of meanings of utterances/ words. This accounts for the rise of the sciences of phonetics, grammar and etymology (*Nirukta*) in the pre-Pāṇinian period. That thinking about language and its structure began very early is evidenced by the fact that Vedic literature contains innumerable reflections on the physics and the metaphysics of *śabda* (language).

Vedic literature itself contains many references to language — its nature, its constitutive elements, and its relationship to the mind and the reality it talks about (see the list below). In *Ṛgveda*, the earliest Indo-European text, the abundant reflections on language show a deep understanding of the nature and function of language that had already been achieved. Language is very important in the eyes of Vedic thinkers — it is a source of happiness, like the mother's breast (1.164.49); it is a means of attaining the desired ends (1.164.49); it is a revealer of true knowledge of objects (of senses) and of reality (10.71.1), and it permeates every aspect of life, and nothing exists beyond language (10.114.8).

There are innumerable references to language elements, structure and nature in classical non-linguistic literature. Only some are being collected here and references are being given against each:

1. ***Ṛgveda***

   (a) 1.164.34, 49, 37, 24, 39; 10.71.1; 10.114.8;

   (b) 5.44.6; 9.95.2; 1.43.7; 8.76.12; 1.164.10; 10.114.8; 2.21.6; 8.59.63; 4.58.6; 10.98.3; 4.58.6; 8.100.11; 8.75.6; 10.71.2.

   (c) 7.18.1; 10.71.5.

   (d) 1.92.9; 10.98.2.

   (e) 1.164.39, 24, 42; 3.34.5, 1.143.7; 3.38.7; 1.164.41; 4.58.3; 10.71.2.2; 1.164.45; 1.3.10; 1.8.4, 5; 1.6.7; 1.113.16; 8.43.2; 1.3.3; 10.85.43; 10.114.8; 10.54.4.

2. ***Śukla Yajurveda*:** 18.6; 29.10; 1.20; 29.26; 1.15; 6.10; 9.22; 1.3; 8.51; 16.13; 8.21; 13.54; 21.61 (*Mādhyandina-Saṁhitā*).

3. ***Atharvaveda*:** 9.6.11; 11.2.9; 10.9.25; 3.13.2; 12.3.73; 6.97.1; 3.13.1.

4. ***Kṛṣṇa Yajurveda*:** 2.6.3.5; 3.1.3.5; 1.2.1.1; 5.3.12.1; 2.3.10.1; 2.5.3.12.13; 3.5.1.2; 1.2.1.1.

5. ***Brāhmaṇas***

   1. *Aitareya*: 1.2; 3.33; 3.43; 7.30; 7.7.
   2. *Śatapatha*: 14.6.11.1; 14.1.1.13; 10.3.5.1, 2, 4, 6; 1.4.4.7.
   3. *Taittirīya*: 1.1.9.3; 1.1.5.4.
   4. *Gopatha*: 1.27; 1.24.
   5. *Kauśītakī*: 7.7.

6. ***Upaniṣads***

   1. *Aitareya*: *Aitareya Āraṇyaka* 3.1.5; 3.1.6; 3.2.1; 4.1.1.
   2. *Kaṭha*: 1.8; 2.16; 3.15; 3.13.

3. *Māṇḍūkya* 1; 8.
4. *Chāndogya*: 7.2; 7.3.
5. *Taittirīya*: 1.2; 1.6.
6. *Muṇḍaka*: 1.5.
7. *Śvetāśvatara*: 1.7, 8, 9, 10.
8. *Kena*: 1.5.
9. *Praśna*: 6.1.
10. *Bṛhadāraṇyaka*: 1.22.

7. (*a*) *Śārīraka Brahmasūtrabhāṣya:* 4.2.1; 4.3.14; 1.3.28.

   (*b*) *Vivekacūḍāmaṇi:* 94; 98; 243; 245; 249; 250; 251; 287; 370; 393; 410; 480; 492.

8. *Mahābhārata:* Śānti-Parva, 283-92; *Rāmāyaṇa* 3-29.

The *Ṛgveda* makes a clear distinction between ordinary language (*bhāṣā*) and good desirable speech (use of language): it lays great stress on using language to communicate truth (5.44.6), on veracity, that is "saying what it sees" (10.35.8; 9.95.2; 8.59.3); good speech is original and creative (6.76.12), sweet (1.182.4; 2.21.6; 8.59.3), lucid (*pravāhamaya*) and clear (4.58.6; 10.98.35; 5.63.6); it must be purposeful and profound (1.164.10) and rich in meaning (4.58.6), laced with carefully reflected thoughts and therefore capable of ensuring welfare of the people (8.100.11); it is "a great gift of gods to men" and should be employed without blemish (7.18.1). We reproduce here the Ṛgvedic hymn of *vāk* (10.125) in which speech (goddess) celebrates her own power and majesty in an effusive monologue:

Verse 1 : I travel with the Rudras and Vasus, with the Ādityas and all Gods of wonder, I hold aloft both Varuṇa and Mitra, Indra and Agni and the pair of Aśvins.

Verse 2 : I cherish and sustain high-swelling Soma, and Tvaṣṭā. I support, Pūṣan and Bhaga. I load with wealth the zealous sacrificer who pours the juice and offers his oblation.

Verse 3 : I am the Queen, the gatherer up of treasures, most thoughtful, first of those who merit worship. Thus, Gods have established me in many places with many homes to enter and abide in.

Verse 4 : Through me alone all eat the food that feeds them, each man who sees, breathes, hears the word outspoken.

They knew it not, but yet they dwell beside me. Hear one and all the truth as I declare it.

Verse 5 : I vainly myself announce and utter the word that Gods and men alike shall welcome.

I make the men I love exceedingly mighty, make him a sage, a *ṛṣi* and a brāhmaṇa.

Verse 6 : I bend the bow of Rudra, that his arrow may strike and slay the hater of devotion.

I rouse and order battle for the people and I have penetrated earth and heaven.

Verse 7 : On the world's summit I bring forth the Father: my home is in the waters, in the ocean

Thence I extend over all existing creatures, and touch even yonder heaven with my forehead.

Verse 8 : I breathe a strong breath like the wind and tempest, the while I hold together all existence. Beyond this wide earth and beyond the heavens I have become so mighty in my grandeur.

In the complex symbolism of this hymn, language is adored as a fit object of worship, a force co-present with everything in this wide world, a sustainer of life, a source of munificence, a cognitive instrument, the secret of a man's power and knowledge, a social force, the very basis of existence.

The *Brāhmaṇas* also contain many references to language and related facts. The *Kauṣītakī Brāhmaṇa,* for example, eulogises "the speech of northern India, particularly of the region known as Kuru-Pāñcāla . . . as the best speech and hence that region is described as the resort of *pāṭhya svasti,* Vāk goddess (*Kauṣītakī Brāhmaṇa,* 7.6. Anandasrama Series, 1911). Elsewhere, speech (*vāk*) is classified into three varieties: the divine (of Vedas), the human (when the priests chant and instruct it) and demonic, *rākṣasī* (the language of an excited person or lunatic). Relation between speech and mind is another subject of reflection in the *Brāhmaṇas*. Speech, it is said, is impossible without mind — "speech is preceded by the mind because speech expresses what is comprehended by the mind" (*Pañcaviṁśa Brāhmaṇa,* Kashi Sanskrit Series No 105, Varanasi 1926). As compared to the mind, the sphere of speech is smaller, limited — "mind is, as it were, unlimited, speech is limited . . . hence speech is less comprehensive than the mind" (*Śatapatha Brāhmaṇa,* 1.4.4.7). Again, the mind expresses itself through speech — hence, "speech is the canal of the mind" (*Jaiminīya Brāhmaṇa*).

The Upaniṣads have numerous reflections on the nature of human language — both its physics and metaphysics. The second *Āraṇyaka* describes *prāṇa* (breath; conscious and unconscious energy that supports life) to be at the root of speech and designations, on which the knowledge of the whole universe rests. The relationship of inhaled, life-supporting breath and speech (language) comes in for more reflection. The third *Āraṇyaka* tells us that *Kauntharva* saw a union of speech and *prāṇa* — *vāk prāṇena saṁhitā iti kauntharvaḥ* (3.1.6). Further, we are given the insightful observation that "when one recites or talks, breath enters speech and speech swallows *prāṇa*. On the other hand, when one entertains no idea or is in deep sleep, then speech dissolves in breath, *prāṇa* swallows speech" (3.1.6). Breath and mind are intimately related and the mind follows the course the other takes. And since breath is the root of speech, there is a correlation between the speech and the mind. In one of the Vedic hymns (*Śāntipāṭha*) the seer prays that his senses should rest in his mind and his mind should rest in his speech and that both should get established in truth. As *Praśnopaniṣad* says — a man who speaks untruth, exposes his root, withers up and perishes (as a tree with roots exposed) (6.1).

In many symbolic and poetical passages, the Upaniṣads dwell on the relationship of self and language — "The wise should merge the speech in the mind, and that (mind) in the intellect, the intellect in the Great Self, and that (Great Self again) in the Self of peace (*śānta-ātman*)." The third *Āraṇyaka* of *Aitareyopaniṣad* contains the secret doctrine of the "whole speech" — earth, fire, *Ṛgveda*, eye and *prāṇa* are considered *sparśa*s (mutes); middle space, air, *Yajurveda*, ear and *apāna* as *uṣman* (sibilants) and sky, sun, *Sāmaveda*, mind and *vyāna* as *svara*s (vowels). This reflection on the alphabet is followed by a highly poetic passage in which the human body is likened to a lute, a counterpart of the divine lute in an extended analogy. Reflections on the symbolism of *Oṁ* also belong here. *Praśnopaniṣad* gives an accurate phonetic analysis of this symbol of *Brahman* as a phonetic entity with three *mātrā*s (prosodial instants) — *A, U, Ṁ*. These are the three *mātrā*s of *Oṁ* when blended together in significance and sound, they truly represent the universal *Brahman*. *Māṇḍūkyopaniṣad* says "All this world is the syllable *Oṁ*." According to Vedic thought, *prakṛti* has a sound symbol, and that is *Oṁ*. As no idea can be dissociated from the denoting word or name, so no object can be thought of without its sound symbol. In linguistic thought also, the relation between *śabda* and *artha*, sound and meaning, is inseparable. So in that sense, *Oṁ*, an all inclusive sound (*a* is the first letter of the alphabet, *ṁ* is the last, and *u* involves the whole tract), is the most appropriate name for the universe, visible and invisible.

Some Upaniṣads give the first expression to limits of language. *Māṇḍūkyopaniṣad* says that absolute truth is realized only from a plane higher than language and thought and therefore, all the descriptions of this absolute, ultimate reality could be only in negative language, with negative prefixes. *Kenopaniṣad* says that; that which speech cannot reveal, but what reveals speech — know that (the *ātman*) also as *Brahman* and not this that people here worship. *Māṇḍūkyopaniṣad* also says that the absolute truth is realized only from a plane higher than language and thought. This truth is apprehended in the fourth level of consciousness -- super-consciousness, *turīya*, a state beyond the familiar three states of wakefulness, dream and sleep.

So *Bṛhadāraṇyakopaniṣad* sings praises of speech — "Speech is *Bṛhatī*. . . . Speech is *Brahman*. . . . This is also *sāma*. Speech is *sāma*. . . . Whatsoever is known is of the nature of speech; for speech is known. . . ." *Chāndogyopaniṣad* similarly says — "without speech who could explain right and wrong; good, evil; pleasant, unpleasant? Speech explains all."

II

Besides these references and reflections in philosophical and metaphysical texts, there are also in existence directly linguistic works pertaining to phonetics, etymology, and morphology that attest the existence of a long tradition of linguistic inquiry before the golden age of Pāṇini, Kātyāyana and Patañjali. Moreover, Yāska's *Nirukta*, Pāṇini's *Aṣṭādhyāyī* and Bhartṛhari's *Vākyapadīya* contain many references to the earlier grammarians, phoneticians and theorists of language in the context of some very significant linguistic controversies. For example, Yāska refers to Śākaṭāyana-Gārgya controversy about the origin of nouns (names) in section 1.12 of *Nirukta*. Śākaṭāyana was evidently a major ancient grammarian who is quoted in the *Ṛk-Prātiśākhya, Vājasaneyi Prātiśākhya, Atharva-Prātiśākhya* and in Pāṇini's *Sūtras*. His name is also associated with *Uṇādi-Sūtra*s which are also based in the claim that all words can be shown to be derived from roots. Śākaṭāyana asserted all words are derived from verb-roots (*dhātus*). Yāska himself subscribes to this view and his etymologies pursue this principle. But he also cites Gārgya whose views on this issue are more balanced. Gārgya says that not all nouns are traceable to verbs but only those whose accent and grammatical form are regular (*Nirukta* 1.12). We should be able to establish that they are derived by regular grammatical processes and the derived word and the root should have a shared meaning as well. Yāska reports this controversy at great length and reproduces the arguments of both Śākaṭāyana and Gārgya.

Yāska quotes another ancient grammarian Auḍumbarāyaṇa on the nature of *śabda* (words) (*Nirukta* 1.1) in the context of the ancient debate about the substance of words and their transitoriness or otherwise. Grammar, Nyāya and Mīmāṁsā, besides *Nirukta*, discuss whether the words are *nitya* (non-transitory) or not. Auḍumbarāyaṇa is of the view that words are objects of senses and, therefore, transitory. If this is accepted then the division and classification, into four types of *pada* as also the process of *prakṛti-pratyaya* (base-affix), conjunction in the derivation of *pada*s (fully inflected morphological forms) also becomes unreal. Patañjali used similar argument to define *kārya-śabda* — an entity made up of separate sequential sounds. For example, in the word *gau:*, the *g*, the *au* and the *ḥ* come into existence at different temporal moments, superseding each other. Truly, therefore, the sounds are destructible, non-permanent. And yet the arrangements of these transient sounds (words) are used to name objects and are fit means of ordinary communication — the same word is successfully used to designate the same object by different people, at different times and in different places. To account for this and to explain how in spite of phonetic variation, the word is understood to designate the same object, an ancient grammarian, Sphoṭāyana, quoted by Pāṇini (6.1.123), is supposed to have originally proposed this concept. Patañjali postulated indirectly the concept of *sphoṭa* in his definition of *śabda* (*Mahābhāṣya, āhnika* I). This insight was later developed into the powerful *sphoṭa* theory by Bhartṛhari. Grammarians accept *sphoṭa* as the instrument of meaning. A word is made of more than one syllable/sound, all of which are transitory and cannot therefore denote meaning either together or severally. So, *sphoṭa*, an entity beyond the transitory sounds, has to be accepted as the revealer of meaning. Yāska also quotes Vārṣyāyaṇi on the six aspects of Being (*Nirukta* 1.2). This ancient grammarian said that *bhāva*, the meaning of verbs, has six *vikāra* (variations): birth, being, change, accretion or development, decay or decline and death or destruction.

Pāṇini also quotes many early grammarians on different aspects of grammar. The following grammarians are cited in the example *sūtra*s listed against each:

Śākaṭāyana	3.4.111
Gārgya	7.3.99
Northern Grammarians	7.3.46
Apiśali	6.1.92.
Kāśyapa, Gālava, Gārgya	8.4.67
Bhāradvāja	7.2.63
Cakravarman	6.1.130
Śākalya	6.1.127
Sphoṭāyana	6.1.123

And finally, Bhartṛhari, in the context of the *khaṇḍapakṣa-akhaṇḍapakṣa* controversy and of the *padavādins* who believed in the reality of individual words, quotes Auḍumbarāyaṇa (*Vākyapadīya* 2.57-58). Auḍumbarāyaṇa believed in the reality of sentence alone and asserted that sounds being transitory, the words constituted by these sounds are also unreal constructs.

III

Also, some texts continue to be available which attest the existence of three kinds of linguistic inquiry:

A. Phonetics (*Prātiśākhyas* and *Śikṣās*)

B. Etymology (*Nighaṇṭu* and *Nirukta*)

C. Morphology (*pāṭha* tradition).

Phonetics

Phonetics was the first science to develop in response to the need to preserve intact and to articulate accurately the Vedic hymns (*mantras*). Yāska refers to the strong phonetic tradition in his *Nirukta* ch. I, when he says that merely correct pronunciation, without a comprehension of the meaning of the text, is vain and of no use. But then this exclusive focus on sound must be considered a later aberration — but, originally and in its long history of phonetic studies produced a brilliant understanding and a highly sophisticated analysis of the sound structure of human language, its phonetics and phonology. Attention may be drawn to three major Prātiśākhya texts, *Ṛk-Prātiśākhya, Taittirīya Prātiśākhya* and *Vājasaneyi Prātiśākhya,* as examples of achievement in this branch of linguistic inquiry. Four dimensions of the sound system of language have been investigated:

1. Origin, production and nature of speech.
2. Classification of and enumeration of speech sounds.

3. System and representation of speech sounds.
4. Sounds in context and types of sound change.

Vājasaneyi Prātiśākhya describes the mechanism and process of speech production in eleven *sūtras* (5-15) of chapter 1. The same is described by *Pāṇīnīya Śikṣā* in nine *ślokas* (6-14). The *Vājasaneyi Prātiśākhya* starts its description by promising to describe what is not known — that, is the nature of speech sound. The air from the chest comes out through the glottis and takes the form of sound through the instrumentality of a flute or a conch, etc. And when human effort is applied to it in the form of will, mind and energy (in the form of manipulation of instruments of articulation), it takes the form of speech. This air, therefore, is modified in three places before it takes the form of speech — chest, throat and mouth. As it reaches the throat, it passes through the glottis, which may be open (*vivṛta*) or closed (*samvṛta*). And then in the mouth, it is modified by various articulators into the form of individual, separate speech sounds. The *Pāṇinīya Śikṣā* describes the same process of speech production but draws analogy between speech sounds and musical notes. Sanskrit phoneticians also engaged themselves with the question of nature of speech sounds. They make a distinction between sounds that are not speech-sounds (such as that of blowing of conches) and speech sounds proper. Another issue that they debate is whether speech-sounds are created (*utpanna*) or made manifest (*abhivyakta*) — accordingly the speech sounds are *anitya*, transient, or *nitya*, without a known beginning and end. Mīmāṁsā School believes in the non-transience of speech sounds which they claim are always immanent or inherent in the air just as fire exists in the loadstone. They are merely made manifest by the vocal organs. The *Śābara Bhāṣya* on *Mīmāṁsāsūtra* (1.1.12) says that the already existent sound requires a push (an excitement) causing the conjunction and disjunction, which makes sounds manifest. The Naiyāyikas on the other hand say that the speech-sounds depend on causes and — "a thing resulting from a cause and liable to destruction is not a permanent entity" (*Nyāya-Sūtra* 2.2.13). All theorists acknowledge sound as a quality of space as, something that results from "the disruption of the great elements." All theorists also acknowledge the role of air — speech as a modification of the act of breathing. So when we speak we have to interrupt breathing. The air with its contact with vocal organs becomes speech. Most also agree that speech production is a physical as well as a mental process. As the *Pāṇinīya Śikṣā* avers — "having intellectually determined the object to be communicated, the self (*ātman*) urges the mind, in order to give expression, to vocalize the thought rising within. The mind, so stimulated, acts on the physical energy (fire) which in turn brings about a movement in the region of internal air. The internal air thus moved gets upward, receives extension in the heart region, undergoes changes in the throat, strikes the palate, comes back to give rise to different kinds of sounds in the mouth." Bhartṛhari says — "air under the influence of the mind gets itself materialized into audible sound . . . it is the life breath, *prāṇa-vāyu*, that gives rise to all sounds" (*Vākyapadīya* 1.115). The mind is associated with speech both as a physiological entity and as a psychological entity. In speech, mind does not merely serve as an instrument — it plays a creative role as well. What is called "inner speech" is a direct reflection of the mind — the mind reveals itself in the visual images of words. Verbal images appearing before the thinking mind as visible pictures are interpreted as visible presences of the objects. These images leave lasting impressions — *saṁskāras* — and the mind is capable of reproducing them when a similar excitation gives rise to it. In the course of receiving the impressions through the medium of sensory organs, the mind is apt to assume, though temporarily, the particular form of the object.

Brief reference may also be made to a theory of speech enunciated by Bhartṛhari, one that is rooted in the Upaniṣadic thought. According to this theory, there are subtle elements of sounds like fine ethereal fluids, incomprehensible for their extreme fineness, lying inside and outside all material bodies. This sound, identified by some with the all-pervading space, is manifested by its own self and comes to our comprehension when it reaches our auditory organs. This theory corresponds in its main features with the one already enunciated in the Upaniṣads — *vāk* (word, speech) possesses two-fold aspects, originating as it does in the vital life-breath (*prāṇa*) and intellect (*buddhi*).

The Vedic literature, the philosophers and the grammarians also distinguish four kinds, or levels of language — *parā*, *paśyantī*, *madhyamā* and *vaikharī*. The first three are non-manifest, though real as even a little reflection on the various stages that precede speech will show. Only the fourth, *vaikharī*, is manifest speech constituted in sound. *Vaikharī* is articulated speech, divided and divisible and is manifest when the air rising up in the fourth stage strikes the vocal organs.

The phoneticists carried out precise analysis, descriptions and classification of speech sounds on the basis of place and manner of articulation and their observations are available, recorded, in Prātiśākhyas and Śikṣās, for example of *ai/au* and the closer *a* which forms the first element of the narrower diphthong *e/o*. This interpretation is supported by a passage in the *Mahābhāṣya* "where the *saṃvṛta a* of *e/o* is specifically contrasted with the more open *ā* of *ai/au*."

We now present here Varadarāja's Table of Sanskrit Speech Sounds as organized in Varadarāja's *Laghusiddhāntakaumudī* in Table B (i) and (ii). In Table A, we present Kātyāyana's *Varṇamālā* and in Table C, we present Pāṇini's *Pratyāhāra Sūtras*.

Table A : Varṇasamāmnāya

Vājasaneyi Prātiśākhya

VARṆA

SVARA		*VYAÑJANA*			
Mūla	*Sandhyakṣara*	*Sparśa*	*Antastha*	*Ūṣma*	*Ayogavāha*
a ā a^3	*e* e^2	*k kh g gh ṅ*	*y*	*ś*	≍*k* ≍*p*
i ī $ī^3$	*ai* ai^2	*c ch j jh ñ*	*r*	*ṣ*	(*anusvāra*) *visarga*
u ū u^3	*o* o^3	*ṭ ṭh ḍ dh ṇ*	*l*	*s*	*hū* (*nāsikya*)
r̥ r̥ r̥^{3}	*au* au^2	*t th d dh n*	*v*	*h*	*kū, khu, gū, ghū* (*yama*)
l̥ l̥ l̥^{3}		*p ph b bh m*			
= 15	= 8	= 25	= 4	= 4	= 9
		Total			= 65

Table B (i) : *Laghusiddhāntakaumudī*

Classification of Speech sounds according to the places of articulation

Velar or Guttural	*a k* k^h *g* g^h *ṅ h ḥ*
Palatal	*i c* c^h *j* j^h *ñ y ś*
Retroflex or cerebral	*r̥ ṭ* ṭ^h *ḍ* ḍ^h *ṇ r ṣ*
Dental	*l̥ t* ṭ^h *d* ḍ^h *n l s*
Labial	*u p* p^h *b* b^h *m p* p^h
Nasal	*ñ m ṅ ṇ n*
Palato Velar	*e a i*
Labio Velar	*o a u*
Labio dental	*v*
Root of the tongue	≍*k* ≍*kh*
Places of articulation	Speech Sounds

Table B (ii) Classification of Speech Sounds according to the manners of articulation:

Intra-Buccal Efforts	Closed			Slight Closed	Slight Open		Open	Saṃvṛtaḥ (+effort)
Terms	STOPS			SEMI VOWELS	SIBILA-NTS		VOWELS	
Speech sounds	*K* K^h *C* C^h *ṭ* $ṭ^h$ *ṭ* t^h *P* P^h	*g* *ṅ* *j* *ñ* *ḍ* *ṇ* *d* *n* *b* *m*	*gh* *jh* *ḍh* *dh* *bh*	*y* *v* *r* *l*	 *s* *ṣ* *s*	 *h*	*a i u* *ṛ ḷ e* *o ai au*	*e*
Extra-Buccal Efforts	S.A. Asp. Lax Breath Voiceless	S.A. Tense Resonant Voiced	Asp. Tense Reso. Voiced	S.A. Tense Reso. Vd.	Asp. Lax Br. Vl.	Asp. Tense Br. Vd.	acute - grave circumflex accents	

S.A. = Sight Aspiration Br. = Breath Asp. = Aspirated

Vl. = Voiceless Reso. = Resonant Vd. = Voiced

Kātyāyana (fifth-sixth century BC) is the founder of the *Varṇamālā* system, followed now in all Indian languages with language specific changes.

Table . C Pāṇini's Pratyāhāra Sūtras

These are the fourteen *sūtras* that traditionally preface *Aṣṭādhyāyī*

1. *a i u ṇ*
2. *ṛ ḷ k*
3. *e o ṇ*
4. *ai au c*
5. *h y v r ṭ*
6. *l ṇ*
7. *ñ m ṅ ṇ n m*
8. *jh bh ñ*
9. *gh dh ḍh ṣ*
10. *j b g d d ś*
11. *kh ph ch ṭh th c ṭ t*
12. *k p y*
13. *ś ṣ s r*
14. *h l*

IV

Etymology (Nirvacana)

In the *Taittirīya Upaniṣad* enumeration, *Nirukta* is the fourth of the six Vedāṅgas. It is a science of fixing the meanings of Vedic words. *Nirukta,* a text by Yāska, is itself a commentary on *Nighaṇṭu,* a classified list of Vedic words compiled by Yāska himself. In order to fix the meanings of those words, Yāska takes a verb root related to the given word in meaning and, as far as possible, in phonetic form. This is the foundation of *Nirukta.*

Nighaṇṭu itself is perhaps the earliest attempt at lexicography, representing an effort to arrange words in sets and subsets on the basis of meaning. However, it is not a complete lexicon of Vedic words — only those words have been collected which are ambiguous or opaque or participate in synonymy with other words. These words are arranged in the following manner:

Chapter 1-3 : 1341 simple words, synonyms arranged in different sections according to meaning

Chapter 1: 17 sections about nature	415 words
Chapter 2: 22 sections about man	516 words
Chapter 3: 30 sections about different abstract concepts and qualities	410 words
Total	1341 words
Chapter 4: relatively opaque homonymous words arranged in 3 sections	278 words
Chapter 5: names of gods arranged in 6 sections	151 words
Total	1770 words

The words are listed in the form in which they appear in the texts — some words are repeated in the same form on account of meaning difference. 265 such words are repeated.

Nirukta does not comment on all the words collected in *Nighaṇṭu*. Yāska comments also on words that do not appear in *Nighaṇṭu*. Further there are the words that appear contextually in the process of giving an exposition of some *Nighaṇṭu* word. 660 words — 230 of the 1341 words of Chapters 1 to 3 and all the 430 words of Chapters 4 and 5 — have been etymologized. Besides 638 words not belonging to *Nighaṇṭu* have also been etymologized. These non-*Nighaṇṭu* words are of these kinds :

(i) those that are synonymous with *Nighaṇṭu* words,

(ii) contextual words, i.e., words that appear in the context of a given etymology (see, for example, section 2.5 of *Nirukta*),

(iii) words that appear in the *mantra* that is cited to exemplify the use of a *Nighaṇṭu* word,

(iv) words that appear in the *nirvacana* of these *mantra* words (see 1.20), and

(v) words that resemble the etymologized words in some interesting way, as for example *bhīṣama* in section 1.20.;

making a total of 1298 etymologies.

What is the structure of a typical *Nirukta* entry? Yāska takes a word and straight away derives it from a verb root. He gives the meaning of the verb-root and from that he states the meaning of the derived word. Then he illustrates the use of the word in that and that meaning by citing some Vedic hymns first or by giving a historical, social, geographic or philosophical background or information of the word followed by a Vedic hymn in which the word is used. Sometimes, in problematic contexts, where there is a controversy or room for controversy, in the true tradition of logical disputation, he first states faithfully the other opinion (*pūrvapakṣa*) and then provides powerful arguments against that and establishes his own point of view. In this scientific spirit, the entire text is composed.

The organization of *Nirukta* in relation to *Nighaṇṭu* is like this:

Nighaṇṭu Chapter	1	-	*Nirukta* Chapter 2
	2	-	Chapter 3, section 1-12
	3	-	Chapter 3, sections 13-22
	4	-	Chapters 4, 5 and 6
	5	-	Chapters 7 - 12

Etymology proper begins in chapter 2, section 2. The whole of chapter 1 and section 1 of chapter 2 are devoted to a discussion of issues that are of theoretical importance for the discipline — (1) primacy of meaning, importance of knowledge, and the meaningfulness of Vedic *mantras*, (2) parts of speech, (3) the verb-root principle, (4) language variation, its causes, forms and effects, and (5) principles of *Nirvacana* (etymology). In the preface to chapter 5, *Daivata Kāṇḍa*, he further discusses, (6) types of hymns, and (7) philosophy of gods.

Yāska is not only an etymologist and a semanticist but also a philosopher-grammarian. His monotheism anticipates later philosophic formulations such as Advaita Vedānta, Śūnya Advaita of Buddhists and Kashmir Śaivism and enables him to rationally explain the multiplicity of gods as an expression of a single principle immanent in the universe. As a grammarian, he has definite views on some old controversies. For example, he believes that while most nouns are derived; from verbs, there are some nouns that are not. Yāska's greatest contribution, however, is his first effort at developing a method for the interpretation of texts. This was his response to the materialist-sceptic assertion that the Vedic *mantras* are meaningless. The defence that began with Yāska achieved full expression later in Jaimini's Mīmāṁsā which is a system of analysis and interpretation of texts. Yāska's contribution to this exegetical system is his systematization of etymological analysis.

Pāṭhas

Besides, there is evidence of a very ancient *pāṭha* tradition, the method of enumerating exhaustively the verb roots and the nominal stems. Two kinds of *pāṭha* methods are available: (1) total enumeration, and (ii) typical enumeration. The verb roots, being finite, are classified extensively in the various *dhātupāṭhas*. The nominal bases, being open-ended, are enumerated typically; that is, typical classes and sub-classes are representatively enumerated. The *pāṭhas* are highly organized and classified lists. Bhartṛhari in his *Vākyapadīya* refers to the *padavādins*, the morphologists, who were evidently the authors of these enumerations.

3

Śabda (Word) in the Indian Tradition

THERE is a long history of thinking about words (*śabda*) in Indian thought. The grammarians have reflected on the reality of "word," its nature, its definition, its meaning, its relationship to meaning, its place in grammar, its difference from *pada*.

Yāska (ninth century BC) has discussed in *Nirukta* the *khaṇḍa-akhaṇḍa* (part *vs.* whole) controversy. Upholders of the holistic (*akhaṇḍa*) view accepted the reality only of the sentence, *ukti*. The words they say are not independently real and "exist," that is have meanings, only in an utterance. In a sentence, the words do not exist independent of each other, coalesce through *sandhi* to constitute a *saṁhitā*, their *rūpa*, form, changes and they are not recognizable separately. There are three arguments for this view:

(i) sounds, *dhvani*, are *anitya*, transient — they come into being, are audible for some time and then are destroyed. How can an entity made up of a series of transient elements be real (*nitya*)? Yāska attributes this view to Auḍumbarāyaṇa who considered sounds and words as objects of senses, that is material objects, and as such subject to birth and decay (see, *Nirukta* 1.1).

(ii) in speech, words coalesce with words before and after — *sandhi* takes place and the forms of words change. Words that constitute an utterance cannot be separately identified — *saṁhitā* is an unbroken chain like the flow in a river. (Older manuscripts and books reproduce the Saṁhitā texts.)

(iii) Even from the point of view of meaning, a word is a part of the sentence as use is the arbiter of meaning. Bhartṛhari (fifth century AD) gives many illustrations to establish this : (a) when a mother says to the child, "See the food is not eaten by the crows" the word "crows" means in this case "animals and birds;" (b) the utterance "The sun is set," depending on who the speaker is, can mean "it is time to worship" (an ascetic to another), "it is time to make love" (a lover), "it is time to go out to steal" (a thief to another).

Yāska holds the opposite view. Accepting the reality of words, he divides (*Nirukta* 1.1) all words into four classes — *nāma* (substantives), *ākhyāta* (verbs), *upasarga* (prefixes), *nipāta* (indeclinable particles). Bhartṛhari (fifth century) accepts both the *khaṇḍa* and *akhaṇḍa* points of view — according to the partitive point of view we move from an awareness of separate words to the holistic meaning of a sentence, and according to the other point of view comprehension proceeds from the holistic sentence-meaning to a cognition of the meanings of separate words (*Vākyapadīya* 2.57). According to one point of view, words are real and *saṁhitā* is a construction; according to the other point of view, *saṁhitā* is real and words are inferred realities.

That sentence is the primary entity of meaning in communication and that words are also real in the sense that they have a primary denotation became a basic assumption of the tradition of grammar. The second issue is the nature (*svarūpa*) of words. There are three standpoints reported and discussed by Bhartṛhari in *Vākyapadīya* 1.107. The Mīmāṁsakas believe that when a speaker has a desire to communicate something, his effort produces vibrations in his breath (*prāṇa-vāyu*, the life-breath) and it is the breath that moves up and striking against the palate, the teeth and the lips becomes audible as sound. The Jains believe that atoms have the power to produce any effect. Bhartṛhari reports "atoms in which powers of conjunction and division reside have the power to produce effects, a power which through division manifests as shade and light and which through conjunction becomes *śabda*s (words)" (*Vākyapadīya* 1.108, 110). But according to the grammarians, the *antarajñātā* (the knowing self) itself is present as the potential of words to denote — the knowledge existing in the self, in order to express itself, takes the form of words (*Vākyapadīya* 1.112). This is the opinion of Patañjali. The mind in the form of the inner cognizing self (*antaḥkaraṇa*), becoming immanent in the breath, with the help of bodily-energy comes outside the body in the form of words (*Vākyapadīya* 1.115).

This principle of the grammarians became the basic assumption of Indian linguistic thinking. No meaning can be expressed or communicated without words: "It is certain that all meanings and their differences are creation of words" (*Vākyapadīya* 1.119). "There is no knowledge in this world which is graspable without words. Hence, all knowledge appears coextensive with words" (*Vākyapadīya* 1.123). In the grammatical tradition, therefore, knowledge is language and language is knowledge.

The question whether word is a form of air or of knowledge is a question of its definition. Words have two aspects — sound (based in air/breath) and meaning (based in the mind). It is not easy to define *śabda*. This word stands for many things in the grammatical and the philosophical tradition. In grammar, *śabda* (word) and *pada* (fully inflected form) are often used interchangeably. It is, therefore, necessary to define *śabda* and to distinguish it from *pada*. Yāska uses both *śabda* and *pada*. When he is referring to the derivation of words as grammatical units, he uses the term *pada* — "These are the four kinds of *pada* : *nāma, ākhyāta, upasarga, nipāta*" (*Nirukta* 1.1). Also when he refers to words used in the texts, he uses the term *pada* — "Give an exposition of *padas* (fully inflected forms) in which the sound and grammatical changes are in accordance with meaning" (*Nirukta* 2.1). Yāska's grammatical classes do not correspond to the semantic classes — the adjectives and nouns are in one class, the *nāma*, because in Sanskrit the adjectives and nouns are declined (change their form to express) according to the nominal grammatical categories as is true of some modern Indian languages as well, as for example in Panjabi : *caṅgā muṇḍā* "good boy," *caṇgī kuḍī* "good girl," *mīṭhā amba* "sweet mango," *mīṭhe amba* "sweet mangoes."

So, functionally, that is from the point of view of inflection (grammatical formation), nouns and adjectives constitute the same class. "Mango" is a word (*śabda*) in the dictionary, and in actual use in speech or writing, inflected appropriately as in "mangoes are delicious," it is a *pada*. The difference between *śabda* and *pada* is the difference between a word and its inflected form. Yāska uses the word *śabda* as well in some specific senses. While reporting Auḍumbarāyaṇa's principle, he says if words are *anitya* (transient) how can we divide them and assign them to four classes (*Nirukta* 1.2). In this comment *śabda* is a linguistic form with which meanings get expressed. And when inflections are added to the words in the process of derivation, the final *siddha rūpa*, the fully inflected form, is *pada*. In the next context when he is explaining why we use language to talk about objects, Yāska again uses the term *śabda*: "Being all-pervasive (as sound) and having a subtle (non-physical) aspect (of reference to objects), words are used for naming in the worldly usage" (*Nirukta* 1.2). According to this words are names, of some object or the other. Their meaning is an object, *padārtha*, a specifically denoted object such as table, tree, wind, breath, goodness. Yāska's science of exposition proceeds on the assumption that words are meaningful linguistic units. He takes the fully inflected form (*pada*), separates the *vibhakti*s from the word and then demonstrates the derivation of the word on the basis of its meaning from the verb-root. In establishing his principles of exposition, Yāska divides *pada*s into two sets: (i) basic such as happy, charity, height, and (ii) the derived such as happiness, charitable, heighten. For purpose of exposition, says Yāska, "The *pada* is analysed into *śabda*, word + (*pratyaya*, derivational affix) + *vibhakti*, inflectional affix. After that the etymology/exposition of words should be given" (*Nirukta* 2.2). It is clear that Yāska maintains a distinction between *śabda* and *pada* — *śabda* is the basic word (base) without any affix, derivational or inflectional. Thus, the *pada ūcāiyān* is = *ūca* (adjective) + *ī* (derivational affix for forming a noun) + *yān* (inflectional affix for plurality). Thus, distinguishing between *pada* and *śabda*, Yāska gives this definition of *śabda* : "That meaningful unit of language which is used in the world to refer to objects and which is manifested by uttered sound is *śabda*" (*Nirukta* 2.2).

Pāṇini in his *Aṣṭādhyāyī* (seventh century BC) uses the word *śabda* only once in 1.3.34 where this word is used in the sense of sound. Since it is a grammar of *pada-siddhi* there is no occasion to use the word *śabda*.

But Patañjali in his *Mahābhāṣya* (second century BC) calls Pāṇini's grammar *Śabdānuśāsana*, the discipline of words. In the first section (*āhnika*) he asks in his characteristic simple dialectical style — "(discipline) of which words (*keṣām śabdānām*), of actual worldly usage (*laukikānām*) or of compositional texts (*vaidikānām*)?" And he himself rejoins, "Both." And he gives examples of words of both the spoken language and of the textual language. Words in actual spoken language are cited in their third person, nominative singular forms — cow, horse, man, elephant, parrot, deer. Words from texts are cited in the form in which they are employed in the instances cited — *agnimīḷe purohitam, agna āyāhi vitaye*, etc. Next he gives a definition of *śabda*, the linguistic sign. He asks — "'cow,' now what is the word in this?" Is it the object with tail, horns, etc.? No, he says that is *padārtha*, object. Is it black, brown, white, etc.? No, that is the attribute. Is it the similarity, oneness, that obtains in all such objects? No that is class or universal. Is it the movement of eyes, body, etc.? No that is action, activity. Then what is a word? *Śabda* (word) is neither particular nor universal nor attribute nor action. It is, says, Patañjali in his remarkably accurate definition of a linguistic sign — "That which when manifested in articulated sounds brings to the hearer's mind the cognition of cow-individuals characterized by the attributes such as tail, hump, horns, etc. is *śabda*" (*Mahābhāṣya* 1.1).

This definition of *śabda* has become established as the standard definition in the school of grammarians and as the foundation of Bhartṛhari's theory which says that the linguistic sign has two dimensions:

Śabda

sphoṭa
(conceptual (*amūrta*)
meaningful unit)

dhvani
(phonemic form)

Sphoṭa is derived from the root *sphuṭ* and means "that which gets expressed," "that which increases and expands." The grammarians mean by this that essential word which when it takes the form of sound denotes a meaning/object. Subramania Iyer comments :

> *Sphoṭavāda* explains the process of transfer and reception of meaning . . . infinite phonetic variation, transience of speech-sounds, sequential structuring of language and the non-

> sequential and non-discrete reality — in spite of all this meaning gets expressed and comprehended.
>
> — K.A. Subramania Iyer 1969:160

Word and meaning have a given relationship which is as follows, according to Bhartṛhari:

- ***Śabda*** (linguistic sign)
  - *sphoṭa* (meaning bearing constant)
  - *varṇa-samūha* (sound)
- ***Artha*** (meaning denoted)
  - *śabdārtha* (meaning denoted)
  - *vāstavārtha* (referred object)

Varṇa-samūha (sounds) constitute the manifest form of the word while *sphoṭa* is the non-manifest form of the word. The manifest word (articulated sound form) creates in the hearer's mind a memory, a picture, an impression (*saṁskāra*) of the non-manifest *sphoṭa*. In Bhartṛhari's theory, the uttered word creates in the hearer's mind the impression (*saṁskāra*) of both the abstract phonemic shape and the radical word, the meaning-constant. In terms of the mental impression, we grasp the meaning. How does *dhvani*, the non-manifest word, evoke *sphoṭa*, the manifest word? What process is involved in the evocation of meaning by a word? Bhartṛhari in an effort to define this specifies a number of possible mental operations:

Dhvani	is to	***Sphoṭa***
as illuminator (*prakāśaka*)	is to	the illumined (*prakāśya*)
expresser (*vācaka*)	is to	the expressed (*vācya*)
grasper (*grāhaka*)	is to	the grasped (*grāhya*)
effect (*kārya*)	is to	the effecting cause (*karaṇa*)
instrument (*nimitta*) (*pratyāyaka*)	is to	the object (*pratyaya*)

Again the relationship between a word and its meaning is "given" in the sense that we do not know when this word was used in this meaning and nor is there any logical or legal basis for the word to have its assigned meaning. This relationship is *siddha*, established. The word has been, and continues to be, used in this meaning. This holds true for the normal words of a language, not for coined words or terms. But the life, history and field of usage of even the neologisms and technical terms coined specially become non-immediate and their origin and meaning become a subject of research after passage of some time.

What is the domain of *śabda-racanā* (word formation)? Word formation is the formation of phonological words. This is of two kinds — (i) in the derivational system of grammar, and (ii) in the world of usage. In the derivational system, both nouns and verbs are derived from other (basic) nouns/adjectives and verbs. Nouns are formed from (i) other nouns or adjectives, and (ii) verbs. Feminine nouns are formed from masculine bases. Verbs are formed from other verbs and in principle can be formed from nouns as well. All these represent word formation through grammatical processes. Words are also formed in the world of usage (*loka*) either through innovative naming or through the processes of combining *prakṛti* (bases) and *pratyaya* (affixes). This latter mechanism combines native and non-native bases with native and non-native affixes. Besides languages borrow words from other languages. Though there are no borrowed words in Sanskrit, there are any number of borrowed words in modern Indian languages. In grammar, all this domain of word formation precedes the domain of inflection, that is words are first formed/derived and then they are inflected.

We can display all this in this way :

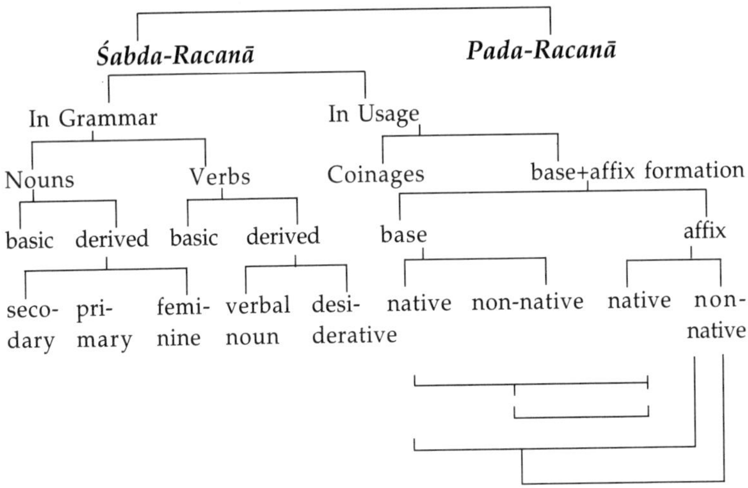

It is clear from this that word formation, except for coinages and borrowing, is a grammatical process and can be described in a rule-bound manner. Pāṇini's rules are a model for such a description — Pāṇini has made rules for 38 kinds of *taddhita* derivations, 8 kinds of feminine formation, 25 kinds of *kr̥danta* and 4 kinds of verb derivations. It is these processes that are the mechanisms for word formation in the usage as well. Moreover, these processes and these rules, it is reasonable to assume, will be found sufficiently explanatory for the word formation in modern Indian languages as well.

4

Pāṇini's Model of Grammar

FOUR statements can be made about Pāṇini's grammar:

According to this grammar, language is a system of five successively "higher" units — *varṇa* (sounds), *akṣara* (syllable), *śabda* (word), *pada* (morphological construction) and *vākya* (sentence).

Four principles convert a collection of elements or units of language into structures or principled arrangements: (1) principle of sequence or order; (2) principle of linearity; (3) principle of centripetal control; (4) principle of hierarchy of organization.

The morphological constructions (*pada*) in a sentence are mutually bound through three systems : (1) of *kāraka* (case); (2) of *samānādhikaraṇa* (equal governance); (3) of *anviti* (agreement).

The grammar identifies the relations among elements and provides a mechanism of overt/covert marking of such relations.

We will now see how this grammar is related to language; that is, how this grammar describes these facts of language structure and how it weaves them into a rule-bound system. Morphology is recognized as the heart of language structure because a sentence/clause is only an arrangement of morphological constructions. Pāṇini's grammar is a grammar of morphology which explains syntactic facts as well.

I

Pāṇini's grammar begins with an enumeration of the sounds of Sanskrit, the *varṇa samāmnaya*. Kātyāyana (third century BC?) in *Vājasaneyi Prātiśākhya* presented another enumeration, the *varṇamālā*, which is the basis of the alphabets of all modern Indian languages. In Kātyāyana's system all sounds are classified into six sets: (1) simple vowels (*mūla svara*), (2) diphthongs (*sandhyakṣara*), (3) stops (*sparśa*), (4) semi-vowels (*antastha*), (5) sibilants (*uṣmana*), and (6) intrusive sounds (*ayogavāha*).

The vowels are divided into simple and complex, classified according to length (short, long and prolated) and separated according to the place of articulation into five sets (gutturals, palatals, linguals, dentals, and labials). The nine primary vowels consist of five simple vowels (*a, i, u, ṛ, ḷ*) and four diphthongs (*e, ei,* and *o, au*). A vowel may be short (*hrasva*), long (*dīrgha*), or prolated (*pluta*). Each of these may be again of two kinds due to the feature, nasality — nasalized (*anunāsika*) or without the nasal sound (*ananunāsika*). Vowels are further discriminated into acute (*udātta*), grave (*anudātta*) and circumflex (*svarita*). These are pitch variations. An acute vowel is produced from the upper part of the vocal organs, grave from the lower and the circumflex arises out of a mixture of the two. Thus, there are eighteen modifications of each of the simple vowels and twelve of each of the diphthongs (as there are no "short" diphthongs).

There are three sets of consonants: stops (*sparśas*) involving complete closure; semi-vowels/intermediate (*antastha*); sibilants (*ūsmaṇa*). The stops (25) are discriminated one from the other on the basis of three features — aspiration, voicing and nasality. Each of the five sets according to the place of articulation comprises five stops with different feature characterization. The first two stops of each set are called hard consonants (surds) as against the other three which are called "sonants." The first stop (*k*) is aspirated and +voiceless; the second (*kh*) is +aspirated and +voiceless; the third (*g*) is -aspirated and +voiced; the fourth (*gh*) is +aspirated, +voiced and the fifth is +voiced, +nasal. The semi-vowels (*y, r, l, v*) are slightly closed — that is, the active and the passive articulators are very close to each other though they are not in contact. In the articualtion of sibilants (*ś, ṣ, s, h*) the articulators are slightly open, more separated than in the case of the semi-vowels. In the Indian analyses, the opposition is not between -aspiration and +aspiration; the opposition is seen as one between weak aspiration and strong aspiration and the first, the third, the fifth stops and the semi-vowels have weak aspiration while the second and the fourth stops have strong aspiration. In addition, Sanskrit has two nasal sounds — *anusvāra* and *anunāsika*. *Anusvāra* (a nasal sound) is denoted by a dot placed above the sound after which it is pronounced. *Anunāsika,* (nasalized vowel) is denoted by a dot in a semi-circle placed aboves the sound after which it is pronounced.

Anusvāra is an intrusive sound, *ayogavāha*. *Ayogavāha* sounds are sounds which are produced incidentally as a result of the adjacency of sounds coming one after another in the speech continuum. A sort of hard breath is known as *visarga*. It is denoted by two dots (:) placed after the letter after which it is to be pronounced. The *visarga* is a substitute in speech for a final *s* or *r*. *Jihvāmūlīya* and *upadhmānīya* are terms given to a sort of semi-*visarga* before *k, kh* and *p, ph* respectively. It is denoted by and may be regarded as the spirants of *ka-varga* (*k*-group) and *pa-varga* (*p*-group) respectively. The table below lists all the sounds according to their place and manner of articulation.

glottal	*a ā* a^3				*h ḥ*
guttural			*k kh g gh ṅ*		*h ~k*
palatal	*i ī* i^3		*c ch j jh ñ*	*y*	*ṣ* (.), (:)
retroflexs	*ṛ ṝ* r^3		*ṭ ṭh ī īh ṇ*	*r*	*ṣ hu*
dental	*ḷ ḹ* l^3		*t th d dh n*	*l*	*s ku*, etc.
labial	*u ū* u^3		*p ph b bh m*	*v*	*h ~p*
glotto - palatal		*e, e* *ai, ai*			
glotto - labial		*o, o* *au, au*			

These sounds are represented by syllabic signs, the Devanāgarī alphabet (consisting of 42 letters or *varṇa*s, 9 for vowels and 33 for consonants). It is to be noted that the minimum unit of utterance is a syllable, *akṣara*. A vowel or a vowel plus one or more than one consonant is a syllable. A vowel can be pronounced independently but a consonant can be pronounced only with the help of a vowel. The consonants therefore are written with a nether stroke (*halanta*, literally "consonant-terminator") — as Against *k* which in the system of Pāṇini stands for the syllable *k+a*.

II

Pāṇini enumerates the sounds/letters in a different manner — he forms fourteen sets (*sūtra*s) with shared phonetic attributes and orders the sets in the order of decreasing vocalicity. In the *sūtra* column, as we have explained in the preceding paragraph, each consonant and semi-vowel is to be read as if followed by a vowel. For example, *n* is to be read *na*. Each group of sounds below is closed by a capital letter/ sound which marks the closure of the set and does not belong to the set:

Sūtra	Abbreviated as (Siglas that include this class of sounds)	Class of sounds
1. *a i u Ṇ*	*aṆ*	Simple vowels
2. *ṛ ḷ K*	*aK iK uK*	'sonant' vowels
3. *e o Ṅ*	*eṄ*	diphthongs
4. *ai au C*	*aC iC eC aiC*	diphthongs
5. *h y v r Ṭ*	*aṬ*	voiced aspirate + semi-vowels
6. *la Ṇ*	(*rA*) *aṆ iṆ yaṆ*	semi-vowel *l*
7. *ñ m ṅ ṇ n M*	*aM yaM naM*	nasal stops
8. *jh bh Ñ*	*yaÑ*	palatal and bilabial voiced aspirates
9. *gh ḍh dh Ṣ*	*jhaṢ bhaṢ*	voiced aspirates stops
10. *j b g ḍ d Ś*	*aŚ haŚ vaŚ jhaŚ jaŚ baŚ*	voiced unaspirated stops
11. *kh ph ch ṭh th c ṭ t V*	*chaV*	unvoiced aspirated stops followed by unaspirated stops.
12. *k p Y*	*yaY maY jhaY khaY*	unvoiced unaspirated stops
13. *ś ṣ s R*	*yaR jhaR khaR caR saR*	sibilants
14. *h L*	*aL haL vaL raL jhaL saL*	voiced fricative

These fourteen sections or groups of sounds (*sutras*) are known variously as *Pratyāhāra-Sūtras*/*Śiva-Sūtras*/*Māheśvara-Sūtras*. Each section ends with an indicatory letter/sound called *IT* (printed in capitals above) which is not a member of the set to which it applies the closure. These markers are functionally important in Pāṇini's grammar — with them *pratyāhāras*, "set denoters"/siglas are generated which enable him to economically specify the domain of application of various rules without having to enumerate every time the members of sets on which those rules operate. A sigla is formed by taking one letter/sound and one of the *IT* sounds — for example, *aC*. In these siglas, any letter with the following *IT* is expressive not only of itself but of all sounds that intervene between it and this *IT*; so, *aC* is = *a, i, u, r̥l̥, e, o, ai, au* and *aK* is = *a, i, u, r̥l̥*.

Pāṇini's grammar employs 43 siglas in his description of what in modern linguistics are called the morphophonemic processes to account for the sound changes that take place in the course of formation of *pada*s (derivation and inflection). What happens is that in the course of formation of words and compounds and in speech, sounds that are adjacent to each other influence each other mutually leading to different kinds of resultant changes which can all be grouped under three general types — *lopa* (deletion), *vikāra* (modification) and *āgama* (addition). Modification in the form of assimilation and dissimilation is the most widespread process. Thus, for example, when we add the prefix *mahā* to *indra* to form *mahendra*, the final *-a* of *mahā* and the initial *i-* of *indra* coalesce and become *e*: *mahā* + *indra* = *mahendra*.

This process is known as *sandhi*. Instead of specifying each such change separately, what Pāṇini does, in order to achieve economy, is to describe the changes as general processes which operate on whole classes of sounds and these classes of sounds are denoted by the *pratyāhāra*s, siglas. Pāṇini's *sandhi* rules state in a generalized form all the possible changes in sounds in context. Five kinds of *sandhi* are identifiable — 1. *svara* (vowel) *sandhi*; 2. *hala* (consonant) *sandhi*; 3. *visarga* (aspiration/breath after *a*) *sandhi*; 4. *natva* (cerebralization of the nasal) *sandhi* ; 5. *ṣatva* (palatalization) *sandhi*. In the first three, the preceding sound is influenced and modified by the succeeding sound, a case of backward assimilation/dissimilation. In the last two, it is the succeeding sound that is influenced/modified by the preceding sound, a case of forward assimilation/dissimilation.

Under each, different changes of sounds are classified and stated as shown below.

Svara (Vowel) Sandhi

The following types are noted :

Yaṇa sandhi (by Pāṇini rule *iko yaṇaci*, 6.1.77) by which *i, u, r, l,* when followed by *a, i, u, r, l, e, o, ai, au,* are replaced respectively by *y, v, r, l*. For example, *apari + āptam = aparyāptam.*

Ayādi sandhi (by Pāṇini rule *eco ayavāyāvaḥ*, 6.1.78) by which *e, o, ai, au* when followed by a vowel are replaced respectively by *ay, av, ay, av*. For example, *mano + e = manave.*

Guṇa sandhi (by Pāṇini rule *ādenga guṇaḥ*, 6.1.87) by which word-final *a* and the immediately following word-initial vowel are replaced by a *guṇa*-vowel. For example, *deva + indra = devendra.*

Vṛddhi sandhi (by Pāṇini rule *vṛddhireci*, 6.1.88) by which a word-final *a* and the immediately following word-initial *e/o/ai/au* vowel are replaced by a *vṛddhi* vowel *a, ai, au*. For example, *sada + aiva = sadaiva.*

Dīrgha sandhi (by Pāṇini rule *akaḥ savarṇe dīrghaḥ*, 6.1.101) by which *a/i/u/ṛ/ḷ* and a following *savarṇa* (homogeneous) vowel are replaced by a lengthened *a/i/u/ṛ/ḷ*. For example, *prati + iti = pratīti.*

Pūrvarūpa sandhi (by Pāṇini rule *eṅgaḥ padāntadina*, 6.1.109) by which *e, o* followed by *a* are replaced by the former *e, o*. For example, *mune + atra = munetra.*

Pararūpa sandhi (by Pāṇini rule *eṅgi pararūpamā*, 6.1.94) by which the final *a* of a prefix merges with the immediately following initial *e/o* of the verb root. For example, *upa+osati = uposati.*

Prakṛtibhāva (no change) (by Pāṇini rule *īdudedadvivacanam pragṛhyam*, 1, 1.111) by which the final *i, u, e* of a form in dual number remains unchanged when followed by an immediately following vowel. For example, *viṣṇu + imo = viṣṇu imo.*

Vyañjana (Consonant) Sandhi

The following types are noted :

Ṣacutva by which dentals, when followed by palatals, are replaced by *palatals* (by Pāṇini rule *sto sacuna scuḥ*, 8.4.40). For example, *sat + citta = saccitta.*

Ṣatutva by which *s* or any of the *t*-set followed by *sh* or any of the *t*-set are replaced by *sh* or a member of the *t*-set (by Pāṇini rule *śaṭuna ṣṭuḥ*, 8.4.41). For example, *mahat + Tika = mahaTtika*. This is a retroflexion rule.

Jaśatva by which voiceless unaspirated stops, when followed by voiced stops, are replaced by corresponding voiced stops (by Pāṇini rule *jhalāṁ jaś jhāśi*, 8.4.53). For example, *ṣaṭa + darśana = ṣaḍadarśana* or *vāk̲ + īśa = vāgīśa*. This is a voicing rule.

Cartara by which a consonantal sound (excluding nasals and semi-vowels) when followed by a voiceless stop is replaced by the first member of its set defined by the place of articulation (by Pāṇini rule *kharica*, 8.4.55). For example, *dig + pāla = dikpāla* and *vipad + kāla = vipatkāla*. It is a devoicing rule.

Anusvāra by which the final *m* of a *pada* when followed by a consonant is replaced by a nasalized vowel (by Pāṇini rule *mo anusvāraḥ*, 8.3.23) and before the next syllable, the fifth sound of the articulatory set to which the next syllable belongs is added. For example, *sam + gati = saṅgati* and *sam + yoga = saṁyoga*.

Anunāsika by which if there is a nasal stop after *y, v, r* then *y/v/r* is, optionally, replaced by its homorganic nasal (by Pāṇini rule *yaro anunāsike*, 8.4.45). For example, *jagat + nāthaḥ = jagadnāthaḥ, jagannāthaḥ.*

Latva by which *t, d* when followed by *l* is replaced by *l* and *n* when followed by *l* is replaced by *nasalized l* (by Pāṇini rule *torli,* 8.4.60). For example, *tad* + *līnaḥ* = *tallīna* and *mahān* + *lābhaṛ* = *mahāllābaḥ.*

Catva by which *s* after *t, d* is replaced by *ch* and *t, d* by *c* (by Pāṇini rule *śaścho # ti,* 8.4.63). For example, *uṯ* + *ṣ̱vāsaḥ* = *ucchvāsaḥ.*

Ngamudāgama : *pada*-final *ng, n, n* are doubled if preceded by a short vowel and followed by any vowel (by Pāṇini rule *namo hrasvadci ngamuninityama,* 8.3.32). For example, *sugan* + *isaḥ* = *sugannisaḥ.*

Tugāgama by which *ch* preceded by a short or a long vowel is replaced by *cch* (by Pāṇini rule *che ca,* 6.1.73). For example, *pari̱* + *chedaḥ* = *pariccheda.*

Suḍāgama by which the final *m* of *sam* prefix when followed by the root *kr̥* is replaced by *anusvāra* or *anunāsika* and is followed by an intrusive *s,* while the prefix *pari* when followed by the root *kr̥* is followed by an intrusive *sh* (by Pāṇini rule *samparyupekṣya karotau bhūṣaṇe,* 6.1.137).

Addition of (intrusive) s : After the *anunāsika* of *pum-, sam-, kan-,* a *s* gets added when followed by the first, second and third letters of the articulatory class (by Pāṇini rules *samaḥsuṭi, pumaḥkhayyampare* and *naṣcavyapraṣan,* 8.3.5-7). For example, *pum* + *kokilaḥ* = *punskokilaḥ, sam* + *kāraḥ* = *saṁskāraḥ, kan* + *kan* = *kanskan.*

Visarga (Aspiration or Leaving off of the Breath) Sandhi

The following types are noted :

Satva — replacement of *visarga* (:) by *s, ś, ṣ* when followed by *c, ch, t* respectively and under various other conditions, (by Pāṇini rules *visarjanīyasya saḥ,* 8.3.34, *va sari,* 8.3.36, *namaspuraso gartyo*). For example: *pūrṇaḥ* + *candraḥ* =

pūrṇascandraḥ, hariḥ + ṭhākuraḥ = hariṣṭhākuraḥ, nadyaḥ + tīraṃ = nadyastīraṃ.

Rutva — replacement of *visarga* by *r* when it is preceded by any vowel other than *a, ā* and followed by a vowel or the third, fourth and fifth sounds of the articulatory class or by *y, r, l, v, h* (by Pāṇini rule *saṣajuṣo ruṛ*, 8.2.66). For example, *niḥ + dhanaḥ = nirdhanaḥ.*

Utva — replacement of the preceding *a* and the *visarga* by *o* when the *visarga* is followed by the third, fourth, or fifth sounds of the articulatory class, or by *y, r, l, v, h* (by Pāṇini rule *haṣi ca*, 6.1.114). For example, *tapaḥ + vanam = tapovanam.*

When the *visarga* is preceded by *a* and followed by *a* the preceding *a* and *visarga* are replaced by *o* and the following *a* is replaced by ṣ or ś. For example, *kaḥ + atra = kostra.*

Yatva and Y-deletion — replacement of *visarga* that follows the words *bho, bhago, adho* and precedes the voiced sounds (stops and sibilants) by *y* (by Pāṇini rule *bhobhagoaghoapurvasya yośi*, 8.3.17) and the subsequent deletion of *y* (by Pāṇini rule *lopaḥ śakālyasya*, 8.3.19). For example, *bhoḥ + deva = bho + y + devaḥ = bhodevaḥ.*

***Visarga lopa* (deletion)** — *visarga* after long *a* and before a vowel or a voiced stop gets deleted. For example, *devaḥ + atra = deva atra* and *aśvaḥ + dhāvanti = aśva dhāvanti*

The *visarga* after *a* and followed by any vowel other than *a* gets deleted. For example, *rāmaḥ + āgataḥ = rāma āgataḥ.*

Exceptions:

The *visarga* after the words *punaḥ, prataḥ, antaḥ, svaḥ, duḥ, niḥ, bhanuḥ* gets neither deleted nor in combination with the preceding *a* does it get replaced by *o* — instead a *r* appears/is added after the *visarga*. For example, *niḥ + guṇa = nirguṇaḥ, punaḥ + gamanam = punargamanam.*

rephalopa — *dirghabhāva r* after *r* and *dh* after *dh* get deleted and the preceding *a, I, u,* if short, are lengthened (by Pāṇini rules *rori,* 8.3.14, and *dhralope purvasya dirgho naḥ,* 6.3.111).

Ṇatva Vidhāna (Retroflexion of the Dental Nasal)

Under various conditions and contexts, the dental nasal *n* is replaced by its retroflex counterpart *ṇ*:

If *n* comes after *r/r* or *ṣ* in the same sentence it gets replaced by its retroflex counterpart.

If a vowel or one or more than one *k*-class or p-class sound or *anusvāra* intervenes between *r/ṣ/r/r* and *n*, the *n* is retroflexed. For example, *hari + nāma = hariṇāma.*

n in specific words and roots is retroflexed in given conditions; thus the *n* of the word *vana* is retroflexed after words such as *āmra* — *āmra + vaṇam = āmravaṇam.*

After the prefix *pari* the *n* of the root *nām* is retroflexed — *pari + nāmaḥ = pariṇāmaḥ.*

Some of the Pāṇini rules involved are *rakṣābhyām no naḥ samānapade,* 8.4.1 and *atkupvangnumvyavayepi,* 8.4.2.

Śatva Vidhāna (Palatalization)

Under various conditions and in various contexts, *s* is replaced by *ś*:

A *s* which is part of a suffix and occurs after vowels other than *a* and *a,* after semi-vowels and after guttural stops is (with a few exceptions) replaced by *ṣ* (by Pāṇini rule *adeśapratyayoḥ,* 8.3.59). For example, *muni + su = munīṣu.*

When *anusvāra, visarga* or *s/ś/ṣ* intervene between vowels other than *a/a,* guttural stops, *r* or *h* and *s,* the *s* is replaced by cerebralized *ṣ* (by Pāṇini rule *numbisarjaniyaśavyarvayepi,* 8.3.58). For example, *dhanun + si = dhanūnṣi.*

After the *upasargas ni-, vi-, pari-, prati-, ati-, adhi-, api-, su-, anu-* the *s* of the verb roots *su, su, so, stu, stubh, stha, seni, sidh, sich, sanj, svanj, sad* and *stambh* is replaced by palatalized/ cereberalized *s*. For example, *s* > *ṣ* in *pratiṣedhati.*

In proper names, the *s* of *sena* after vowels other than *a/ā* is palatalized. For example, *su* + *s̱ena* = *suṣeṇa.*

There are a number of strictly specific contexts in which *s* is similarly replaced by *ṣ*. For example, *mātṛ* + *svāsa* = *mātṛṣvasa, su* + *supta* = *suṣupta, su* + *sama* = *suṣama.*

As already noted, Pāṇini captures these varied, specific changes in the speech stream with general morphophonemic rules such as *jhalām jaṣ jaśi,* 8.4.53, which says — "the *jhal* sounds (all sounds except vowels, semi-vowels and nasals) when followed by *jhaṣ* (voiced and voiced aspirated stops) are replaced by *jaś* (voiced unaspirated stops)." We can present this in an explicit form :

Jhalām followed by	*jhaṣ* replaced by	*jaś*
jh, bh, gh, dh, *kh, ph, ch, ṭh, th, j, b, g, ḍ, d* *kh,ph, ch, ṭh, th,* *c, ṭ, t, k, p, ś, ṣ, s, h*	*jh, bh, gh, ḍh, dh,*	*j, b, g, ḍ, d*

This is, in effect a de-aspiration rule by which *bh* in *labh* > *b* as in *labh* + *ta* = *labdha*. (The *t* > *dh* by another rule, the voicing rule, *jhalam jaṣo ante*, 8.2.39).

How does one replace *bh* by *b* and not, say, by *d*? There is in the grammar the principle of *savarṇa* — a metarule of this grammar that require replacement by the closest analogue, a *savarṇa*, that is, by a homorganic/homogeneous sound.

The first level of grammar is *varṇa*; the second level is *akṣara* (syllable). The third level is of *śabda* (words) which are made of syllables. About the syllabic division of words, there is a rule in Indian phonetics about the segmentation of medial consonant clusters — the first consonant of the cluster belongs to the preceding syllable and the rest of the cluster constitutes the initial segment of the succeeding syllable. Accordingly, *ekstra* (extra) has the syllabic structure — *ek* + *stra*. The discussion in the preceding section shows that the rules of morphophonemic change operate at the level of both the syllable and parts of the syllable.

Syllables constitute *śabda* (words). All words in Pāṇini's system are divided into four classes: *nāma* (substantive, i.e., nouns and adjectives), *ākhyāta* (verb), *upasarga* (prefixes), *nipāta* (indeclinables). *Upasarga*s are words such as *pra, pari-,* which are always used along with a verb or a verbal derivative or a noun showing verbal activity. *Nipāta*s such as *iva, na, ca,* etc., are particles which possess no gender and number, and the case termination after which is elided or dropped. The class includes adverbs, conjunctions, and expletives used in comparative, conjunctive and specifying senses. This classification is originally present in Yāska's *Nirukta* (1.1), a ninth-century BC text of *nirvacana*, etymology/exposition of meaning through derivation. These four classes are assumed in Pāṇini's grammar — many rules refer to the different classes of words. Functionally, however, all words are divided into two sets — declinable and indeclinable as shown below:

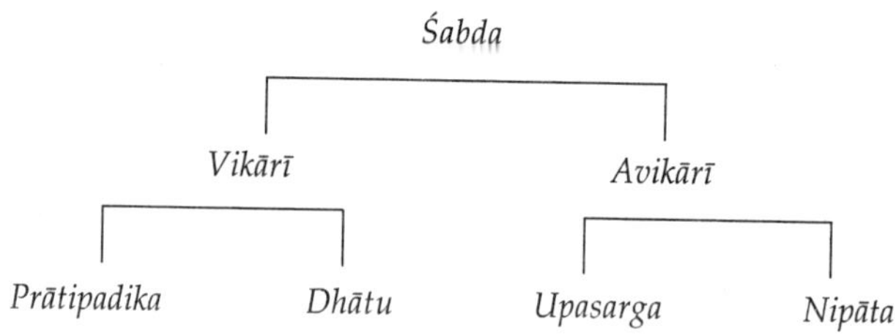

These four functional classes are present in Pāṇini's grammar, and in its ancillary texts, in the form of lists/lexicons. The *prātipadika*, nominal stems, are enumerated, exhaustively and typically, in the *Gaṇapāṭha* and the *dhātu*s are classified and listed in the *Dhātupāṭha*. The *upasarga*s and *nipāta*s are listed in the *Sūtrapāṭha* itself (and 1.4.56-97).

IV

The next level of organization is *pada* (morphological construction). Formation of *pada* from *śabda*, *pada-siddhi*, is the domain of grammar. A *pada* is formed by a conjunction of *prakṛti* (base) and *pratyaya* (affix):

Pada

subanta (ending in nominal inflection) | *tiñanta* (ending in verb inflection)

The grammar of Pāṇini is, therefore, an affixation model, that is, *pada*s are derived through a process of affixation of *pratyaya* to *prakṛti*.

Derivationally, all *pada*s are divided into two sets:

There are eight kinds of *pada* :

1. Nominal base + nominal inflection — *kumāra*.
2. Nominal base + feminine affix + nominal inflection — *kumārī*.
3. Nominal base + *taddhita* affix + nominal inflection — *gārgī*.
4. Nominal base + *taddhita* affix + fem. aff. + nom. aff. — *gārgī*.
5. Verb base + verb inflection — *pācati*.
6. Verb base + *kṛt* affix + nominal inflection — *pācaka*.
7. Verb base + *kṛt* affix + fem. affix + nominal inflection — *pācikā*.
8. *Samāsa*, compound, e.g., *sukhduḥkhe, prajāpatiḥ*.

The bases are of two kinds: (1) primary (*mūla*), and (ii) derived (*vyutpanna*). Primary nominal bases are listed — some exhaustively, some typically — in the *Gaṇapāṭha*. Derived nominal bases are of three kinds:

(i) *kṛdanta*, nominals derived from verbs. For example, *pācaka*, cook from the verb root *pac*, "to cook."

(ii) *taddhita*, nominals derived from nouns/adjectives. For example, *vaiṣṇavaḥ* < *viṣṇu*, *māthuraḥ* < *mathur*.

(iii) *Samāsa*, compound. For example, *bahuvrīhi*.

The verb roots are listed in the *Dhātupāṭha*. The derived verb bases are of four kinds:

(i) *ṇijanta* (causative) — for example, *kṛ* > *karoti* > *karayati*

(ii) *sannanta* (desiderative, to express the meaning of "desire to do") — for example, *pipaṭhiṣati*, wants to read, < the root *paṭh*.

(iii) *yaṅgañta* (to express the meaning of "doing repeatedly" or "doing a lot") — for example, *vavrajyate*, goes again and again.

(iv) *nāmadhātu* (verbal noun) — for example, *putriyati*, desires a son.

Affixes are first divisible into two sets (1) nominal, and (2) verbal. Again they are cross-classified as (1) derivational, and (2) inflectional :

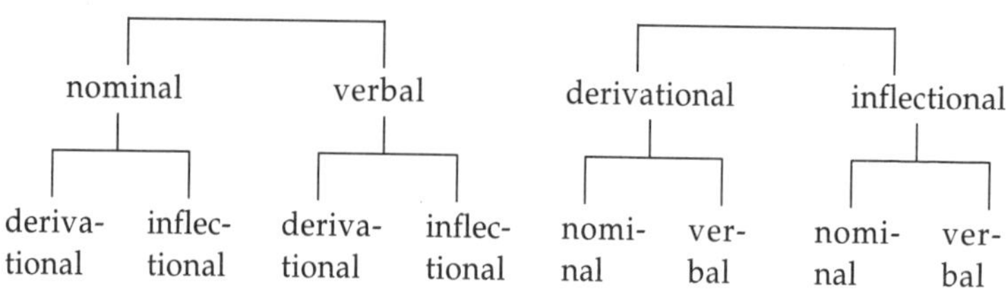

The affixational model looks like this:

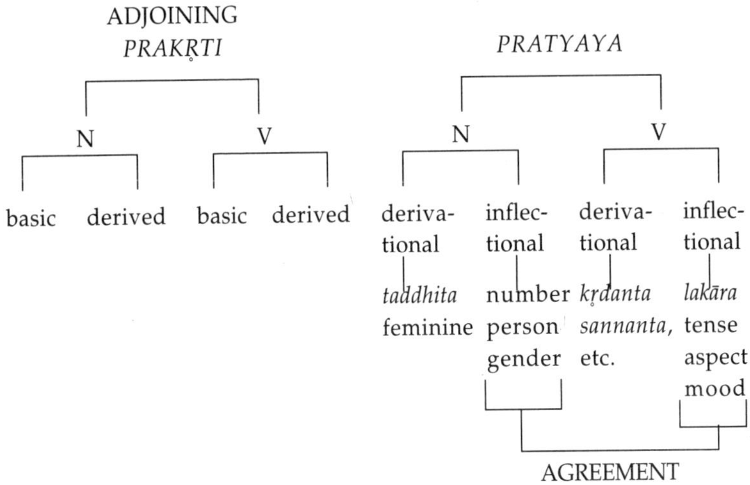

Accordingly, an utterance, *śabda*, is seen as a construction of the following kind :

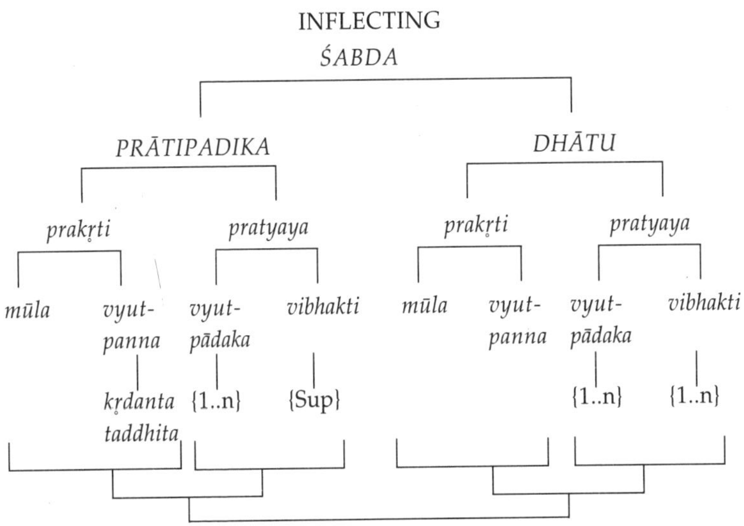

V

The *pada*s are generated by attaching affixes to the bases under given conditions which may be phonological/morphological/

semantic and the operations are enjoined in *sūtras*, rules. Pāṇini's *sūtras* are not self-contained rules. They are stages in a long interlinked operation in which *sūtras* often assume information that has been presented in earlier *sūtras* and may also assume information in the ensuing *sūtras*. The *sūtras* are brief and precise but unambiguous. Consequently, the *Aṣṭādhyāyī* employs the mechanism of context-sharing, *ekavākyatā*, the fact of all the *sūtras* constituting a single statement. Pāṇini uses two major techniques to establish *ekavākyata* of the rules:

> marks (*liṅga*): *saṃjñā* and *paribhāṣā*,
>
> *svarita* accent indicating *anuvṛtti* of the elements so marked

This results in two kinds of interdependency among the rules, inter-domain (through marks) and intra-domain (*anuvṛtti*).

There are three kinds of *sūtras* — definitional, meta-rules and operational. Operational rules are, in turn, of five kinds — *adhikāra*, topic rule (for example, 3.1.1); *vidhi*, injunctive rule (for example, 6.1.77); *niyama*, restriction rule (for example, 1.3.12); *niśedha*, blocking or exception rule (for example, 1.1.10, 1.3.4) and *atideśa*, extension rule (for example, 1.1.56). The operational rules prescribe or proscribe operations of placement, replacement, modification, addition and deletion. The rules are ordered intrinsically, that is a rule applies only when the conditions for its application have been created by the operations of the other rules and if the conditions are not met the rule does not apply. There is also an extrinsic ordering — the rules are placed relative to each other according to some conventions — thus, for example, an exception rule is placed after the general rule and the exception rules are mutually ordered according to the scope of the exception.

Since the *sūtras* are coded in a very abbreviated language, they are interpretable only by following the rigorous conventions of interpretation. For example, given a rule, which is in a *saṁhitā* form, we need to in the given order (1) do *sandhi* re-analysis and restore *padas*, (2) identify *adhikāra sūtra* to secure *anuvṛtta-padas*, (3) insert *anuvṛtta padas*, (4) identify the *vibhaktis* of all *padas*, (5) arrange *padas* in an order based on *vibhaktis* (5, 7, 6, 1), (6) insert the verb "be" (*bhavati*), and (7) assign a meaning to the thus fully reconstructed statement by employing the metalinguistic meaning of the cases of the *padas*. Thus, for example, the *sūtra adguṇa* (6.1.84) is reconstructed through various stages as *ad* (5.1), *guṇa* (1.1), *saṁhitāyām* (7.1), *aci* (7.1), *pūrva-parayo* (6.2), *eka* (*bhavati*) (1.1) to mean "if *a* is followed by *ac* in a continuous text, in place of the preceding-succeeding one *guṇa* vowel (is)."

How does the grammar work? How are the *padas* shown to be *siddha* (well-formed)? Take the example of *ramaḥ* in *ramaḥ paṭhati*. As the verb-form is either independent (in the *bhāva-vācya*) or depends on the form of one of the co-occurring nouns, the noun form is derived/mapped first. Below we show in three columns in successive application the rules that apply, the operation that the rule performs and the result of the application of the rule :

1.2.45	it identifies *prātipadika* (by exclusion)	*rāma* is a *prātipadika*
1.2.46.	specifies the sub-class	*rāma* is a *kṛdanta prātipadika*
1.4.13	identifies it as *aṅga*, inflective base	(*rāma*) (affix)
1.4.14	identifies it as *pada*, syntactic word	(*rāma*) (affix) is *pada*
1.4.21-22	number and number specification	*rāma* is non-dual, non-plural
1.4.23	*kāraka* belongs to *prātipadika*	*rāma* is so marked
1.4.54	*kāraka* specification	*rāma* is *kartā*
1.4.101	assignment of person	*rāma* is third person
1.4.102	assignment of number	*rāma* is singular

1.4.103	assignment of the required affix from the triad of case affixes	matching affix is selected
1.4.104	case affixes are termed *vibhakti*s	(*rāma*) (affix/*vibhakti*)
3.1.2.	place the "affix" after the base	*rāma* = *vibhakti*
4.1.2	*sup* (case) affixes are listed and selection enjoined	*rāma* = *su*
1.3.2.	*u* of *su* is a marker	*rāma* = *su*
1.3.9	of that *lopa*, deletion	
1.1.60	*lopa* is non-visibility	*rāma* - *s*
8.1.16	in syntactic words, *pada*s	*rāma* - *s* is a *pada*
8.2.66	replace *s* by *ru*	*rāma* - *ru*
1.3.2	*u* of *ru* is it	*rāma* - *r*
1.3.9]	it is elided	*rāma* - *r*
1.1.60]	elision is non-visibility	
1.4.110	terminal pause defined and assigned	*rāma* - *r*
8.3.15	replace terminal *r* by *visarga* (:)	*rāmaḥ*

VI

A number of generalizations can be made about the process of derivation. First, there are given stages in the process: the element is identified; its grammatical categories are mapped one by one; accordingly the affix (*vibhakti*) is selected; the affix is then replaced by the actual surface realization. Also notice the explicitness of this grammar — nothing is left to judgement. For example, a rule, 1.3.9, enjoins *lopa*, elision. But what is *lopa*? Another rule, 1.1.60, defines *lopa* for us as "non-visibility" (not deletion). Also notice that some rules or sets of rules apply recursively, that is again and again. What gives the grammar its rigour and precision is its metalanguage — all the knowledge of the structure of Sanskrit is coded in explicitly defined categories which constitute the metalanguage of this grammar. This language of grammar is classifiable as :

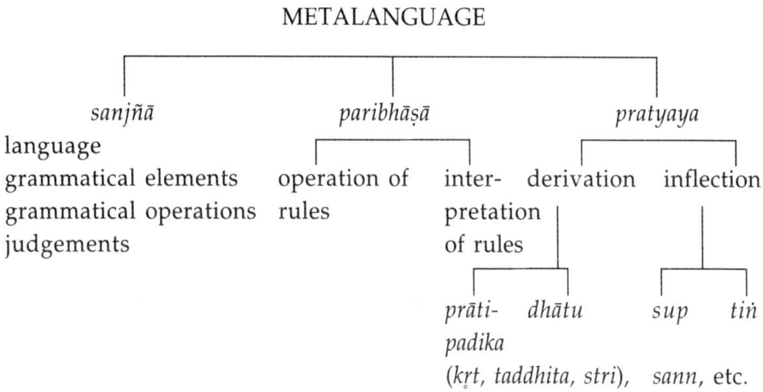

What the grammar does is to establish *rāmaḥ* as a well-formed *pada.*

The grammar acts as a filter — a well-formed *śabda* "passes through" grammar by successively meeting the requirements of the relevant rules. An ill-formed utterance, on the other hand, would get blocked at some stage or the other. Pāṇini's grammar is an explicit, structural grammar, comprehensive and rule bound: through a set of explicit instructions it analyses an utterance as a structure of well-defined elements that are defined by their paradigmatic and syntagmatic relations. It has exercised a strong formative influence in the construction of modern linguistics via de Saussure who was a Sanskritist and taught Sanskrit as a professor of Sanskrit at Geneva before he came over to Sorbonne. It has served as a model for grammars of many languages — Persian, Tibetan, Tamil, Prākṛt besides many Indian and central Asian languages. In the nineteenth century, its replacement by the Latin model under the influence of English education has contributed towards a "de-intellectualization" of the Indian tradition. However, on account of its appropriateness for computational grammar formalism, the *Aṣṭādhyāyī* has come to be studied in a big way all over the world in the departments of Linguistics and Computer systems. In the days to come, it will become the centre of language and linguistic studies in India.

5

Goals and Assumptions of Grammar

We examine here some key concepts and modes in Pāṇini's theory of grammar in the perspective of general theoretical issues such as (i) the function of grammar, (ii) the context of grammar, (iii) the nature of possible grammar, (iv) the form of linguistic statement, and (v) the assumptions of grammar. In the process, as a methodological principle, our purpose is not to make any comparisons with the contemporary Western linguistic theory but to restrict ourselves to expounding the Pāṇinian system.

I

Aṣṭādhyāyī, the seventh-century BC grammar of Sanskrit has both historical and intellectual value. As Ducrot and Todorov note, "The first text on linguistics available to us is the Sanskrit grammar of Pāṇini. As irony would have it, this book, perhaps the first scientific work in western (sic) history, remains without equal in its field even today." (1981: 45) Intellectually, *Aṣṭādhyāyī* has functioned in the Indian tradition, like "a primary modelling device" for knowledge and has been the source of conceptual constructs for diverse disciplines of study ranging from literary theory to philosophy (K. Kapoor 1994: 19-25).

It is of value to try to understand how and in what social-intellectual context this work came to be composed. It is evident that as a meta-text, *Aṣṭādhyāyī* represents standardization of a culturally central code, the linguistic code. It is also evident, as Professors Lele and Singh note that "classical Hindu grammatical theory originated in a socio-historical context radically different from the one in which classical western grammatical theory arose" (1987: 43-51).

Two facts of this socio-historical context have been noted by us (K. Kapoor 1992): (i) one, the manifest and multiple linguistic diversity in a vast speech area from Kabul to Kāmākhyā, and from Srinagar to Śravaṇabeḷagoḷa, and (ii) the evident movements towards transcendence and systematization in different disciplines — we are referring to the composition of Śāstras, treatises, primary texts in innumerable intellectual fields — architecture, polity, social thought, astronomy, philosophy, literary theory, metrics, etc. In this context of the competing movements of variation and building up of systems that seek to transcend the variation through codification, *Aṣṭādhyāyī* appears as a very powerful and meaningful response.

Faced with rampant diversity (noted by Yāska in *Nirukta*, 1) one expects a normative grammar that defines what Chomsky called "the monolectal view of language" : ". . . if we fix a certain level of acceptability then this internally represented system of grammar generates one set, and we say OK that is language. If we fix the language a little differently, the same grammar generates a different set, and we can say this is the language" (in Huybregts and Rilmsdijk 1982: 107).

However, what we have in *Aṣṭādhyāyī*, is something totally different. We have an internally complex norm, not the norm of one dialect, not the generation of one-set, but of a number of sets, of a number of varieties (dialects) of the language. We have detailed elsewhere (K. Kapoor, 1992) how Pāṇini records and sanctions rich diversity of usage, for example —

(i) the usage restricted to the texts (*vaidikī*), vide *P*.1.1.18, 1.2.34-37.

(ii) characteristic features of contemporary speech, vide *P*. 3.2.107, 6.1.181, etc.

(iii) geographical variation, vide *P*. 2.4.20, 6.3.10, etc.

(iv) "stylistic" variation, vide 6.3.115.

(v) cultural variety, viz., the language of *śiṣṭas*.

(vi) "free variation", or optionality in living usage, vide 6.3.106, 6.4.75, 6.4.117. We noted that there are 339 optionality rules listed by Katre (1968). Pāṇini does not prestige any one of them over the rest.

Clearly Pāṇini's view of language is "polylectal." The polylectal view, according to Trudgill (1983), is oriented to incorporate more than one variety of the same language into a single grammar. As Labov noted (1973):

> We can and should write a single grammar to encompass all (or nearly all), of the dialects of a language since the competence of the (fully adult) native speaker reaches far beyond the dialect he uses himself.

In recognizing varieties, in refusing to prestige one over the other, *Aṣṭādhyāyī* presents an internally multiple standard. It is the only such example of linguistic self-confidence and the related tolerance of linguistic difference. The "level of acceptability," to use Chomsky's words, has been so fixed, as to exclude a single dialectal norm. This reinforces the point so well made by Rajindra Singh and Jayant Lele (1987: 45-48) that *Aṣṭādhyāyī* was not composed to teach others the "correct" grammar, that this grammar was not meant to be an instrument of "denial" and "negation." Contrasting the goals of the classical Graeco-Roman tradition (1) establishing and explaining the language of the classical authors, (2) preserving Greek from corruption by the ignorant and the unlettered, and (3) teaching Greek to barbarians and those of the empiricist Western tradition (the grammar has been taken care of by agents of imperial expansion, appointed or self-appointed to teach the new language to those who speak a lesser one). Professors Rajindra Singh and Jayant Lele say (1987: 47-48), that "*Aṣṭādhyāyī* was not inspired by a desire to take over the world, piece by piece, and to teach the newly acquired people the language of the gods" (*ibid.*: 48). They continue: "Grammar within the Graeco-Roman tradition is a manual that helps you write your language 'correctly,' to learn the other language properly, to teach your language, through intermediaries, to those who you have recently conquered. In the Hindu tradition, even post-Pāṇinian *vṛtti* is not motivated by pedagogical concerns" (*ibid.*: 48). They take care to point out that they are not saying that "Pāṇini's grammar cannot or must not be used for pedagogical purposes," only that "the teaching of Sanskrit could not have been the prime concern of *chez* Pāṇini" (*ibid.*: 47). At this point is recalled, Kiparsky's conclusion that the form of the *Aṣṭādhyāyī* (cf. in particular the technical terms) "is not primarily determined by the practical needs of a learner of Sanskrit and. . . . The *Aṣṭādhyāyī* is, rather, a theoretical inquiry into the grammar of Sanskrit and into language in general" (1979: 214).

What then is the proper nature of this grammar? It is properly an explanatory grammatical description, the kind that modern linguistics has set itself the task of achieving. It merely orders the innate "knowledge" of the Sanskrit native speakers (the grammarian himself being one of them). It is therefore as such, a product of that thriving rationalist tradition which produced other thought-systems, such as the Buddhist, the Jain and the Hindu thought — systems (*darśanas*) as well. In conceptualizing the innate knowledge of the native speakers, the categories and processes and operations of that knowledge, the grammar attains the status of a theory of grammar.

II

Therefore the parameters of this theory and its linguistic-philosophical assumptions and implications need to be worked out with the help of the commentary tradition for these are only implicit in *Aṣṭādhyāyī*, which does not at all discuss any general issues or questions of principles or methods. An inquiry into these helps us build up the conceptual system of Pāṇini's grammatical model. What follows here is only a preliminary discussion of some of these issues.

Consider first of all the definition of grammar. Grammar is not a mere body of rules isolated from linguistic phenomena. Patañjali says *lakṣya lakṣaṇe vyākaraṇam*, i.e., "object indicated/signified and the indicator/signifier together constitute grammar." The *sūtra*s are the "indicator/signifier" and *śabda* (words/utterances) are the "indicated/signified". Both *lakṣya* and *lakṣaṇa* used as technical terms in logic and philosophy as well, are derived from the verb root *lakṣa* which means "to see, to include in its reference or scope". So the *sūtra*s of grammar have as their domain of reference *śabda* (utterances). They are *lakṣaṇa* sufficient, necessary and real characterization of the behaviour of words. By metaphoric extension, the whole grammatical description is understood/described as *lakṣaṇa* (indicator/marker) of language — so Vyākaraṇa is *lakṣaṇa*. Its purpose (described in the first statement *atha śabdānuśāsanam*) is to lay down the characteristics of linguistic behaviour, following the actual linguistic behaviour. Grammar, thus, is a description of language. The concepts of *sūtra* and rule (of grammar) are not equivalent. A rule specifies a particular feature — a *sūtra* signifies the whole class of utterances in which a characteristic may be present. Secondly, a rule (of grammar) is self-contained. An *Aṣṭādhyāyī sūtra* on the other hand is one link in a chain, and is an element in a set of statements that share the same context(s) in a domain. This *ekavākyatā* among *sūtra*s is marked through markers (*liṅga*) such as *samjñā* and *paribhāṣā* and through devices such as *anuvṛtti*. This produces two kinds of dependency among *sūtras*, (i) inter-domain which is established through marks, and (ii) intra-domain which is established through devices such as *anuvṛtti* (understood recurrence) which relates preceding rule of a domain to the following. It emerges from this brief exposition that "grammar" or "rule" in this tradition is not something autonomous, i.e., abstracted from the actual linguistic phenomena; it is in continuity with the phenomena.

Śabda is linguistic phenomena. But what is *śabda* ? Just as we characterize the nature of *lakṣaṇa* (*sūtra*) we have also to understand the concept of *śabda*, *lakṣya* or the object of grammar. The word *śabda* is multivalent. It stands for (i) sound, (ii) words, (iii) utterances, (iv) language, and it also stands for, (v) the linguistic sign. Three of these senses appear to be involved in this question. First of all as the linguistic sign *śabda* is an abstraction and grammar, when we say, it deals with *śabda*, it deals with these abstract forms — it could not be treating of millions of phonetic variants in the speech of a community — it treats "that which when articulated brings to the hearer's mind, certain cognition (of an object)." This is Patañjali's definition of *śabda* — it posits an abstract entity which has a two-fold reality of form and of meaning. The complete theory was later to be developed by Bhartṛhari and designated as *Sphoṭavāda*. So grammar as *śabdānuśāsana* is a discipline of the linguistic system, that underlies linguistic behaviour. These abstract entities exist at all levels of linguistic organization — at the level of sounds, *pada* and *vākya* — and it is these that constitute the linguistic reality handled by grammar, the *svamrūpa* of *śabda*.

The second aspect of this question is — which *śabda* (*keṣām śabdānām*) constitute the object of description? Here *śabda* means "language" or to be specific "language variety." Abstract linguistic entities or system, yes, but of which language, the living speech or the textual language — *laukika* or *vaidikī*? Both, says Patañjali. *Aṣṭādhyāyī* is a description of *bhāṣā* as well as of *vaidikī*. This is different from the prātiśākhyas' goal, for example, the *Vājasaneyi Prātiśākhya*, which expressly restricts itself to the compositional language, for, as it declares, values of the living speech are well-known, a matter of actual practice, and therefore, need no exposition. In this, *Aṣṭādhyāyī* has a more comprehensive goal.

The third aspect of this question deals with the grammatical unit of language. The abstract entities of *prakṛti* and *pratyaya* (bases and affixes) are the primary linguistic entities and exist in their own right and may be enumerated in lexicons and lists. But grammar is not concerned with them in isolation; its concern is the dynamics of affixation, of the attachment of *pratyaya* to *prakṛti*, under given conditions, to yield *pada*. *Pada* is the fully inflected form or utterance and it is meaningful. So the tradition in theories of meaning refers to *sārthaka śabda* as the object of grammatical analysis — and this *sārthaka śabda*, the unit of grammar, is *pada*. Grammar, as *vyākaraṇa*, analyses and synthesizes *pada* to show how the acceptable *pada*s (i.e., "meaningful utterances") are constituted.

But then what is the authority for acceptability or otherwise of forms. Not the grammar — a potter is the source/creator and the "authority" for pitchers and may be requested to create a pitcher to meet a particular need. But the grammarian is neither the creator nor an authority of linguistic forms. Linguistic forms and their employment in particular meanings are sanctioned by *loka*, the universe of usage. *Loka*, usage, in fact is the authority for forms, meanings and the given relationships of form and meaning. However, if *loka* is *pramāṇa*, authority, then what does grammar do? What is the function of grammar? The grammar lays down the *niyama* in regard to forms that are successfully used to communicate the intended meaning. What is *niyama*? *Niyama*, we are informed in

Mīmāṃsā, is a restraint, a restriction, a rule or precept which enjoins what would, in its absence, be only optional. Thus, the given purpose of communicating the intended meaning may be achieved by (i) an acceptable form, (ii) any one of the dialectal variants, or even (iii) erroneous or deviant articulations. In this situation, a typical linguistic situation, the grammar restricts the choice to one or more than one of the possible many. This is almost like ritual injunction — of the many grains or grasses required in a *yajña*, only one is laid down as appropriate. Patañjali calls it *dharmaniyamaḥ* — and interprets it in three ways: *niyama* for *dharma*; *niyama* itself *dharma*; *niyama* that is inspired by *dharma*. This needs explication — *dharma* here is used to mean the inherent purpose, the characteristic features, viz., of fire, "to burn," and of water "to wet" which in the case of language is recognized as capacity for transfer of meaning. Grammar lays down *niyama* so that meaning is successfully transferred — that is Patañjali's first interpretation of *dharma niyama* as the goal or function of grammar. Secondly, restriction to the appropriate option, is in itself the *dharma* or characteristic purpose of grammar. Thirdly, and this is the most subtle of the three interpretations, the grammatical *niyama* is inspired by the need to conform most closely to the abstract linguistic reality and so seeks to identify its closest reflex.

Dharmaniyamaḥ is the identification of, restriction to, *sādhu śabda*. What is *sādhu śabda* is only negatively definable, like all ideal postulates (such as *Brahman*). *Sādhu śabda* is what is (i) not *mleccha-prayoga*, usage of non-native speakers, (ii) not *apaśabda*, dialectal or marked variants, and (iii) not *duṣṭa śabda*, inaccurate usage caused by either physical infirmity or ignorance. (If the cause is physical infirmity, it is ignored; however ignorant usage is to be edited.) Why must the grammar lay down *niyama*, particularly when the intended meaning in any case gets conveyed even if the forms are deviant, dialectal or inaccurate. The answer to this comes from the larger concerns of the Hindu civilization which in its social, cultural and personal dimensions is founded on *niyama* — "do this and only this." Says Patañjali, in a remarkable analogy, that when a man is hungry, his hunger can be assuaged with anything, even dog flesh — in that case a *niyama* is laid down of *bhakṣya-abhakṣya*, of what may be eaten and what may not be. So also between *śabda* and *apaśabda* — one can achieve one's purpose by both, but a man of virtue uses *śabda*, his *vāṇī*, speech, is like nectar, and such a man shall be heard wherever the learned assemble.

This much for the function of grammar. But then how does the grammar realize this function. How does this grammar establish *sādhu prayoga*? It does so by filtering out the *mleccha prayoga*, *duṣṭa śabda* and *apaśabda*. Only the *sādhu śabda* are shown to be *siddha*, a term that means "mature" or "properly cooked/ prepared." A *sādhu* expression will pass through the grammar, will be mapped by this grammar without being blocked, and thus shown to be *siddha*. *Asādhu pada* on the other hand will be blocked at some stage or the other in their derivation. Patañjali located the *sādhu śabda*s in the *śiṣṭaprayoga* — the usage of those men whose worldly goods are constituted by a jar of grain and who, without motive or purpose, devote themselves to a branch of learning and excel in it. Later Bhartṛhari, in his theory of meaning, was to postulate that only the *sādhu śabda* have *sphoṭa*, a universally shared abstraction.

What is this mechanism that filters out a *sādhu* expression? What is the form and content of *Aṣṭādhyāyī*? We may distinguish three things — (a) the universe of a language's lexis, (b) the processes of derivation and agreement, and (c) the form and type of grammatical statements, the apparatus of statement. All the lexis of a language, its *śabdarāśi* is divided into *prakṛti* (bases) and *pratyaya* (affixes) and *vibhakti*s (inflectional endings). *Prakṛti* are classified two-ways into (i) nominal and verbal, and (ii) basic and derived. The *pratyaya*s are classified into nominal and verbal, and the *vibhakti*s are similarly classified:

1. *Śabda*
   - *Prakṛti*
   - *Pratyaya*

2a. *Prakṛti*
   - Basic
   - Derived

2b. *Prakṛti*
   - Nominal *prātipadika*
   - Verbal *Dhātu*

3a *Pratyaya* Derivational Affixes
   - Nominal attaching
   - Verb attaching

3b *Pratyaya*
   - Nominal generating
   - Verb genera-ting

4 *Vibhakti*
   - Nominal closing
   - Verb closing

The grammar enunciates the process of affixation of *pratyaya*s and *vibhakti*s to the *prātipadika*s and *dhātu*s. The bases are enumerated in the lexicons outside the *sūtrapāṭha* while the *pratyaya*s and *vibhakti*s get enumerated or listed in the text itself.

Rules, *sūtra*, define and set-up classes of bases and affixes and lay down conditions of attachment of affixes to the respective bases. *Sūtras*, from the point of view of the operations they lay down or/and domain of applicability, fall into three kinds of oppositions:

- Lexicons (outside the *sūtrapāṭha*)
  - *Gaṇapāṭha*
  - *Dhātupāṭha*
  - *Liṅgānu-śāsana*
- Lists (in the *sūtra pāṭha*)
  - sounds *varṇa samuccaya*
  - affixes
    - *pratyayas*
      - *Kṛt.*
      - *Taddhita*
      - *San*
      - *Strī*
    - *vibhaktis*
      - *Sup*
      - *Tiṅg*

1. unrestricted rule *vs.* exception rule
2. general rule *vs.* idiosyncratic or particular rule
3. prescriptive rule *vs.* proscription rule.

All the rules constitute an ordered set — and some principles of ordering are quite evident. The operational rules are generally sequenced in the order :

general — particular
exception
restriction.

Exception rules themselves are of four kinds — (i) blocking (1.2.15-16), (ii) extension (1.2.17-20), (iii) optional operation (1.2.43), and (iv) highly local exception (1.2.65). Another kind of order that is generally maintained is that of Regular Formation followed by Irregular Formation (6.4.174-175). Still another discernible order is *laukika-vaidika* forms.

The entire body of rules constitutes a single set and a *pada* is mapped practically with reference to rules spread from the first chapter to the eighth. A derivation proceeds through well-marked stages: the identification and classification of the constituting elements (viz., *prātipadika, dhātu,* etc.); introduction of the inflectional categories, their semantic content; introduction of the correlated abstract markers; attachment of the markers (*pratyayas/vibhaktis*) to bases under specified conditions; and finally the processing of final phonetic forms — through various morphophonemic changes.

A form that maps through all these stages is *siddha* and *sādhu*.

III

What are the assumptions of this system? Some of these we have already noted, for example, the fact that *loka,* the universe of usage constitutes the authority for acceptability. Some other assumptions are also inferrable, which we propose only to touch upon here. The inclusion of Vedic in the scope of grammar implies the rejection of the view that some language/ languages are, or become, obsolete. The grammar also assumes that a *pada*, has two dimensions — (a) its own form (*svarūpa*) and (b) its denotation (*artha*). The denotation, the grammar assumes, neutrally, is both *jāti* (universal) and *vyakti* (particular), both *dravya* (substance) and *ākṛti* (form). Howsoever it is, the grammar assumes that the form, the meaning and the relation of form and meaning are given, grammar does not predicate any one of them — *siddhe śabdārtha sambandhe*. This is important — the use of a given *pada* to communicate a given intended meaning is taken for granted before the operations of grammar commence.

IV

Finally how does one rate the Pāṇinian grammatical model as a theory ? As we noted elsewhere (1992: 138-139), the model has empirical adequacy — it describes all the known range of Sanskrit usage. To achieve this comprehensively and with simplicity, Pāṇini has developed an almost unique metalanguage — unequalled in the history of grammatical studies, both Eastern and Western, a symbolic system that progressively reduces linguistic multiplicity to layers of more and more abstract categories. "What is at stake here is the simplicity that results from an abstract hypothesis. . ." (R. Singh and Jayant Lele, 1987: 44). Some of these categories are general enough to be shared with different philosophical systems, such as Vaiśeṣika and Nyāya, and on the other became instrumental in the analysis of literary language as is demonstrated by Bhāmaha in his *Kāvyālaṁkāra*. It has also been already suggested that this grammar with its static and dynamic elements has functioned like a model of all knowledge that has the potential to analyse other symbolic systems (dance and sculpture, for example) and even non-symbolic social institutions. Finally, we have also suggested elsewhere that in its system of hierarchy of categories moving from the physical to the abstract, Pāṇini's grammar anticipates the structure of Advaita thought.

6

Pāṇini's Metalanguage
As a System of Signification

INDIAN intellectual traditions have generally been concerned with development and study of abstract modes of structuring and interpreting realities. The Indian grammarians, for example, worked out a general epistemology that kept the axis of language at the centre, analysed the indivisible relation that holds between language and reality and read in this indivisibility, the inseparability of human consciousness.

I

> The word is both the revealer and the revealed . . . the world is but the words' construct (*vikalpa*) . . . all cognition/knowledge is determinate/is the product of/takes the form of words — *jñānam sarvam śabdena bhāsate.*
>
> — *Vākyapadīya*, I.55, 119, 120, 123

In the grammatical science, therefore, the analysis of language as object, of its categories and operations, amounts to being a statement of the structure and interpretation of both the linguistic and the extra-linguistic reality and an expression of a philosophy.

It has been noted that *Aṣṭādhyāyī* is both a theory and a grammar of Sanskrit. The theory implicit in the grammar envisages a dynamic system in which the surface variety and differences (*bheda*) are dissolved to reveal underlying unities (*abheda*), wherein this has the potential to be that, wherein each has the potential to become the other. Pāṇini's metalanguage is the instrument that articulates and manifests this dynamic view. We recall that Pāṇini's grammar is known in the tradition as *saṁjñaka vyākaraṇa* — a grammar of categories of technical terms. We also know that the Buddhist grammarian Cāndra prepared an *a-saṁjñaka* recension, one specifically "more brief and more explicit" (*laghu-vispaṣṭa-sampūrṇama-ucyate-śabda-lakṣaṇam*). Even a brief comparison with the parallel Pāṇini *Sūtra*s shows how Cāndra simplified the grammatical statements by reordering the content of the rules (cf. *C*, 1.1.13, *P*, 1.1.46), by eliminating the technical terms (cf. *C*, 1.1.10; *P*, 1.1.52) and by paraphrasing the rules (cf. *C*, 11.1.3; *P*, 1.1.70). He reduced the grammar to six chapters, chiefly by abbreviating the first two *saṁjñā* chapters of *Aṣṭādhyāyī*.

This Buddhist attitude to *saṁjñā*s is very significant in that it is an effort to rid the linguistic description of its overwhelming theistic superstructure, and to reduce reality, the linguistic reality, to a system. *Saṁjñā*s reduce phenomena to abstract constructs; they are such designations for physical reality as never occur in actual speech. Significantly, the word *saṁjñā* stands for both (1) the technical terms of grammar, i.e., names for grammatical objects, and also (ii) consciousness (vide Bhartṛhari, *Vākyapadīya*, 1.126 *saiṣā saṁsāriṇām sañjñā bahirantaśca vartate* "this language is the consciousness in animate beings that is the instrument of inter-personal action and interaction"). It is further believed that this consciousness (*saṁjñā*) in animate beings is language (*vāk*) itself (*Vākyapadīya* 1, 127). The names for categories, classes and processes of language are as well constructs of consciousness and, as a whole function as a framework for filtering this reality.

But this is an instance of epistemological integration — as the basic semiotic function of *Aṣṭādhyāyī*, according to Patañjali

(*Mahābhāṣya*, first *āhnika*) is *dharma-niyama*, the identification of a culturally central auditive linguistic code (the *śiṣṭa prayoga*), the establishment of *sādhutva* of language use in the face of *apaśabda* (dialectal variety) and *mleccha prayoga* (non-native usages). The increased elaboration of this code (classical Sanskrit and its many more registers as against the earlier forms, viz., *vaidika*) and its complexity resulting from the rise and development, in contact situations and intellectual needs, of varieties and styles (including the highly nominalized style of the Śāstras) evidently motivated the final codification in a complete metatext, a grammar, the *Aṣṭādhyāyī*. Subsequently the code was renewed through the commentaries and the extension of the theory to other languages — Tamil, Tibetan, Prākṛta and Kannaḍa. Pāṇini's special language, the metalanguage, is a code, partly adapted and partly constructed by him to achieve this codification. This metalanguage, which interprets the linguistic reality that is Sanskrit, is itself interpretable only in the signifying code established by Pāṇini himself.

II

There are two aspects of Pāṇini's metalanguage — (i) the metalinguistic use of ordinary language, and (ii) the technical terminology including that invented specially, specific to the Śāstra. There are ordinary language words that are used in a slightly extended sense, i.e., in a specific technical sense — the terms *vṛddhi* (*P*, 1.1.1) and *guṇa* (1.1.2) are examples. There are terms whose etymological sense is the basis of its specific denotation in grammar — *akṣara* is an example in the sense of syllable and of vowel. The term *nadī* is yet another instance — the word means river in ordinary language and in grammar, it is gender marked feminine; on account of this it is used as a technical term to denote words in the feminine gender ending in *ī* or *ū* (excepting a few like *strī, śrī, bhrū*). Here, the technical denotation is modelled on the ordinary language content and grammar of the word. And there are terms whose ordinary meaning is retained in its technical use, for example *lopa* (1.1.60).

In the same way, ordinary grammar — its categories — are used metalinguistically. Grammar becomes metagrammar. For example, the cases are used metalinguistically in *Aṣṭādhyāyī* — the grammar itself lays down that:

(i) The force of the genitive case is that of the phrase "in the place of" (1.1.49). The genitive case or *ṣaṣṭhī* denotes many sorts of relations — causation, possession, nearness, change, collection, comparison, relation, etc. So when a word in the genitive case is used, how is it understood? This rule lays down that the force of such genitive is to convey the meaning of "in the place of." Thus, in 1.1.3, *ika guṇa vr̥ddhi, ika* which stands for the set, *ī, u, r̥, ḷ*, is in the sixth case. Literally the rule reads — "of *ika* that is *guṇavr̥ddhi*. But "of" by virtue of the present rule of interpretation means, "in the place of," so that the rule 1.1.3 means "in the place of *ika*, there is *guṇavr̥ddhi*." Metalinguistically, then the genitive case (the sixth) marks the place/element which undergoes the operation of the rule. Similarly,

(ii) Rule 1.1.66 specifies the metalinguistic use of the locative case (the seventh): "when a term is exhibited in the seventh case (the operation directed), is to be understood as affecting the state of what immediately precedes that which the term denotes." The seventh case means that the operation enjoined is performed on the word preceding the one marked for the locative. Metalinguistically, the seventh case, the locative signifies the subsequent context. In the rule *ikoyaṇaci* (6.1.77), for example, *aci* is in the locative and the rule reads "in the context of *ac*, i.e., when followed by *ac*, replace *ik* by *yaṇ*, as in *dadhi* + *odanam* = *dadhyodanam*."

(iii) Rule 1.1.67 specifies the function of the fifth case, the Ablative — "it marks the preceding context — the operation is enjoined in the room of that which immediately follows the word marked by the fifth case.

The second aspect of his metalanguage is the special vocabulary employed as a code to denote the elements and operations of grammar. Two kinds of specially invented terms can be distinguished — a term such as *lakāra* is not an actual word, but can be literally interpreted as *l-akāra*, "the shape of/form of *l*." A term such as *aṇ*, on the other hand, is also not an actual word and in addition, completely opaque — it is properly a symbol. The motivation for the use of such specially invented terms, as *aṇ* and *lakāra* is partly, of course, the economy of statement it achieves. More importantly the coded terms represent an analysis of a particular understanding of the domain they stand for. For example, in taking *l* from *kāla*, time, and adjoining it to *ākāra*, form or shape, Pāṇini is declaring that a symmetry holds between time and tense, as tense is the form in which time is represented in language. There are a large number of such terms (more than 200) and they pertain to sounds and affixes and to classes of sounds and affixes, both derivational and inflectional.

These terms are enumerated in the *Aṣṭādhyāyī* itself. *Saṁjñā*s (names for sets and elements) and *vibhakti*s (concepts of nominal and verb inflections) are introduced in the first two chapters. Elements and sets of elements (*pragṛhya*, *sarvanāma*), grammatical operations and categories (*bhāva*, *vidhitva*, *guṇa*, *samprasāraṇa*, *kāraka*), arrangements/structures involved in *siddhi* (*aṅga*, *pada*, etc.), structure of nominal and verb *vibhakti*, and rules to interpret linguistic/grammatical conventions (*ekaśeṣa*) are designated in the first chapter. The *saṁjñā*s, therefore, are not just defined and enumerated — they function themselves to enumerate and classify the elements of language. The second chapter designates elements and sets of elements that result from grammatical processes (*samāsa*, compound, for example), the grammatical processes (*lopa*, elision) and the choice of inflections, etc.

From 3.1.1 to 5.4.160, *pratyaya* (affixes) are introduced. Affixes that are attached to verb-bases (*dhātu*) are enumerated in the third chapter — the primary derivational affixes (*kṛt*) and the inflections (*tiṅ*). The affixes attached to the nominal bases are enumerated in the 4th and 5th chapters — the feminine affixes (*strī*) and the secondary derivational affixes (*taddhita*) attached to primary bases in the 4th chapter, and their attachment to derived bases in the 5th chapter.

In this middle part of grammar, thus, the permitted arrangements of bases and affixes are laid out. The enumeration and designation of affixes, which involves the enumeration of conditions under which the affixes are attached, functions to identify the syntactic arrangements, the *sārthaka pada*.

The *pratyaya*s have conceptual grammatical content but their own form is that of a symbol — they are non-meaningful and non-existent as ordinary language terms. They have a meaning only as part of the grammatical code constituted by Pāṇini, and the key to the code is provided in the grammar itself both in explicit rules, such as for *kāraka*, (1.1.46-75) and through actual practice.

It has been pointed out (cf. K.C. Chatterji, 1964) that Pāṇini took most of the *saṁjñā*s from his predecessors; he defines most of them as they were understood in the tradition (for example, *kṛt*. as defined in *Gopatha Brāhmaṇa*, see K.C. Chatterji, 1964: 101), redefines some to accord with his own need and analysis — for example, his definition of *prātipadika* — "that which conveys sense and is neither a root, nor a suffix is a *prātipadika*. Compounds as well as words ending in primary and secondary suffixes are also *prātipadika*s" (1.2.45-46) — which, in its method of definition by exclusion, differs from the available definitions, and which facilitates mechanical scanning of the *dhātu-pāṭha* and *pratyaya*s to establish an item as a *prātipadika*. Pāṇini's definition also differs in excluding words ending in feminine suffixes from the class of *prātipadika*s. And "Pāṇini does not define technical terms only when they have become established . . . in the system he follows, otherwise he defines terms even though they may have been used by his predecessors" (K.C. Chatterji 1964: 7).

For the symbolic language, for the invented terms like *laṭ*, *loṭ*, it is a moot point whether Pāṇini had, available to him, the practice of his predecessors. In the older Prātiśākhyas, one *Atharvaveda Prātiśākhya,* for example, self-explanatory terms (*parokṣa*, non-present, for *liṭ*) are used. "It would appear . . . that Pāṇini was the first to do away with the *Kālādhikāra* in Sanskrit grammar. It follows as a corollary that Pāṇini was the first to introduce the technical terms, *laṭ*, *liṭ*, etc." (K.C. Chatterji 1964: 16). That is, Pāṇini is to be credited with creating a symbolic language for his discipline, though the principle of brevity in the domain of grammar which inspired these was first fully enunciated by Apiśali, the only predecessor of Pāṇini fairly large number of whose rules have been preserved in subsequent systems (see K.C. Chatterji 1964: 2).

All the technical terms are classifiable as in the Table on page 76).

Saṁjñā

designate -
- elements of language; 1.1.37, 1.1.64
- elements of grammar: *ti, bhāva* 1.4.18 *apādāna* 1.4.24-31 *nadī* 1.4.3-6
- arrangements of language: *saṁketa, avasāna* 1.4.109-110
- arrangements of grammar, *aṅga, pada,* 1.4.13-17
- grammatical processes *lopa, vikāra, samprasā-rana* 1.1.60-61 VI.3.24, 1.1.45

Paribhāṣā

- dealing with operation of rules: *Samartha pada vidhi* 2.1.1
- dealing with interpretation of rules and of categories *sthānivadabhāva* 1.1.56-59 *ekaśeṣa* 1.2.64 *lopa* 1.1.60 *pratyaya lakṣaṇa* 1.1.62-63

Vibhakti
Inflections

- of nomi - nals (sup) 1.4.103-4 2.3.1-47, 50-73
- of verbs (*tiṅ*) 1.4. 101-2 3.2- 3.4

Pratyaya
derivational affixes:

- yielding derived nominals bases *kṛt.* 3.1.93-150 *taddhita* 1.1.76 - 5.4.160 *strī* 4.1.3-75
- yielding derived verbs bases causal, etc. 3.1.5-32

or

derivational affixes

- attached to nominal base (taddhita *strī*)
- attached to verb bases (causal, etc.)

III

As we have noted, the derivational and inflectional affixes are of special interest, metalinguistically, as they are represented by specially invented symbols (*kṛtrima*). These are the major inflectional and derivational affixes:

Sub-classes of these affixes on the basis of their common behaviour (such as shared operation or their relative placement) are further given class designations — *kiṭ* and *ṅiṭ*, *iṭ*, *ardhadhātuka* and *sarvadhātuka*, *miṭ*.

Besides among the "invented" (*kṛtrima*) terms, are included (i) the verb roots listed in the *dhātu-pāṭha* — these also, have indicatory markers attached to them, and (ii) there are 42 *pratyāhāras* (abbreviated symbols denoting classes of sounds that undergo shared morphornemic changes/grammatical operations). The *pratyāhāras* are:

aṇ	*uk*	*cay*	*jhal*	*ral*
am	*eṅa*	*khar*	*jhaṣ*	*ṣar*
al	*ec*	*car*	*may*	*ṣal*
aś	*aic*	*jaś*	*yam*	*haś*
iṇ	*khay*	*jhay*	*yar*	*hal*

and are generated by rules in *Aṣṭādhyāyī* (1.3.3, 1.3.9, 1.1.71).

We shall be concerned here with *pratyaya*s and *vibhakti*s and terms for them that are highly structured sequences with a definite signifying code. We may call them metasigns, "signs about signs of language." It is to be noted that the *pratyaya*s are "causal conditions" for the changed forms that result from affixation. (In philosophy, the term *pratyaya* means "causal condition" see, B.K. Matilal, *Logic, Language and Reality*).

When we look at the list below, we notice that each metasign is made up of one or more of three elements, (Indicatory)-Nuclear-(Indicatory) in which the Nuclear may

Some *saṁjñās* (*ti*, *ghu*, *bhā*, etc.) and all *vibhaktis* and all *pratyayas* are symbols, that is specially invented terms with a meaning fixed by the code of grammar. From the point of view of "inventedness," the following classification is suggested by Patañjali (*Mahābhāṣya*, ed Kielhorn, vol. 1, p. 223, II.3-4):

- *akṛtrima*
  "terms that are current in the language and that are, as a consequence, self-explanatary"
  - natural words in ordinary sense
  - terms descriptive of *kṛt.*, *bahuvrīhi*
- *kṛtrima*
  "terms not current in speech but coined to meet the peculiar demands of particular sciences"
  - entirely invented (*ṭi*, *ghu*, etc.)
  - abbreviations of longer words with or without additions

The *kṛtrima* category is of special interest — almost all *vibhaktis* and *pratyayas* are subsumed under this.

Vibhakti

- N
  - *su-au-jas*
  - *am-auṭ-śas*
- V
  - *tip-tas-jhi*
  - *sip-thas-tha*
  - *mip-vas-mas*
  - *ta-ātām-jha*

Pratyaya

- N-attaching
  - *Taddhita*: 1. *aṇ* 2. *iṣṭhan* 3. *yat* 4. *yak* 5. *tva* 12. *matrap* 13. *ṭhaña* 14. *vini* 15. *sāti* 16. *tarap*
  - *Strī*: 1. *ṭāp* 2. *ṅīp* 3. *ṅīn* 4. *ṅīṣ* 5. *kyap*
- V -attaching
  - *Kṛt* : 1. *tavyat* 2. *aniyar* 3. *ṇyat* 4. *yat* 5. *yaṅa*
  - *Ṇijanta etc.*: 1. *ṇic* 2. *san*

		6. tal	17. *ṅit*	6. *kelimar*	
ṭa-bhyām-bhis	*thās-āthām-dhvam*	7. *ṣyaña*	18. *ṇit*	7. *klā*	4. *kyac*
ṅe-bhyām-bhayas	*it-vahi-mahit*	8. *matup*	19. *kit*	8. *ghaña*	
ṅasi-bhyām-bhayas	(by Pāṇini 3.4.78)	9. *cha*	20. *ṭha*	9. *lyuṭ*	
ṅas-os-am		10. *vati*	21. *ḍhak*	10. *aṅ*	
ṅi-os-sup		11. *manic*	etc.	11. *ṇini*	
(by Pāṇini 4.1.2)				12. *śānac*	
				13. *kyap*	
	Lakāras:			14. *ṇvul*	
	laṭ, liṭ, luṭ, lr̥ṭ,			15. *tr̥c*	
	leṭ, loṭ,			16. *tumul*	
	laṅa, liṅa, luṅa, lr̥ṅa			etc.	

be made of one or more than one sound — the feminine affixes *ti, tap,* the *taddhita* affix *aṅ*, and the *kr̥t* affix *a*, are examples of the possibilities.

Which sound or sounds are indicatory, and the rest nuclear, is identifiable by rules 1.3.2 to 1.3.9, which say:

Initial position (*it*)	Middle position	Final position (*it*)
1.3.6: The initial *ṣa* of an affix		1.3.3: All consonants except *ta, tha, da, dha, na, sa* and *ma* in *vibhaktis*.
1.3.7: *ca, cha, ja, ñya, ṭa, ṭha, aa, dha, ṇ*		
1.3.8: *la, śa* and *ka, kha, ga, gha, ṅa* (except in *taddhita* affixes)		

Given the affix, its nuclear and indicatory elements are rule-identifiable:

— In the *vikarṇa, śaP - śa, P*
— In the *kr̥t, tavyaT — tavya, T*
— In the *taddhita aṆ — a, Ṇ*

These indicatory sounds (*It*) are dropped after the affix is attached to the base — thus "a" is the nuclear element of the affix — *aṆ*

Vāsudeva aṆ = Vāsudeva - a

Then what is the value (need) of these indicatory sounds? The *It* markers signify the causal and the consequent conditions of attachment — i.e., they signify (i) the bases or the types of bases to which the affix is to be attached, and/or (ii) the changes that are consequently triggered or blocked in the base, and/or, the affix itself. Thus *Ṇ* of *aṆ* indicates that the first vowel of the base to which *aṆ* is attached will be replaced by a *vr̥ddhi* vowel, while the actual affix *a* itself will be replaced by *visarga*(:) —

Vāsudeva - aṆ = Vāsudeva - a = Vāsudevaḥ

The *It*-markers have value in a signifying code that is set up in the grammar explicitly or is inferable from the actual operations of grammar. Generally *it (eti gacchatiti it)* is "attached to roots, suffixes, augments, substitutes, etc,. to indicate their accentuation or some grammatical operation in connection with them or to distinguish them from similar other things . . ." (K.C. Chatterji 1964: 156). Pointing out that "there is nothing arbitrary . . . in the technical terms of Sanskrit grammar," Prof. Chatterji shows how Pāṇini has very carefully and with reason selected the sounds or syllables to be used as *anubandhas* (cf. his discussion of the choice of *ś* as *anubandha*). A series of rules (1.1.46 t. seq.) lays down the values of these markers —

1. Affixes with *t* or *k* respectively precede or follow the element about which they are enunciated (1.1.46). Thus, *kit* is to be added after the *pada* while it is to be placed before the *ardhadhātuka* affix.
2. *mit* augments are placed immediately after the final vowel of a word (1.1.47).
3. A substitute with *ṅg-it* takes the place of the final sound of the original expression (1.1.53) — *mātṛ-ānaṅg* = *māt-ā* = *mātā*.
4. A substitute consisting of more than one sound, and a substitute having an indicatory *S* take the place of the whole of the original expression (1.1.55).
5. The sounds of the *pratyāhāra aṇ* (all vowels and semi-vowels, and a term having *ū* as its *it*, refer to their own form as well as to their homogeneous (*savarṇa*) sounds (except when they are used as affixes) (1.1.69).
6. The sound which has a *t* after or before it, besides referring to its own form, refers to those homogeneous sounds which have the same prosodial length of time (1.1.70). Thus *at* is *a* only, not *ā*.

7. *it -t* causes *vṛddhi* of the first vowel — *pac-i* = *pāci* (VII.2. 116).

8. The *it - t, ṅg* of the terms for moods and tenses are attached respectively to primary and secondary endings and indicate respectively that the *āgama* will come in the beginning (for T) and that the *ādeśa* will oust the final (for *ṅg*).

Again, when a whole class of affixes is treated as *ngit*, it means that certain changes that would have otherwise taken place (gunation) are blocked (1.2.1-4). Similarly *kit* causes the elision of the penultimate nasal (1.2.5). These values emerge from the practice of grammar. The signification of terms is often determined in this manner. The *yary pratyāhāra* (7.3.101) for example, encompasses nine sounds, but Pāṇini refers to the subset of four sounds only (cf. 7.3.101). How do we know that it is this subset which is the signified? The interpretation is secured by practice vide the rule: *sthanaḥ antaratamaḥ* (1.1.50).

The following *it*-values are obtainable according to Sri K.C. Chatterji (1964: 156-65):

ś = applicability to *sārvadeśa* (all roots) in the case of a substitute, and *sarvadhātuka* in the case of a *kṛt* affix.

m = the penultimate vowel will not undergo lengthening before the causal suffix (cf. *P*, 6.4.92).

kh = the nasal *m* is to be inserted after stem's ending in vowels.

ṅ = *ātmanepada*.

t = (i) quantity of the vowel; (ii) *svarita* accent.

p = the suffix or ending is strong.

k = the ending or suffix is weak.

ṛ = augment of *n* in the strong forms and the formation of the feminine with *i*.

Specifically with reference to the *taddhita*-affixes one notes the following values —

1. *ñ* and *n* signify *vṛddhi* of the first (*ādi*) vowel.
2. *k* also signifies *vṛddhi* of the first (*ādi*) vowel.
3. *y* and absence of initial *it* signify modification of the final sound of the base.
4. For the bases ending in *-n*, an initial *-it* signifies deletion of the final *-n* of the base.
5. *ṭh* signifies the substitute *ik*.
6. *ph, ḍh, kh, ch, gh* signify respectively the substitutes, *āi, eya, ina, īya, iy*.
7. The final consonantal *it* signifies changes in the vowels — *guṇa* or *vṛddhi*.

That this signifying code is a part of the tradition, a shared code, has been noted by K.C. Chatterji :

> There is hardly any doubt that Pāṇini introduced several new indicatory (sounds) and that the value of some of the old indicatory sounds was changed or augmented, but a careful comparison . . . leads to the conclusion that most of the older anubandhas were retained by Pāṇini and that in most cases the indicatory significance is the same in Pāṇini as in the older grammarians. — 1964: 165

IV

We have here thus terms that are symbols in the proper sense of having a value ascribed to them by a given code. Each symbol is made up of an actual affix that is attached to the base and the deletable environments. As a whole it stands for a concept and also for the correlated actual sound that is to function as the affix. This is the first level of its structure. At the second level, the actual sound to be affixed also becomes an abstract element *saṁketa* (sign) that stands for a number of concepts for a number of correlated actual forms (sounds) that are actually realized in real speech or usage. While at the first level the *it* sounds indicate (i) the bases to which the affix shall be attached, and/or (ii) the changes that it shall trigger, at the second level its attachment to the given base becomes the "cause" for the realization of given meanings, with each given meaning correlating with a given form, i.e., changes in the sound shape of base and of the affix.

To illustrate, consider the *taddhita* affix *aṇ*^{2}. First of all, it is in distributional opposition to the *pratyāhāra aṇ*^{1} and to the *kṛt-pratyaya aṇ*^{3} (attached to *dhātus*). It is also in opposition to all the other *taddhita* affixes — *iṅg*, etc. The structure of *aṇ*^{2} (*taddhita* affix) as described above can be shown thus :

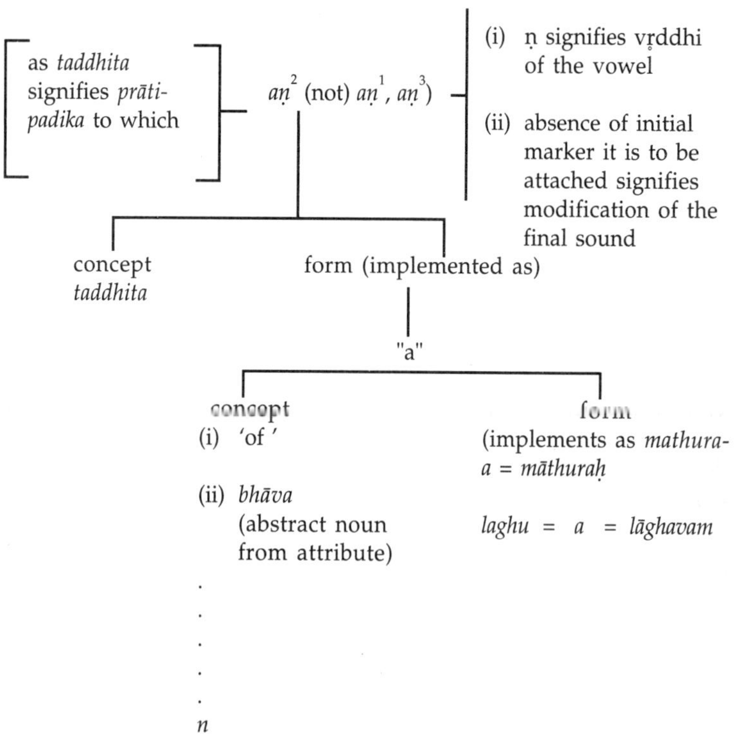

By creating such symbols, Pāṇini articulates the domain of secondary derivation — of the related entities. The tradition uses two terms, for sign — *saṁketa* and *lakṣaṇa*. *Lakṣaṇa*, sign, is "that which assumes the form of a limit (*avadhi*) (*Vākyapadīya* III.7.24). Also when a certain thing has the power to produce a certain effect, it can become its sign (*lakṣaṇa*) also. For example, the rising of the clouds becomes the cause (*hetu*) of our understanding that it will rain. Even that which is a limit becomes a sign only if it causes the knowledge of something. In *vṛkṣam anu vidyotate vidyut*, *vṛkṣa* is a sign. Irrespective of the consideration whether it produces lightening or not, it is taken as the point of indication of lightning. Lightning flashes from the tree, after reaching the tree. (This is an example of *P*, 1.4.90.)

It is asserted in the *vṛtti* on *VP* (III.7.24) that "a sign (*lakṣaṇa*) is of many kinds. Sometimes, a thing is a *lakṣaṇa*, because it is a limit as the tree in the case of lightning. Sometimes it makes the cause to be known as in the case of smoke. Sometimes, it makes the effect to be known, as in the case of clouds." (*Vṛtti* on *VP* (III.7.24)).

In *Tarka*, logic, *lakṣaṇa* of *lakṣaṇa* is given as "that which is devoid of the three defects of *avyāpti, ativyāpti,* and *asambhava* is called *lakṣaṇa*."

Saṁketa is a more restricted term — it appears in the discussions of theories of grammar and language. With reference to meaning, it is said that *saṁketa* = *vācya-vācaka sambandha*. In Pāṇinian grammar, rules are called *lakṣaṇa*, as they signify linguistic realities, domains of actual linguistic behaviour. These symbols of metalanguage are complex signs — in that they make the concept, the conditions and the actual form known.

V

All the individual metasigns are part of an overall system — they cohere in the overall articulation of the domain of language. Pāṇinian theory of grammar envisages the structure of language as an ascending hierarchy of inter-category and intra-category relations, from the base/"real" level of physical reality, the materiality of language, through intermediate levels of transcendental categories of increasing abstraction, till one reaches the highest abstraction — *Śabda Brahman* — where the linguistic reality loses its autonomy and merges in the larger cosmos.

The entire *śabdarāśi* is seen as falling into three classes — *prakṛti, pratyaya* and *vibhakti. Prakṛti* encompasses bases, the given entities, the *prātipadika*s and the *dhātu*s, both of which are of two kinds — "basic" and "derived." The *pratyaya*s are the dynamic elements which when attached to the base establish the relationship between the basic entity and the corresponding entity. *Vibhakti*s, inflections, when attached to the bases, result in *pada* — the *sārthaka śabda. Prakṛti* is the inert lexical mass, while both *pratyaya* and *vibhakti*s are the dynamic life elements. *Pratyaya*s (derivational affixes) are seen as arranging themselves into two classes, from two points of view — (i) according to the bases to which they get attached, and (ii) according to the padas they relate (*kṛt*, for example, attaches to a verb root but relates the root to a primary nominal). Similarly the *vibhakti*s are of two kinds — (i) nominal (*sup*) and (ii) of verbs (*tiṅ*). *Vibhakti*s attach to the bases — both basic and derived — and are the "living" elements that transform the inert lexical mass into the reality and concreteness of utterance. Once the *vibhakti* is attached, the *pada* or the *sārthaka śabda* is *siddha* (completed; matured). If we look upon *pratyaya*s as simply producing new *prakṛti*, then *vibhakti* is a class distinct from the two:

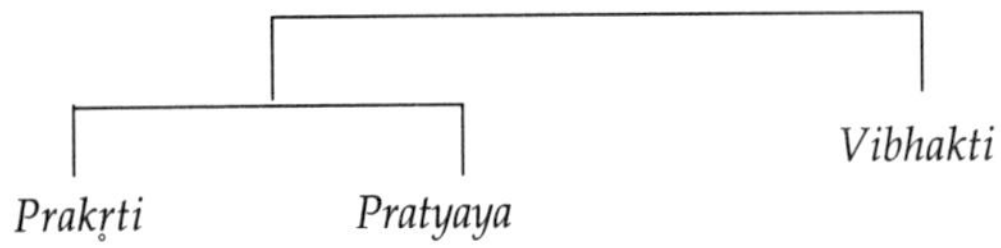

From the point of view of the process of affixation, however, *prakṛti* forms a distinct class:

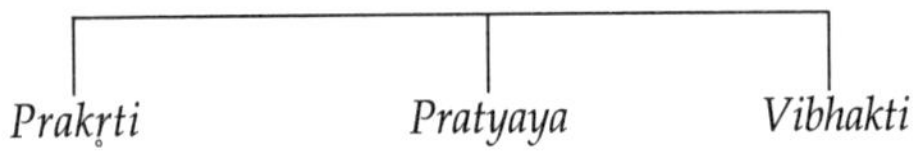

The *siddhi* process can be represented like this :

Prakṛti	*Pratyaya*	*Vibhakti*	= *Pada*
Nominal basic			
	- *pratyaya* (*strī*/	- *vibhakti*	= *Subanta*
basic +	(*taddhita*) derived	(*sup*)	
verb root	- *pratyaya* (*kṛt*)		
	= derived		
verb root			
	- *pratyaya*	- *vibhakti*	= *Tiṅanta*
root +	= derived	(*tiṅ*)	

In a very general representation, the over-all analysis of the linguistic reality may be presented thus:

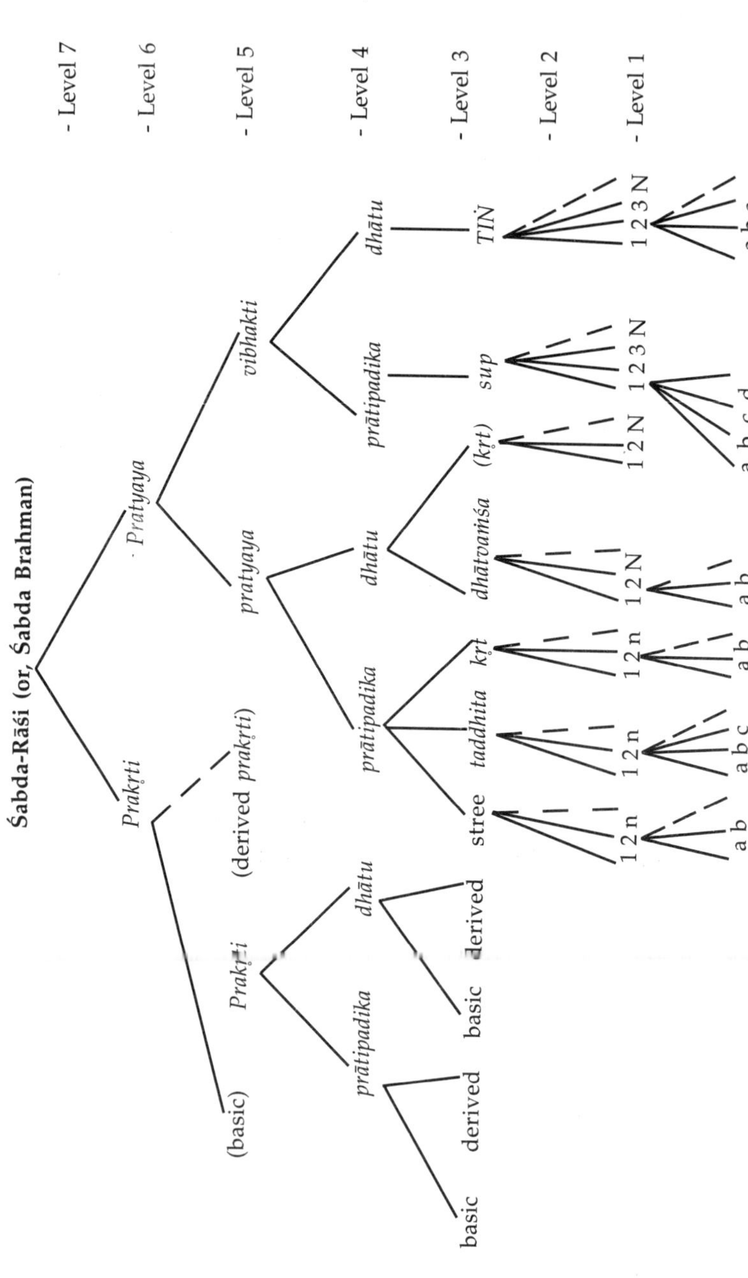
Śabda-Rāśi (or, Śabda Brahman)
- Level 7
- Level 6
- Level 5
- Level 4
- Level 3
- Level 2
- Level 1
Prakṛti
Pratyaya
(basic)
(derived prakṛti)
pratyaya
vibhakti
Prakṛti
prātipadika
dhātu
prātipadika
dhātu
prātipadika
dhātu
basic
derived
basic
derived
stree
taddhita
kṛt
dhātvaṁśa
(kṛt)
sup
TIṄ
1 2 n
1 2 n
1 2 n
1 2 N
1 2 N
1 2 3 N
1 2 3 N
a b
a b c
a b
a b
a b c d
a b c

VI

It is now possible to see how language is perceived to be structured in an ascending hierarchy of inter-category and intra-category relations. There are seven levels of conceptualization (see chart Śabdarāśi on p. 88) from recognition (level 1) through interpretation (level 2 to 6) to assignation or identification (level 7). Two kinds of relations among categories are perceptible — class membership and class opposition. Categories belong to a super-category (at different levels) and categories are in opposition to other categories (at the same level). This is how the system is structured.

Level 1 is the level of observable, concrete or physical reality of speech. At this level, there is multiplicity, variety and diversity, i.e., difference or *bheda* is the characteristic of this reality. For example, the seven plural-signifying forms of English *-s, -z, -iz, - em , -ren, - en, o* constitute the diverse physical reality of plurality. If we posit an element "X" of which we assume these seven actual entities are reflexes, we are moving to the second level and the first of the levels of conceptualization. "X" is never actually "heard" or seen in the language, yet it is very much present as that something in terms of which all the seven elements make unified sense. "X" is abstract in the sense that it is not physical and is not particular. As we ascend the hierarchy of language structure, the categories become more and more "abstract" (in the sense of more and more general, i.e., encompassing larger chunks of phenomena). As we "ascend" we progressively transcend the multiplicity and the difference till we reach the level of "no-diversity," "non-difference."

We may illustrate this with reference to the SUP! affixes — in the following Chart *Abheda*.

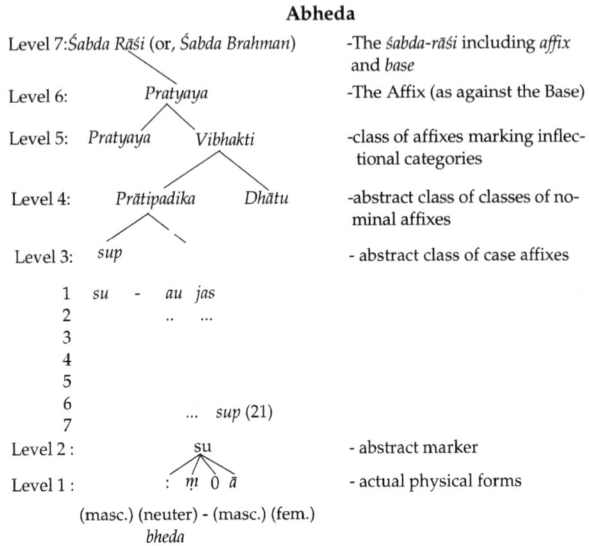

This is the conceptual structure of linguistic reality.

VII

It is a moot point whether the understanding of linguistic reality was extended to all reality or that a particular philosophical understanding of reality preceded this grammatical analysis of Sanskrit. It may be noted that the non-dualistic world-view is an ancient conception in the Indian tradition, and that Yāska's discussion of the reality of gods suggests this conception rather directly. For, after all, we can ask ourselves what does constitute, in fact, the reality of an object? What is the reality of linguistic objects, of the third person, singular, masculine *vibhakti -aḥ*, (:)? Is its reality constituted by, exhausted by, this physical puff of air? What about what it signifies? The "third" person, merely, singular? It has no actual physical existence, this concept, but it is *nihita*, inherent in this phenomenon. What about the notion of *kartā*, the independent one? Is it part of the reality of *-aḥ* or not? The total reality of *-aḥ*, it must be conceded, is constituted by all the layers of its existence, for the *saṁskāra*, the conceptual impression, of the categories of all the levels, is an inextricable part of the meaning (reality) of this object.

And if we forget, for the moment, that we are talking of linguistic objects, it is easy to analogise the structure of reality on this model. Reality is a continuum from the physical to the abstract — each link in the chain is real yet incomplete without the other and each is bound with the other. The conceptual framework leads from *bheda* to *abheda,* from difference to non-difference through several intermediate stages of abstractions, with degree of abstraction determined by the domain signified. Language at the level of lexis is the instrument of expression of *bheda,** while at the level of structure, it expresses the *abheda* of all existence.

Śrī Bhaṭṭoji Dīkṣita commented on this conclusion of the grammarians thus:

> Just as one is said to have received through accidental fortune the much-coveted jewel *cintāmaṇi* in his search after shells (*sūkti*), so the grammarians while dealing with the nature of words, preached the doctrine of absolute monism of the Upaniṣads and ultimately found Brahman as the essence of *vāk.*

Bhartṛhari later completely harmonized (*Vākyapadīya,* Kāṇḍa I) the grammatical speculations with Advaita philosophy — all words and meanings are different aspects of one and same thing. *Mahāsattā* permeates all — *sattā* represents the real essence of all things: it seems to be manifold in consequence of the diversity of objects; it is to be regarded as the *summum bonum* which is denoted by all words, all *prātipadika,* all verbal roots and suffixes like *L* and *Tal.*

The *sattā* as spoken of above is the eternal Supreme Self of the *śabdādvaita.*

---

* The principle of *vāk* fashion creates or fashions out the manifold forms out of the waters of the infinite Ocean of the ultimate Reality — *Hymn of Durghatamas, Ṛgveda,* 1.164.41.

7

Language as Epistemology
Explanation in the Pāṇinian Grammar

IT has been noted that "what is striking about *Aṣṭādhyāyī* is that it is a theory and grammar of Sanskrit at the same time. In the Western tradition, the theory of language has been left to philosophers, ..."[1] It is possible to approach this question of grammar as a theory of language in the perspective of the Western linguistic problem of "explanation." The effort to evaluate statements about language in terms of "scientific explanation," an expression of teleological anxiety, is founded on an assumption of the exclusively physical reality of language, on the reality of linguistic physical objects, an assumption that has its genesis in the Western preoccupation with the written word — Saussurian phonocentrism being but an episode in the general drama of scriptal obsession. But physical objects are themselves mere constructs — "cultural posits," and their status is akin, as Quine opines to, "Homer's gods. . . ." "For my part," he continues, "I do *qua lay* physicist believe in physical objects and not in Homer's gods. . . . But in point of epistemological footing the physical objects and the gods differ only in degree, and not in kind. . . ."[2] The purpose of such myths being evidently epistemological — working a structure into the flux of experience, linguistic or else — there

1. Jayant Lele and Rajendra Singh, 1987, p. 47.
2. W.V.O. Quine, *From a Logical Point of View: Logico Philosophical Essays*.

is no denying of the possibility and the respectability of other posits that are not necessarily physical, and that are more in harmony with the other culture. In the oral culture of India, for example, it has always been easier to accept the illusory quality of the word and to posit abstract underlying reality behind the surface forms.

Another major difference in the Indian and Western perception, and one that is pertinent to the present discussion, is one that concerns the conceptions of dynamism and change. Even at the risk of making a generalization, one may say that the Indian perception is simultaneous while the Western perception is linear or chronological. Chronology, or history requires segmentation of events and ideas and a study of their change and evolution. Simultaneity on the other hand regards all things as subsisting side by side both in space and time. The Indian world-view is thus fundamentally synthesizing and does not see things in isolation or in evolving sequence.

> Western dynamics, for example, continually expresses itself in setting problems, the single object being generally regarded as a static entity; India, on the contrary utilizes the fundamental notions of statics, in stating its leading questions, but at the same time conceives the object dynamically as passing from its origin to decay . . . without becoming clearly recognized and distinguished as a static existence separated from other cosmic phenomena. . . .[3]

Against Western anthropology, India posits cosmology.

In the Indian tradition, therefore, language has been studied in relation to the larger reality. The fundamental concern of the Indian grammarian is the relation that holds between language and reality. Language is no doubt important as ontology and has been studied as such, as it is for example,

3. Betty Heimann, *Indian and Western Philosophy. A Study in Contrasts*, 1937, p. 19.

in Pāṇini's *Aṣṭādhyāyī*, but it is also important as epistemology. The word, says Bhartṛhari is both the revealed and the revealer.[4] The world is but the word's construct (*vikalpa, jagatkāraṇa*)[5] and all cognition is determinate.[6] The correspondence between linear, sequential and discrete language on the one hand and non-linear, non-sequential, non-discrete reality[7] on the other is never perfect or straight-forward, yet the reality is cognized through, shines through the illusory forms of words — *brahma tatvam dravya śabda vācyam,* i.e., "the word predicates the essential reality." From this the complete identification of word and object is but a step. "Since the period of the Hymns, the word is one of the forces which govern nature, and Brahman is nothing else in its essence than the word par excellence. . . ."[8] From this the *Brahman* expands into "a sort of supreme essence, representing the very basis of all being. . . ."[9] In grammar it becomes the notion of the eternity (*nityatva*) of the word[10] which then has led to the postulation of a phonic-semantic substratum, a sort of prototype of all words which is at the source of the actual word, and is called *sphoṭa* a kind of fusion before fission.[11] It is this which carries the meaning of the word in association with its given form. This conception is an attempt to explain how a group of inert,

---

4. Bhartṛhari, *Vākyapadīya,* I.55.
5. *Ibid.*, I.120, p. 125. See also the Hymn of Dīrghatamas, "the principle of *Vāk* creates or fashions out the manifold forms out of the waters of the infinite Ocean of the ultimate Reality," I.164.41.
6. *Ibid.*, I.123, p. 133.
7. Bhartṛhari, *op. cit.*, I.48, p. 65.
8. *Ibid.*, I.131, p. 140.
9. Louis Renou, *The Civilization in Ancient India*, tr. from the French by Philip Spratt, Calcutta: Sushil Gupta Ltd., 1956, p. 31.
10. Bhartṛhari, *op. cit.*, I.23, p. 35.
11. *Ibid.*, I.45, 46, pp. 62-63.

momentary sounds can form an intelligible and permanent value. And on the metaphysical plane, *sphoṭa* is an aspect of "verbal *Brahman*," a transcendent principle which, as we said above, controls the world of words.

All this constitutes the foundation of *Aṣṭādhyāyī*, which is a Śāstra. Chomsky's attention[12] and Bloomfield's judgements[13] are now well-known. The term *śāstra* is used "to denote the branch of study which is treated on a scientific basis. It means that by which something is taught . . . its doctrines are recorded in aphorisms. . . ."[14] The method of exposition "consists of enunciation (*uddeśa*), definition (*lakṣaṇa*) and examination (*parīkṣā*)."[15] The *Aṣṭādhyāyī* is a system of five texts[16] with the *sūtra* (book of aphorisms) as the central text that consists of 3995 rules which together constitute a single body of rules (*ekavākyatā*) though it is arranged in eight chapters, each chapter having four quarters. The *Aṣṭādhyāyī* is a particular theoretical description of the Sanskrit language. To make possible an algorithmic, generative description, the Grammarian has arrived at a highly complex analysis of Sanskrit, complex in terms not only of the number of categories of grammar, the grammatical concepts that are needed to formulate the rules, but also in terms of the different degrees of abstraction of these categories and in terms of the hierarchical internal relationship that holds within the given conceptual systems: such as that of the *sup vibhaktis* (*kāraka*-affixation). The grammar thus is a grammatical explanation in the sense that ". . . it suggests an explanation for the fact that . . . a speaker of the

12. See N. Chomsky, *Aspects of the Theory of Syntax*, Preface.

13. See Leonard Bloomfield, *Language*, 1933, p. 33.

14. Varadachari, A *History of the Sanskrit Literature*, p. 183.

15. N.S. Junarkar, *Gautama: The Nyaya Philosophy*, 1978, p. xii.

16. (i) *Pratyāhāra Sūtras*, (ii) main body of rules, *Sūtra Pāṭha*, (iii) *Gaṇa Pāṭha*, (iv) *Dhātu Pāṭha* (v) *Liṅgānuśāsana*.

language in question will perceive, interpret, form or use an utterance in certain ways and not in other ways."[17]

Aṣṭādhyāyī — a theoretical description — explains — the facts of Sanskrit language

What is the nature of this explanation ? Decides *sādhutva* of utterances. Cf. Patañjali's *Paspaśa* (the first *āhnika* of *Mahābhāṣya*)

fig. **1**

So the undoubted interest in metaphysical questions and postulates does not detract from the scientific merit of *Aṣṭādhyāyī*. The point is that the ultimate concern in the Indian tradition is different — nature of language acquisition faculty or linguistic competence is not the goal of language analysis, but the structure of reality. The picture of levels of explanation therefore is different. This is Botha's picture of levels of explanation in the Western linguistic theory:

Level	Explained phenomenon	Explanatory Mechanism
grammatical explanation	properties of sentences	law-like generalizations about linguistic competence
internal (general linguistic) explanation	properties of linguistic competence	law-like generalizations about language acquisition faculty
external explanation	properties of language acquisition faculty	law-like generalizations about the human mind

fig. **2 Levels of Explanation (Rudolf P. Botha, p. 225)**

The Indian picture of explanation is evidently different — instead of "linguistic competence," we have "elements of language-structure" (the question of innateness is redundant),

17. Chomsky (1970: 428) quoted by Rudolf P. Botha, 1980, p. 202.

and instead of "language acquisition faculty,"[18] we are concerned with "structure of larger reality":

Level	Explained Phenomenon	Explanatory Mechanism
grammatical explanation	properties of *śabda* utterances	law-like generalization about language structure
internal (general linguistic explanation)	properties of language structure	law-like generalizations about larger reality
external explanation	structure of larger reality	concepts of Advaita

fig. **3 Levels of Explanation in the Indian Tradition**

Evidently, while the Western grammatical theory relies crucially on psychology, the Indian grammatical theory relies on metaphysics or philosophy.

If we consider the last right-box in *fig.* 2, it becomes plain that explanation is a matter of endless deferment — there is no ultimate explanation. Each "explanation" or "reason" itself becomes the explanandum requiring yet another explananus. If at all, the ultimate explanation or foundation has to be sought in some philosophic postulate. The Indian grammarian finds this in terms of the non-dualist world-view,[19] in a view that had its first clear formulation in the age of tremendous intellectual upsurge from tenth to sixth century BC in the great

18. However, it must be clearly noted that Indian thought *presumes* the fact that language is a mental faculty, *mānasa vyāpāra*, is in fact inseparable from cognition and cognitive processes. (cf. *Vākyapadīya*, Kāṇḍa I)

19. In a deliberate preference for the term non-dualist, we are referring the general trend of the monistic thought that has been there, and has developed since the period of the hymns. See Mādhavācārya's *Sarvadrśanasaṁgraha*. See also S. Radhakrishnan, *Indian Philosophy*, vol. 1 (Chapters 2 and 4) and vol. 2 (Chapters 7-8).

plains of north India and found its apogee in Ādi Śaṅkara and its final expression in the Viśiṣṭādvaita of Rāmānujācārya. In its simplest deductive terms, this world-view distinguishes between the multiple, diverse, changeful surface reality and the underlying changeless, one essence. This view is transferred to the linguistic object, and language is seen as consisting of a multiplicity of surface forms which are successively, hierarchically reducible to underlying forms, and ultimately to one abode:

sup P. 1-4-104
Twenty-one *vibhaktis*
P. 4-1-2
multiplicity of *Kāraka* (Case) affixes

fig. 4

The ultimate reality of the *kāraka* affixes, is the abstract postulate — *Sup* — it is the Real, it remains unchanged during the presence of modification, as people give different garbs to it in the course of language use, and it is "that wherein change comes and goes. . . ."[20] This is so because the actual affixes, of a class, individual refer to one meaning, "which shines out in many forms as the thing denoted."[21] Behind the surface forms, there are layers of abstract entities, with expanding domains, entities that have no physical existence, but which exist, quite really in our consciousness.

In order to give a definition to this "grammatical explanation" of the universe of Sanskrit, we briefly enunciate some aspects of "scientific explanation."

"Explanation" involves exploring/reasoning why certain linguistic constructs are:

---

20. Mādhavācārya quotes Bhartṛhari with approval to this effect. Cf. Cowell and Gough, *op. cit.*, p. 304.

1. "acceptable" or unacceptable.[22]
2. Scientific explanation has the structure of a logical argument.
3. The explanans consists in (i) Grounds and (ii) Reasons (or, in (i) Law like generalizations and (ii) Factual reasons).
4. Language particular rules and general rules (principles of linguistic theory) together constitute the Grounds, while the grammatical concepts in terms of which the rules are formulated constitute Reasons.
5. It is possible to classify explanations on the bases of objects, reasons and logical relation betwen parts of the argument.
6. Interscientific explanation

> . . . The sciences can be arranged in a hierarchy such that explanation of facts in one is given, in terms of the description of facts in another.
>
> — Harre, 1967, 101

> Such explanations may be given in every individual science or form of inquiry which is directed at a two-levelled reality.[23]

It now remains to relate, briefly here, the explanation in the Indian grammar, to these characteristics of scientific explanation. First, it is evident that the Indian grammarians were quite clear about the function or purpose of their inquiry. They were in the course of enunciating *śabdānusāsana* — deciding the *sādhutva* of *śabda* (utterances). Patañjali in the

---

21. Bhartṛhari, *Vākyapadīya*, III.3.87.
22. These points are based on Rudolf, P. Botha, *op. cit.*, pp. 185-237, and Bernard Comrie, *Language Universals and Linguistic Typology*, 1981.

paśpaśa āhnika of *Mahābhāṣya* makes this quite clear, and carries out an elaborate discussion of *sādhutva* (roughly but not quite aptly "acceptability").[24]

Secondly, there is evidence of the explicit recognition that the structure of the grammatical explanation is logical in the terms of *lakṣya* and *lakṣaṇa* and common to the notions of "explanandum" and "explanans." In fact, Patañjali in the description cited above uses the term *lakṣaṇa* for a rule of grammar.

Thirdly, the explanans take the form of *utsarga* and *apavāda* (general and exception rules). The rules of *Aṣṭādhyāyī* are "law-like generalizations"[25] the Grounds, while the *saṁjñā*s (the categories of grammar) constitute the Reasons, or the defining vocabulary of the rules (they are all placed together in the beginning of the grammar).

Fourthly, it is possible to argue that *Aṣṭādhyāyī* exhibits a particular "depth" of a grammatical explanation by virtue of the fact that several rules of *Aṣṭādhyāyī* (*kāraka*s, phonological rules like that of de-aspiration, etc.) have, or are at least claimed to have, applicability to human languages in general. (Also, a philosophical foundation renders the 'Reasons' more fundamental.)

Fifthly, an examination of the rules and operations of

23. Botha, *op. cit.*, p. 196.

24. Patañjali, *Mahābhāsya*, Part I, explanator, Yudhiṣṭhira Mīmāṁsaka, 1979, pp. 14-18.

25. There are several kinds of rules: definitional and operational, general and restricting, general and exception, local and meta. These rules enjoin general operations of identification, deletion (*lopa*) modification (*vikāra*) and addition (*āgama*) involving phonetic, phonological, morphophonemic, syntactic and semantico-syntactic and such other linguistic phenomena.

Aṣṭādhyāyī shows the existence of all types of grammatical explanation.

Sixthly, and finally, the ultimate explanation in Sanskrit grammar is "interscientific." Two levels of reality — the linguistic and the universal are correlated and the linguistic reality is sought to be explained in terms of the conceptual structuring of the visible reality. There are these expanding circles or waves of explanation: facts of language are explained by rules; rules are explained by the nature of the structure of human language; this linguistic structure is explained by the reality (existence) that is to be communicated by the human vocal apparatus; and this "reality" is explained in terms of the monist or non-dualist world-view.

We conclude by invoking the high priests of modern linguistics. Bever has formulated the general philosophical assumptions to determine the status of linguistic judgements. Among them he mentions — "Specific factual phenomena are often the result of interactions among different (physical, psychological, biological) systems.[26] Further, both McCawley (1974) and George Lakoff (1974a, 1974b) have argued the empiricist point of view. Lakoff says:

> I take linguistics to be the study of natural languages in all of its manifestations. . . . It includes not just syntax-semantics . . . as well the study of the relationship betwen language and thought. . . .[27]

This is a very close approximation of the Indian position.

The foundation of Indian grammar thus is different from the comprehensive general philosophical position called Rationalism by generative grammarians.

---

26. Cf. Botha, *op. cit.*, p. 234.

27. See, *ibid.*, p. 235.

8

Pāṇini Vyākaraṇa
Questions of Theory and Order

BOTH *Nirukta* and *Vyākaraṇa* developed in response to the twin, imperative, communicative needs of interpreting and maintaining the culturally and intellectually important Śruti-texts and produced a rich, three-fold analysis of language: as a physical object, as a cognitive structure, and as a cultural object. This grammatical tradition of Sanskrit does not explicitly formulate the question of universals or universal grammar, evolving as it did in a necessarily hermetic intellectual and linguistic context, and was concerned with communication and transfer of meaning, essentially within one geographically continuous speech community — its concern with speakers of non-native languages (*mleccha prayoga*) being purely secondary. But the rigorous analysis of one language, in this case Sanskrit, being one of the two methods of arriving at linguistic generalizations, creates a theory with the potential to apply to other languages as well — certainly to Indian languages, as witnessed in Tolkappiyar's Grammar of Tamil (third century AD) and Hemacandra's Grammar of Prakrit (eleventh century AD) and Nāgavarma's *Karnataka Bhāṣā Bhūṣaṇa* (twelfth century) and Keśirāja's *Śabdamaṇidarpaṇa* (thirteenth century) for Kannaḍa. The very phylogenetic relationships between Sanskrit and Modern Indo-Āryan languages (see Chart 1) predict affinities of structure and, therefore, the pertinence of applying Sanskrit analysis to Indian languages. While the relationship with modern Indo-Āryan languages is evident and obvious, even the Draviḍian languages, have very close lexical and structural affinity with this analysis:

1. the same *Vājasaneyi Varṇamālā* system accounts for the sound systems of these languages;
2. there is a high degree of derived/adapted vocabulary; and
3. the same morphophonemic, derivational and inflectional conceptual systems are applicable to them, as shown for Tamil, for example, by Sri P.S. Subrahmanya Sastri in his "History of Grammatical Theories in Tamil and Their Relation to the Grammatical Literature in Sanskrit" (*The Journal of Oriental Research*, Madras, 1934).

As a theory of grammar founded in an inflectional language, it accounts for the grammaticality (well-formedness) of utterances and word-formation in terms of processes of derivational and inflectional affixation, and agreement (*anvaya*). Assuming an internally complex norm in the utterances, this grammar accounts for the internal structure of *pada*, the inflected word or compound, of phrase, and of the clause. The utterance-set it accounts for, is the language size set and also the various dialects that are included in the set — the Vedic textual usage (VI.3.109), the geographic variety (VI.3.32), the historically earlier usage (VI.1.123, 127, 130), language of the *chandas* (VI.1.126), of the contemporary texts in the uninterrupted flow of speech (VI.4.141) and the speech of *śiṣṭas*. Its object language is both *vaidika* and *laukika* (*Mahābhāṣya*, 1.1) both the language of the texts and the contemporary, current speech (*bhāṣā*). But then Vyākaraṇa is not a Smṛti of the manifest use of language, of *vaikharī* alone but of the system that informs all the three *bheda* (forms) of *vāṇī* (*paṣyanti, madhyamā, vaikharī*), of *param padam* (*Vākyapadīya,*

Chart 1: Modern Indian Language and Sanskrit

0. *Bhāṣā*: *Prākṛta* and *Saṁskṛta* are tell tale words

Prākṛta

Saṁskṛta word/terms: every language at any given time has Prakṛta and Saṁskṛta forms. (The English in T.S. Eliot's *The Waste Land* or in Dickens' novels is *Saṁskṛta* not *Prākṛta* English).

1. Sanskrit Spoken by people: Lg. of speech; changeable (First Prākṛt)

Sanskrit in the Vedas: compositional language; fixed.

↓ over a period of time, changed and became

2. Pāli (palli = village/market (2nd Prākṛt)

Texts of Prākṛt : Jaina Literature

Texts of Pāli: Buddhist Literature

↓ Over a period of time changed and became

3. Apabhraṁśas (spoken language of the people, such as cowherds)

↓

4. Modern Indian Languages (approx. eleventh century onwards)

This chart is based on, Sri Kishoridas Vajpeyi's theory in his Hindi *Śabdānuśāsana*

1.143), of structure of language which is articulated in different forms, uses and varieties.

How does one rate it as a theory ? First of all, it has evident empirical adequacy — it describes the known range of Sanskrit usage, as we have already indicated above, albeit the description does posit elements that do not actually exist — affixes like *tavya* and *tva* do not actually occur in the speech of the Sanskrit speakers but are abstract elements posited to denote given types of operations and other elements such as *gh* that denote, in turn, a class of abstract elements (*tarap*, and *tamap*, the comparative superlative affixes). Again we know that Pāṇini's grammatical description shared some of the categories of different philosophical systems such as Vaiśeṣika and Nyāya on the one hand and, on the other influenced the development of poetics as well, as is attested by Bhāmaha's tribute to the grammarians in his *Kāvyālaṁkāra Sūtra Vṛtti*. Further, as is borne out in *Vākyapadīya*, this theory of description fitted in very well with the non-structural dimensions of language, such as cognition and communication. Also, it has been suggested (see, K. Kapoor, 1991) that Pāṇini's grammar with its basic postulates of "affixation," "base," "affix," "deletion," "modification," "augment," inter- and intra-category relations, and "hierarchy of structuration," has functioned like "a primary modelling device" and has been employed/has the potential of being employed to other symbolic systems (dance and sculputre, for example) and non-symbolic social institutions. Finally, we know for certain that in its description of Sanskrit, mediated through a hierarchy of categories, this grammar anticipates (is an analogue of) the structure of Advaita thought.

We now move to the mode of grammatical description and questions of order. An outline of this analysis is presented in Chart 2. How is this information organized (or to be organized)? The *Aṣṭādhyāyī* topic order is presented in Chart 3, very broadly which states the relationship and order between different parts of analysis.

The grammar re-analyses the *śabda-rāśi*, the universe of words, into two — the base and affix. The class base, includes all the four lexical classes redefined into two grammatical types — the nominal and the verb-root. The form of *pratyaya*, affix is the grammarian's construct for inflectional and derivational categories. The over-all model of grammar may be described

Chart II: Analysis of Sanskrit

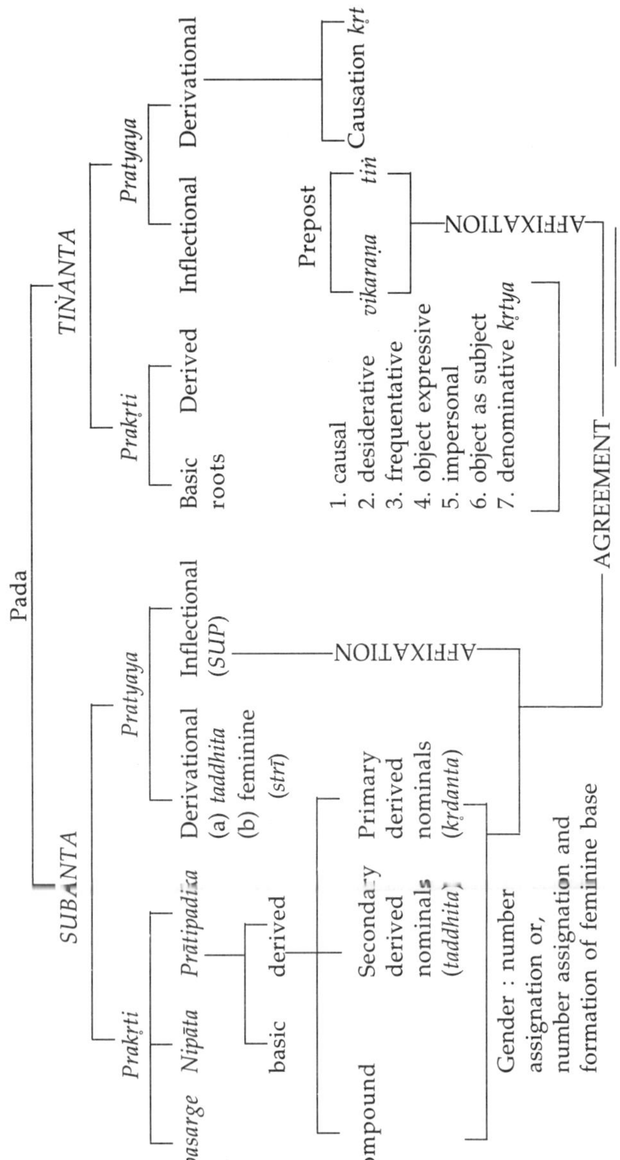

Chart 3: Stored Information

In Chapters 1 and 2 (*Saṁjñās*) *Terms* or *Categories*

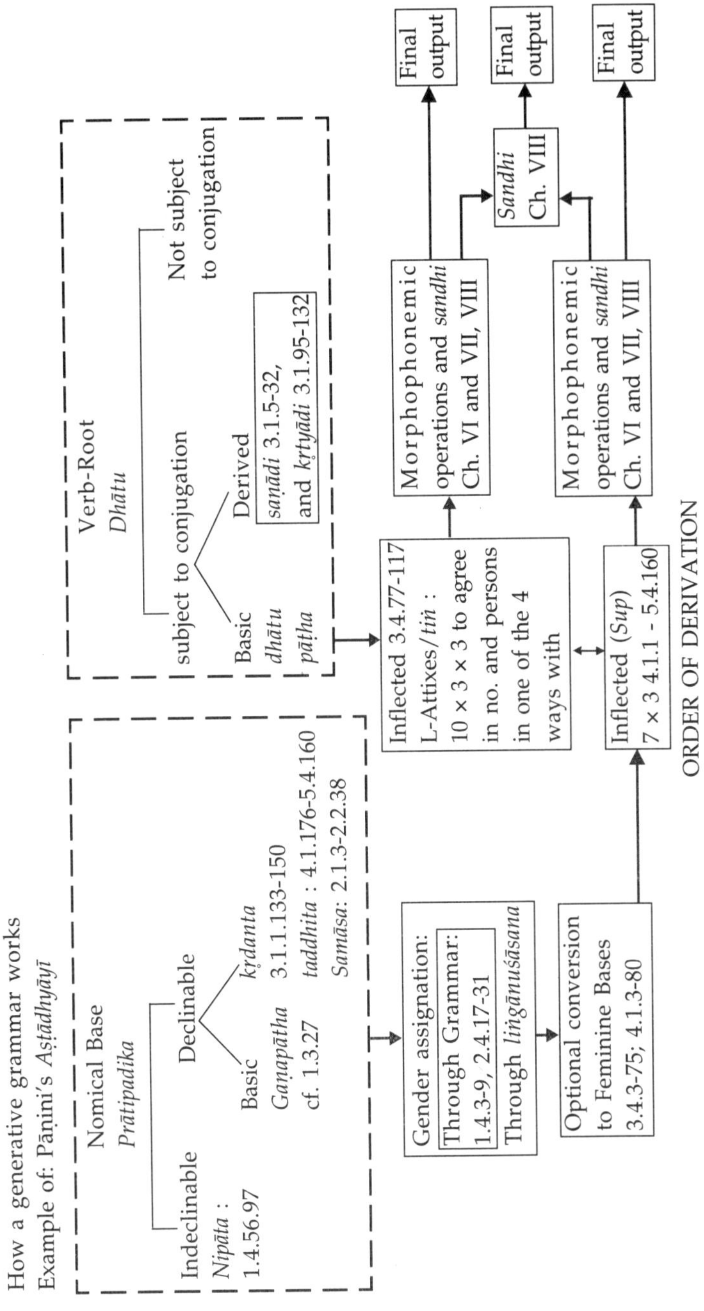

as the Affixation Model — all the operations in this grammar are based on the process of affixation in which the affixes, while themselves undergoing change may also bring about a change in the base. Five major grammatical operations are involved — (1) classification of bases; (2) derivation/formation of bases, (3) conversion of bases; (4) inflection of bases and (5) achieving agreement of two major bases.

Three kinds of equipment is available — (i) lexicons (outside the grammar, *sūtra-pāṭha*); (ii) lists (inside the grammar), and (iii) rules or *sūtra* (which are functionally divisible into seven kinds : *adhikāra* (3.1.1), *saṁjñā* (VI.1.2.45), *paribhāṣā* (1.1.3), *vidhi* (3.2.123), *niṣedha* (1.3.4), *niyama* (3.4.111), *atideṣa* (1.1.55)).

	Lexicons		Lists	
	Referred to in Grammar	Not referred to in Grammar	Nominal Related	Verb-Root Related
1.	*Varṇasamuccaya*		*Sup*	*Tiṅ*
2.	*Gaṇapāṭha*	*Liṅgānuśāsana*	*Taddhita*	*Kṛtkṛtya*
3.	*Dhātupāṭha*		*Strī* (Fem.)	*San-Vikaraṇa*

The following lists and lexicons are available:

All this information is made accessible through rules. The tradition refers to all the grammatical operations by the term — *pada-vidhi* or *pada-siddhi*, i.e., the grammar shows, demonstrates the structure, the building up, of fully inflected forms. Seven kinds of affixation/derivation is to be noted:

A. From the nominal-base (*prātipadika*)

1. *Subanta* (*puruṣaḥ*)
2. *Strī-pratyaya* (*kumārī*)
3. *Taddhita* (*mathurāḥ*)

B. From the verb-root (*dhātu*)

4. *Tiṅanta (paṭhati)*
5. *Kṛdanta (kāraka, paṭhitva)*
6. *Kṛtya-pratyaya (paṭhitavyam)*

C. From two nominal bases:

7. *Samāsa (devagṛham)*

There is an obvious internal order among these operations — first there is derivation of bases and then, inflection; again the inflection of nominal bases must precede, in sequence, the inflection of verbal bases. The *prakaraṇa-krama* (order and treatment of topics) of *Aṣṭādhyāyī* becomes intelligible in the light of these dependencies.

A scholarly editor, Sri Nand Kishore, in his recent reprinting of the Vṛndāvana edition of *Aṣṭādhyāyī* (1990) has identified 258 *prakaraṇa* (major topics treated). These can be reduced, in a hierarchy, to the major themes or subject-matter of the eight chapters which can be organized into four functional divisions :

Division 1

- Classification and enumeration of base and categories (*Saṁjñā*): Chs. 1 and 2.

Division 2

- *Prakṛti-Pratyaya* analysis (enumeration) and derivation of bases: Chs. 3 to 5
- Verbal bases and derivation of primary nominals: Ch. 3
- Derivation of secondary nominals: Ch. 4-5

Division 3

- Synthesis of *Prakṛti-Pratyaya*: Chs. 6 & 7 and 8.1
- Changes affecting the bases (*prakṛti*): Ch. 6
- Changes affecting the affixes (*Pratyaya*): Ch. 7

- Reduplication: Ch. 8.1

Division 4

- *Sandhi* (euphonic combinations and resultant changes): 8.2 to 8.4

Chart 3 shows the relationship order among different kinds of *siddhi*.

The actual statements (*sūtra*, rules), too, are ordered; though the motivation of ordering is not always apparent. This is an area where considerable understanding, study and research is still needed. Pāṇini's order has been defended by the commentary tradition and the traditional scholars say it seems to break down when rules related to the same topic, which are placed at two or three different places, are brought together, as for example, in *Siddhānta-Kaumudī*. The logic of treatment is not always apparent, though one vaguely apprehends it everywhere — thus, in the first two chapters that give definitions, the internal order of the defined terms needs to be worked out. Again, these definitional rules are so sequenced that to define some category, certain terms are used which are themselves defined later in the chapter (viz., 1.1.28 and 2.2.26). At the same time, one clearly discerns an order in the operational rules. The operational rules are generally sequenced in the order:

general - particular
exception
restriction

Exception rules themselves are of four kinds — (i) blocking (1.2.15-16); (ii) extension (1.2.17, 20); (iii) optional operation (1.2.43); (iv) highly local restriction (1.2.65) (see also 3.2.1-2 followed by 3.2.3-8).

Another kind of order that is generally maintained is — "Regular Formations" followed by "Irregular Formations," viz., VI.4.174, 175 which come at the end of a body of rules laying down systematic operations. Still another discernible order is *Laukika-Vaidika*. And when affixation is enjoined with respect to a set of affixes, for example, the *parasmaipada* affixes, the general order of *upadeśa* is —

1. when used
2. when not used
3. when optionally used.

Part of the difficulty of interpretation comes from a complexly organized and highly abbreviated mode of statement. For example, the terms seem to be employed as indices to link the related rule. For example, the use of the term *ṛtva* in 3.4.18. How do we know it is indeclinable? We scan. Rule 1.1.40 has the same term *ṛtva*. At that point, the term *avyaya*, indeclinable, comes as *anuvṛtti* from rule 1.1.37 and operates up to 1.1.41. Again the rule of economy of statement is always obeyed. The set with fewer items is listed; and the larger class is implied as "the rest" and not enumerated (see, for example, *ātmanepada* and *parasmaipada* contexts in 1.3.12-93). Again the metalinguistic uses of cases, the omission of the verb, and the subjecting of the language of statement to the enjoined rules of grammar and phonology require that the rules be read by reconstructing them completely.

For each rule, one has to : (i) do *sandhi*-reanalysis and establish separate *pada*, (ii) identify the *adhikāra sūtra*; (iii) identify *anuvṛtti*; (iv) insert *adhikāra, anuvṛtti padas*; (v) identify the *vibhaktis* of all the *padas*, (vi) arrange the padas in a particular *vibhakti*-order; (vii) insert the verb "be," (viii) interpret the rule by using the metalinguistic meaning of cases. For example:

1. ād *guṇa* (6.1.84).
2. + *adhikāra* + *anuvṛtti* + "be" = ād 5.1, *guṇa* 1.1, *saṁhitāyām* 7.1, *aci* 7.1, *pūrva-parayoḥ* 6.2, *ekaḥ* 1.1, (*bhāvati*).

3. The *padas* arranged in 5-7-6-1 *vibhakti* order: āt 5.1 *aci* 7.1 *saṁhitāyāṁ* 7.1 *pūrvaparayo* 6.2 *ekaḥ* 1.1 *guṇaḥ* 1.1 *bhāvati* = If *a* is followed by *ac* in a continuous text, in place of the preceding-succeeding, one *guṇa* vowel becomes.

The Pāṇinian grammar assumes the speaker's *vivakṣā*, intention/desire to say/communicate something. The grammatical operations begin only after that. Say, the intended/expressed utterance is "Rāma reads" (*rāmāḥ paṭhati*). The grammar will decide whether this is well-formed or not by deriving the utterance through the rules. But which rules apply and in what order depends on the knowledge of the operator of the grammar. In other words, the rules which apply have to be selected and they have to be applied in one order. Many scholars have argued that the sequential order of the *Aṣṭādhyāyī* should be made the basis of the order of application except in the case of rules which apply more than once. The latter case suggests that something, such as the presence of some item/"term" in the output of the application of a body of rules, "triggers" the application of rules that contain the said term. Any example derivation will show that this is often true in which case the "term" becomes the index for the application of rules. Such "intrinsic" order is indifferent to the "extrinsic" order of rules in *Aṣṭādhyāyī*. The following body of rules are necessary for the *siddhi* of *vācaḥ* (1.3; *cakārānta strī-liṅga bahuvacana prathamā*):

Stage 1 — 1.2.45
Stage 2 — 1.4.21-23, 54
Stage 3 — 4.1.1-2
Stage 4 — 3.1.1-2
Stage 5 — 1.4.100-103
Stage 6 — 2.3.47
(Stage 7)/(Stage 2)
Stage 8 — 1.3.7, 1.3.9

Stage 9 — 1.4.14, 8.2.66, 8.1.16
Stage 10 — 1.3.2, 1.3.9
Stage 11 — 1.4.109, 8.3.15 (8.3.14)

When we actually work out this derivation we feel that there is some kind of reverse or anticipatory ordering at times (1.4.100-102 in respect of 4.1.1-2; 1.4.14 in respect of 1.4 and 2.3 and 4.1 rules). Secondly, the rules apply in clusters (or "stages") in terms of "product" or "operations." Sometimes the order is free — 3.1.1-2 in respect of 4.1.1 and 4.1.2. May be we have to make a distinction between the priority of some knowledge in respect of some other and the use we make of that knowledge any time or any number of times. Thus, 1.3.7-1.3.8 is prior, though we apply it only after the relevant item subject to those operations actually makes its appearance. So also the knowledge contained in rule 1.4.109. Also, in the application of rule, we have to make reference to the lexicons as well — thus, the very first rule (1.2.45) above assigns the item to a class by the process of exclusion from two lists.

Let us briefly consider the derivation of *paṭhati* (in *rāmaḥ paṭhati*).

Rāmaḥ would be generated, first, as a third person, singular nominative.

Then, the generation of *paṭhati* begins separately, as a separate operation up to a point.

We first note/instruct that this form, *paṭhati* is a formation from the verb-root *paṭh.*

Rule 1.3.1 (*bhūvādayo dhātavaḥ*) ascribes *paṭh* to the *dhātupāṭha*, and thereby terms it, designates it as a *dhātu* = *paṭh* (+ *dhātu* 1.3.1).

This requires scanning of the *dhātupāṭha* — by 1/222. We elicit the form *paṭham;* as such, it is an *upadeśa*, an item listed, articulated by Pāṇini. So = *paṭha* (+ *dhātu* + *upadeśa*).

Rule 1.3.2 (*upadeśe ac anunāsika it*) applies to *upadeśa*. By this, *-am* is designated as an *anunāsika-ac* it

= *paṭha* (+ *dhātu* + *upadeśa* + *anunāsika-ac IT*)

The rule is general — it says: "the final *anunāsika-ac* in an *upadeśa* is designated as *IT* — is functionally *IT*." To judge where it applies to *-a* of *paṭha*, we need to recall (i) what is *ac*, and (ii) what is *anunāsika*? Then a matching operation follows, leading to the recognition of the final *-a* as *aC anunāsika* and its consequent designation as "*IT*." So the rule, for its implementation requires fore-knowledge which may or may not be available in the *Aṣṭādhyāyī*. Thus, what is *upadeśa*? (to judge whether *paṭha* is *upadeśa* or not). The text does not define it. Evidently, the *Vaiyākaraṇa*, the grammarian KNOWS that any item recited in the text or enumerated in one of the lists is an *upadeśa*. This knowledge is based in the discipline's conventional knowledge and is external to the text.

The sigla *ac* stands for a class, whose members are enumerated from the *Śiva-Sūtras* by applying rules available within the text — the rule 1.1.71, a rule placed earlier in the text which is recalled now and this rule 1.3.2, itself (interestingly) and the subsequently placed rule 1.3.9, which applies obligatorily to the output of rule 1.3.2. The enumerated members are matched with the object item, which is noted to be a variant of one of the members. Somewhat like *upadeśa*, we know *aC* is a technical term that has a given meaning in the treatise/discipline.

Is this "variant" *anunāsika*? It is, for the *anunāsika* is defined by a rule placed earlier — 1.1.8.

So, this rule requires three kinds of knowledge —

1. of something external to the text
2. of rules placed earlier/later and their application
3. of a definition (*saṁjñā*) placed earlier in the text.

The effect of the complexly stated rule is to designate the *-am* of *paṭha* as *IT*.

The next rule to apply, 1.3.9 (*tasya lopaḥ*) has to apply to the product of application of 1.3.2. But what is *lopa*? What does it mean?

Rule 1.1.60 (*adarśanam lopaḥ*) is recalled and applied. Here too, if 1.3.9 applies, 1.1.60 has to apply. So *paṭham* = *paṭh*.

PAṬH = PAṬH + LAṬ

Under 3.1.91 (*dhātvaḥ*) *adhikāra sūtra* (Topic Rule), rule 3.2.123 (*vartamāne laṭ*) provides that to express the present tense, we choose *laṭ*-affix. Why *vartamāna*, the present? This is not dictated by grammar — it depends on the speaker, his *vivakṣā*.

By 3.1.1 (*pratyaya*) and 3.1.2 (*paraśca*), the affix *laṭ* is positioned after *paṭh* = *paṭh* + *laṭ*.

At this point, the speaker's choice is made in another matter — the *laṭ*-affix is to agree with *kartā* or *karma*? Rule 3.4.69 (*laḥ karmaṇi ca bhave cakarmakebhayaḥ*) with *anuvṛtti* of *kartṛ* from 3.4.67, it is provided that the *lakāra*s in verb-roots (the topic rule 3.1.91 is effective still) may agree with *kartā* or *karma* for transitive verbs. *Paṭh* is transitive and allows *kartā-laṭ*, which is chosen here with (*ramaḥ paṭhati* in mind).

PAṬH + LAṬ = PAṬH + L

By 1.3.3 (*halantyam*) *ṭ* is IT which is made invisible by 1.3.9 leaving *lam*. By 1.3.2 *am* is *IT* and is made invisible by 1.3.9 leaving *l*: *laṭ* = *l*.

PAṬH + L = PAṬH + TIP

By 3.4.77 (*tasya*) in place of *l*, come 18 affixal elements by Rule 3.4.78 (*tiptasjhi*) which by 3.1.1 and 3.1.2 are also placed after *paṭh*.

paṭh +	*tip*	x	x	*ta*	x	x
	x	x	x	x	x	x
	x	x	*mas*	x	x	*mahi(ng)*

By 1.4.98 (*laḥ parasmaipadam*), the affixes that replace *l* are designated as *parasmaipada* except that by 1.4.99 (*tananavātmanepadam*), the second set of nine affixes (*taṅ-pratyāhāra*) are designated *ātmanepada*.

By 1.3.78 (*śeṣat kartari parasmaipadam*), the *dhātus* that have not been said to take *ātmanepada*, for *kartā*, for them *parasmaipada* affixes are chosen. So *paṭh* takes *parasmaipada*-affix. But which one of the 3 × 3 affixes?

By 1.4.100 (*tiṅastrini trini prathamā madhyamottamaḥ*), each horizontal set of 3 each is designated, *prathamā*, *madhyamā*, *uttamā*. By 1.4.108 *śeṣe prathamaḥ*) excluding the person spoken to (*yuṣmad*) and the speaker (*asmad*), the rest, as in the case of *rāma* in *rāma paṭhati* take *prathamā-puruṣa*. So, the first triad *tip-tas-jhi* becomes available. By 1.4.101 (*tanyekavacanadvivacana-bahuva-cananyekṣaḥ*) horizontally the affixes in the triad are sequentially designated as singular, dual and plural respectively. *Tip* is singular. Thus, by 1.4.22 (*dvayekayord-vivacanaikavacane*), in the case of the desire to express one entity, as here, the singular affix is chosen.

So, we get *tip* = *paṭh* + *tip*.

PAṬH + TIP = PAṬH + ŚAP + TIP

By 3.4.113 (*tinsit sarvadhātukam*) under the domain of the Topic Rules 3.1.1. 3.1.2 and 3.1.91 *tip* affix is designated as *sarvadhātuka*.

Under 3.1.67 (*sarvadhātuka*), in the case of a *sarvadhātu* affix, by 3.1.68 (*kartr̥-śap*) if it is *kartā*-expressive, *śap* is placed between the verb-root and the affix, yielding = *paṭh* + *śap* + *tip*.

PAṬH + ŚAP + TIP = PAṬH + A + TI

By the application of 1.3.3 twice, the two *-p* of *śap* and *tip* are designated as *IT*. By 1.3.8 (*lasakvataddhite*), *s* of *śap* is also designated as *IT*. Then the rules 1.3.9/1.1.60 apply thrice.

They could apply thrice in two ways -

1. 1.3.9 followed by 1.1.60
2. 1.3.9 followed by 1.1.60
3. 1.3.9 followed by 1.1.60

or

1.	1.3.9	4.	1.1.60
2.	1.3.9	5.	1.1.60
3.	1.3.9	6.	1.1.60

The first one appears psychologically more plausible order. We are left with —

PAṬH + A + TI = PAṬHATI

Some general observations on the above derivation are in order. Designation or categorization is the key operation. Once an element is designated as *X* or *Z* by a designating rule, i.e., assigned to a class, it immediately triggers one of the two operations — (i) it initiates scanning of some list or lexicon, or (ii) it makes the designated item the object of the body of rules pertaining to the class to which the item has been assigned in which case pertinent operations enjoined by those rules are set in motion depending on the item meeting the requisite conditions.

Further, particular rules such as 1.3.2 require, for their interpretation and application (i) knowledge of concepts not available within the text (viz., *upadeśa*), (ii) recall of related rules (placed before and/or after the rule under reference), (iii) recall of concepts defined prior to the particular rule, the knowledge of rules available elsewhere to and/or explicate a class referred to by a technical term that is part of the vocabulary of the particular rule. Interestingly, the rule, in which this questioned term appears, may itself also be applied in the explication of the term.

Next, evidently a kind of relationship of dependency prevails among the rules. Thus, for example, if 1.3.2 applies, 1.3.9 must apply subsequently, and when 1.3.9 applies, 1.1.60 must apply. Such sets of rules as 1.3.2-1.3.9-1.1.60 constitute operational sets and could be very extended sets.

Again, it is quite clear that many rules apply more than once in a single derivation. Rules pertaining to sequencing/ positioning and *IT-saṁjñā* rules, including IT-deletion rule, apply more than once.

Finally, the question of *prakaraṇa-krama,* the sequencing of topics. Restricting oneself to the topics involved in this derivation, we notice the following order of treatment :

A. 1. *ātmanepada/parasmaipada*: meaning and conditions (1.3.12-93) of selection.

   2. *vacana* (1.4.21-22)

   3. *puruṣa* (1.4.105-108)

B. agreement or choice (3.4.69-72)

C. actual affixes (3.4.77-78)

A sets out the concepts that build up the system. B states conditions that govern the choice of particular forms, and C is the set of forms from which the choice is made. This is the order of statement which is to be distinguished from the order of application and the two do not necessarily correspond. A in particular seems to constitute *smṛti* in the treatise, which is often recalled in the course of derivation. But then the whole treatise is known as a *smṛti*-text which is held in the mind as a whole by its operator, the *vaiyākaraṇa*. Within that, there is a body of rules which constitute the background of knowledge in which the actual operations — enjoined by the operational rules — take place, and these operational rules are naturally sequenced after the conceptual or definitional rules. The derivational system, therefore, has a certain psychological reality.

At the conceptual level, the rules (or clusters of rules) operate in five phases — (i) identification of a unit (by matching, or by markers); (ii) naming or designating the unit; (iii) operations required by the designated term (affixation of x, y, z, etc.); (iv) modifications that follow (replacement, deletion, elision); (v) end product (and the cycle begins again).

As we proceed through the grammar in its sequential order, we store information that causes/controls *x* operations when *y* conditions are met. When we reach such a point, we pause and recall the information and carry out the operations. A very general break-down of the derivation of *vācaḥ* would look like:

FOR THE DERIVATION OF VĀCAḤ

Identification of nominal base, no. person, case	-Affixation : no., person, case = *SU*	Deletion of *IT* - "*u*" = a "*Sa*"	- So - replacement by "*ra*"	Deletion of *IT* - "*i*" = *ra*	Replacement by :
	↓	↓	↓	↓	
	Saṁjñā IT - Saṁjñā definition	called *x*	IT-definition	called *y*	

This is how the grammar organizes the description in the form of definitions-instructions-output. It is a gigantic intellectual construct that challenges the young Indian minds to extend it and adopt it to modern Indian languages.

9

Reconstituting Aṣṭādhyāyī Materials as Data Base

CURRENTLY five kinds of Computational Linguistic work is centered on *Aṣṭādhyāyī* : (1) analysis and description of Sanskrit structure; (2) developing learning/teaching systems within the Pāṇinian frame; (3) inferring from *Aṣṭādhyāyī* (as a proto-Grammar) universal features and properties of language and of knowledge representation to draw lessons both for language analysis and language representation; (4) computerizing and storing the text; (5) its study as a primary model of knowledge (semiotics).

The fourth area may be modified into — (4) study and storing of *Aṣṭādhyāyī* as a text/as a Śāstra. A full access to the text should be made possible by reconstituting/organizing it into a computer text system.

A tentative proposal is being made here for preparing an *Aṣṭādhyāyī* text as a computer aided/learning and instruction system in the Indian (and wider, if possible) context. This will be an expanded text stored and made available in several ways:

1. The need for such a text as a teaching/learning aid is self-evident — it will be used by a wide range of users — students and scholars of Indian languages, linguistics, semiotics and of Sanskrit language and grammar. It will be of particular use to Indian students belonging to different languages who are able to read only one particular script.

2. The text should be made flexible by appropriate staging to allow its use by an average learner and at the same time making advanced materials accessible to advanced learners and scholars.

3. The text may be made available in the first stage in 11 Indian languages in their respective scripts. It may also be prepared in English. These eleven Indian languages could be: Punjābī, Hindī, Assamese, Beṅgālī, Oriyā, Telugu, Tamil, Kannaḍa, Malayālam, Marāṭhī, Gujarātī.

4. No particular effort or special language will be required to transfer this text into the machine. The real problem is designing an appropriate structure for such a text. This involves an understanding of —

   (a) the way a reader studies or understands this grammar,

   (b) the difficulties he encounters or is likely to encounter,

   (c) the nature of the text,

   (d) the available materials in the tradition,

   (e) the method (*paddhati*) to be adopted, and

   (f) the traditional Śāstra-*paddhati*.

5. With reference to the six issues listed above, it may be suggested with reference to each of the six that —

   (a) The reader proceeds from knowledge about the text (history, general organization, content, method of reading rules, other relevant information) to the study of the text. This order may be adopted.

   (b) The major difficulty is — (a) the metalanguage and the (b) devices of brevity (*adhikāra*, *anuvr̥tti*, esp.), and (c) technical terminology (see *fig.* 2)

Object of knowledge in Pāṇini grammar

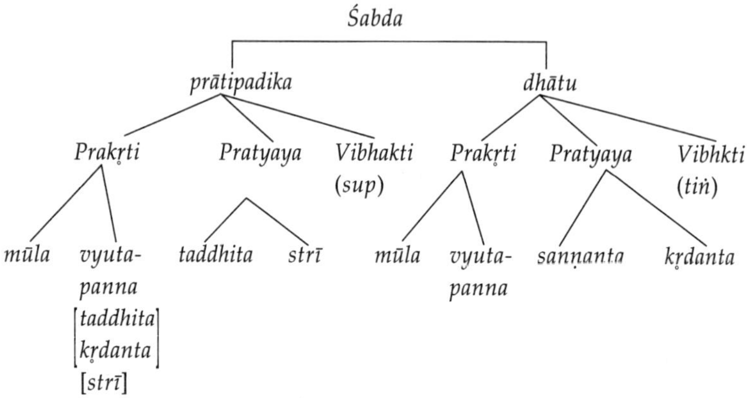

which may have to be handled separately and clearly besides *IT-saṁjñā* rules).

(c) Its features as an oral text have to be taken into account; absence of exposition/instructions for implementation, for example. These have to be supplied. And pitch marking for *adhikāra*.

(d) *Vārttika* and *Mahābhāṣya* to be treated as part of the text, and optionally incorporated after or along the pertinent rules.

6. (ia) The presentation of the *Aṣṭādhyāyī-sūtra*s will be in (ia) Devanāgarī Sanskrit, and (iib) correspondingly in the independent scripts of the eleven languages.

Classification of Pāṇini's Vocabulary

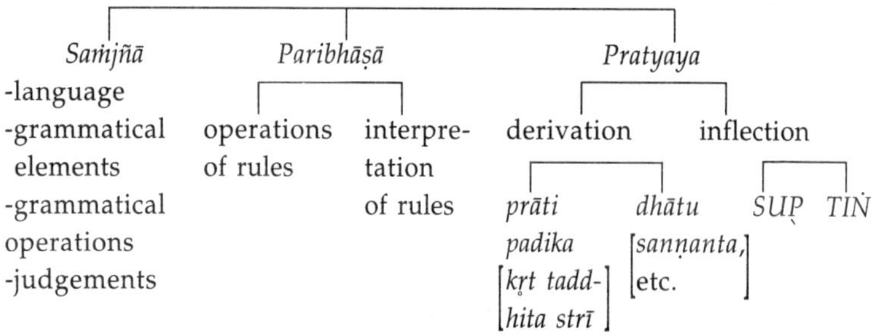

(b) The essential method would consist of: (i) explicit reconstitution of the *Aṣṭādhyāyī-sūtra*; (ii) *pada-artha*; (iii) *tattvārtha* through elucidation — based on *vārttika* and *Mahābhāṣya* wherever needed and available. This may be presented in two levels (a) simplified for average reader, and (b) scholarly for advanced students and scholars. Further — (iv) *sādhāraṇa-bhāṣā-ṭīkā*; (v) *uddharaṇa, pratyuddharaṇa*; (vi) *vākya-prayoga*, (vii) reference to further portions of texts, if necessary.

For an actual example of wonderful pedagogical method, please refer to Sri Dayananda's *bhāṣya* on 1.1.9. (*Aṣṭādhyāyī bhāṣya*, pp. 20-26). This may provide helpful principles for proper exegesis.

(c) Further exposition of the rule would be through *vārttika-bhāṣya* and then a summing up. *Vārttika-bhāṣya* portions will also have the same choice of scripts as the *Aṣṭādhyāyī-sūtras*, and will be exegetized in the same way.

7. The traditional method of interpretation (*Śāstra-paddhati*) employs the following devices:

A. (i) *Śruti*
(ii) *Darśana/Smṛti*
(iii) *Itihāsa-Purāṇa*

B. (i) *Sārvabhauma-siddhānta*
(ii) *Saṅgati (prasaṅga)*
(iii) *Paribhāṣā-nyāya*
(iv) *Laukika-nyāya*
(v) *Vyākaraṇa*
(vi) *Nirvacana*
(vii) *Śabda-śakti*

The methods from B(i) to B(vii), in particular, are relevant for grammatical exegesis and have been employed in the tradition. *Sārvabhauma-Siddhānta* of Pāṇinian grammar will go into the introduction (based perhaps on Mādhavācārya's 13th Chapter) to the text. *Saṅgati* requires relating the philosophical foundation of grammar to Vaiśeṣika-Sāṁkhya thought, and other systems. It also requires establishing continuity or discontinuity among different parts of the text. Attention may be drawn to different *nyāya*s (*paribhāṣā* and *laukika*) when they are involved in the determination of meaning.

8. The Reconstruction would consist, for each *sūtra*, of (see chart)

   (i) analysis into *pada*

   (ii) restoring a*dhikāra-anuvṛtti* elements

   (iii) identifying the *samāsa* (compound) (if required)

   (iv) marking the *vibhakti*s of each *pada*

   (v) re-ordering the *pada* in —

   5-7-6-1

   5-7-1

   6-1-7

   case-orders as required.

   (vi) translating the *sūtra* into English, Hindī, Panjābī, Gujarātī, Marāṭhī, Kannaḍa, Malayālam, Tamil, Telugu, Oriyā, Beṅgālī and Assamese.

9. Support texts will be separately included: *Dhātu-pāṭha*, *Gaṇapāṭha*, *Pratyāhārasūtra*s, *Liṅgānuśāsana* and *Uṇādisūtra*s. Also *IT-Saṁjñā* rules, and Pāṇinīya *Śikṣā* as well (in original Sanskrit, and in script choices), with provision for recall and display along with the pertinent *sūtra*.

10. Indices (for reference)

    1. Alphabetical list of *sūtra*s
    2. Thematic grouping of *sūtra*s (65 themes according to Siddhānta-Kaumudī).
    3. *Pratyāhāra* list and *Pratyāhāra*-generation programme
    4. *IT-Saṁjñā*s dictionary
    5. Dictionary of affixes
    6. Dictionary of technical terms
    7. Typical declension paradigms (83 paradigms)
    8. Typical conjugation paradigms (23 paradigms)
    9. Typical Examples of each of the seven kinds of *siddhi*
    10. *Sandhi*-enumeration and corresponding rules
    11. Concordance of *pada* in *Aṣṭādhyāyī*.
    12. Enumeration of representative, frequent nouns and verbs for declension and conjugation paradigms.
    13. Supplementary texts : The following four texts -
        (i) Kātantra
        (ii) Cāndra
        (iii) Hemaśabdānuśāsana
        (iv) Jainendra text

    Further, the power of this system will increase enormously if explanatory comments in major *Ṭīka*s on different *Aṣṭādhyāyī* rules are made available as reference system for each rule that has been commented upon.

The material looks like this (see the diagram on page 126).

Prolegomenon to Aṣṭādhyāyī text for Computer Aided Study

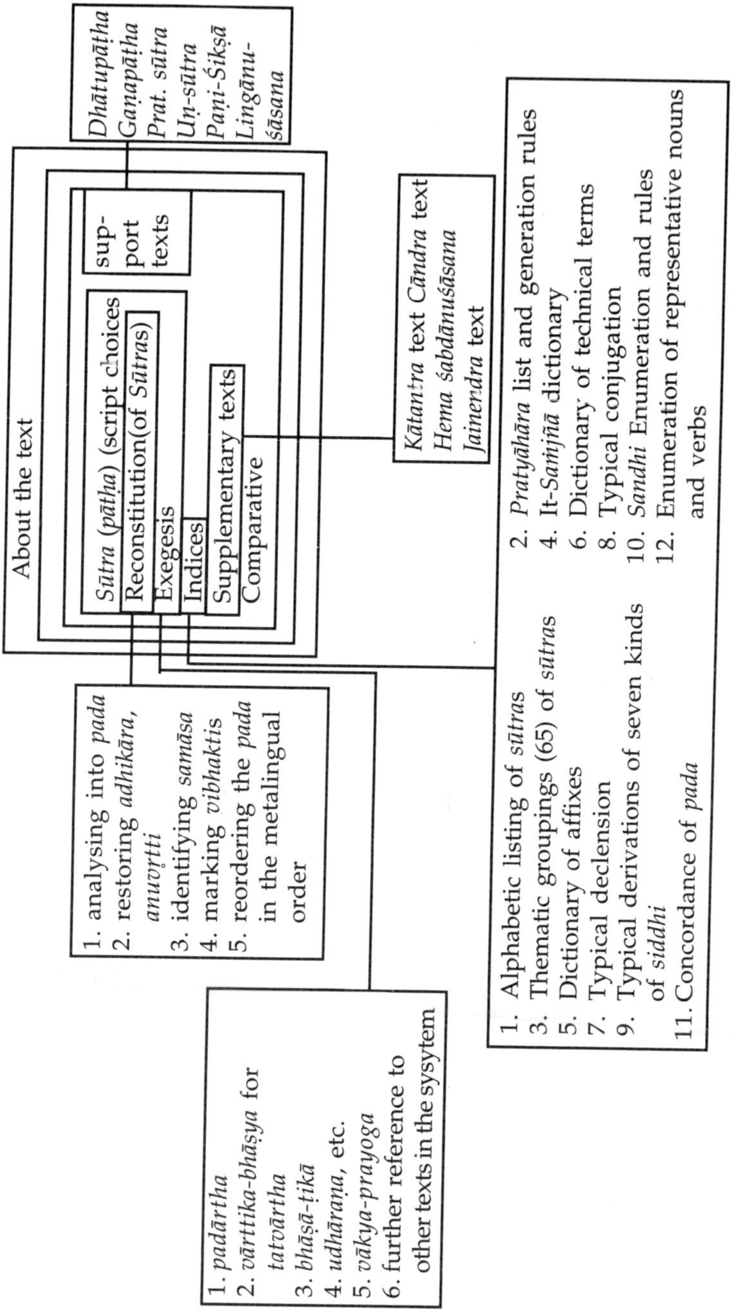

10

Who are/were the Padavādins?
A Note

B.K. Matilal : "Just as the Padavādins (those who regard the word as the primary indivisible unit) consider word constituents, such as roots and suffixes, to be mere fictitious abstractions from words, so also the Vākyavādins (those who regard the sentence as the indivisible unit) consider words to be imaginary abstractions from the sentence.

— *Vākyapadīya*, III.1.1.

"What holds at the syntactic level also holds at the semantic level. Thus in the beginning of the fourth chapter of the third book (*kāṇḍa*), Bhartṛhari rephrases his theory as follows:

For the grammarians (i.e., for the *Vākyavādins*), the word-meanings are fictitious constructions from the sentence-meanings (which are to be regarded as wholes), just as for the Padavādins (the Mīmāṁsakas?) the meanings of roots and suffixes are mere abstractions from the indivisible word-meanings. The sentence-meaning, according to Bhartṛhari, is an indivisible *saṁvit* — one whole cognitive content — from which different word-meanings — also called ontological categories — are abstracted for imaginative construction."

— *Logic, Language and Reality*, 1985, p. 379.

Observations

A look at the *Vākyapadīya* text shows that 3.1.1 does not mention Padavādins or Vākyavādins — it only talks of analysis of *vākya* into *pada* and of *pada* into *prakṛti* and *pratyaya*. Nor does it talk of "imaginary abstractions." Nor do 3.4.1-2 talk of "fictitious constructions." (It is III.3.86-88 which postulate Reality as "beyond all differentiation" and the communicative necessity of words, *padas*.) Again no reference is made to Padavādins or Vākyavādins.

The suggested possible identification of *padavādins* with Mīmāṁsakas is perhaps not valid — in fact Mīmāṁsakas are Vākyavādins, as they started a detailed study of sentences. The terms *padavādins* and *vākyavādins*, in Bhartṛhari's context, must refer to sub-schools of grammarians.

In *Vākyapadīya* (II.41-65), particularly *kārikās* 56-59, first the view that sentence is a, *samghaṭa*, a collection of words (in a given sequence) is presented (*kārikās* 41-53), i.e., sentence meaning is the aggregate of meanings of constituting words; then in *kārikās* 54 onwards, the *vākya-sphoṭa* view is presented, and here the controversy about the reality or prior existence of words, or otherwise, is referred to — the *khaṇḍapakṣa* that upholds the *saṁhitā*, a continuous text/utterance, as the secondary entity contingent on prior and independently existing *padas*, and the *akhaṇḍapakṣa* that upholds the reality of the *saṁhitā* and the derived status of *padas*. The *kārikā* 58 in *padaprakṛtiḥ saṁhitā* (*Ṛk-Prātiśākhya* 2.1) refers to this. Prof. Iyer in his comment (p. 28) says -

> The *vṛtti* also refers to the statement of the *Ṛk-Prātiśākhya* and says that some held the *padapāṭha* of the Vedas to be eternal and the connected text *saṁhitāpāṭha* to be of human origin while others held just the opposite view.

The next *kārikā* (59) reports Patañjali's view that the *saṁhitā* is the "natural" (or prior, or essential, or independent) text and the *padapāṭha* is man-made, i.e., contingent. Prof. Iyer explains:

> The very fact that Patañjali says that the authors of the *padapāṭha* have to follow the rules in doing their work shows that, according to him, that text is man-made. His words are : *na lakṣaṇena padakārā anuvartyāḥ; padakārair nāma lakṣaṇam anuvartyam* = "Rules are not to be framed according to the text made by the authors of the *padapāṭha;* it is the latter who have to follow the rules."

In other words, Patañjali is in favour of the *akhaṇḍapakṣa.* See *M. Bha.* II, p. 85.1.4.5,

Puṇyarāja is quoted in the comment on *kārikā* 41 to the effect that "the *saṁghaṭa* view is held by the *abhihitānvayavādins.*" In *kārikās* 44-45, the contrary view of *anvitābhidhāna* is cited. Thus the *khaṇḍapakṣa-akhaṇḍapakṣa* controversy extends into the theory of meaning as well, and this is recorded by Prof. K. Kunjunni Raja in his *Indian Theories of Meaning* (Adyar: 1963, pp. 203-13).

There is evidence for the existence of a strong *pāṭha*-tradition from the earliest times, in the Śrutis and *Brāhmaṇas* and in Yāska's *Nirukta.* (Please see Introduction to *Nirukta,* 1-4, 7 chapters Pt. Shri Shivnarayana Shastri, editor/translator/commentator, Delhi, 1972, pp. 22-40.) (Sanskrit text with Hindi translation, introduction, commentary). As Prof. G.B. Palsule's work shows there were Pre-Pāṇinīan *dhātupāṭhas* (*The Sanskrit Dhātupāṭhas, A Critical Study,* Poona: University of Poona. 1961). We also know that the Saṁhitās were broken down into *pādas* which were then put together in different permutations — *jaṭāpāṭha, ghanapāṭha, kramapāṭha,* etc., as devices to maintain the texts unviolate.

It appears, therefore, that before Pāṇini, grammatical analysis based itself on *padas* — to account for *padas* was to account for language. The phoneticists held this view — witness the *Ṛk-Prātiśākhya* which uses 281 technical terms to sort out various facets of the construction of *saṁhitā-pāṭha* from *pāda-*

pāṭha. [see, Indira (1973), *Prātiśākhyon Mein prayukta Pāribhāṣika Śabdon kā Alocanātmaka Adhyayana*, Banaras: Bharatiya Vidya Publications, (Hindi)]. Subsequently, it would appear, the insight developed that *vākya*, an utterance, is the proper unit of language analysis (*akhaṇḍapakṣa*). The ritualists (those who believed in the efficacy of *mantra*s properly articulated), the metricians, and the musicians by virtue of their object of study could have been in possession of this insight before the grammarians.

Yāska in *Nirukta* (I.17) also notes that *pada*s are the Prākṛta units and he seems to be taking a position in the controversy. Durgācārya's commentary notes that the Prātiśākhya-grammars of specific schools, examined the Saṁhitās by examining the *pada*s. *Nirukta* and *Koṣa* traditions are built around *pada*s. In *Nirukta* (1.4), Yāska explains how padas are to be identified. In 1.2, he mentions Auḍumbarāyaṇa as an upholder of *akhaṇḍapakṣa*.

It is possible to reflect on the movement from the empirically more definite/concrete *pada* to relatively abstract *vākya* as part of the larger Indian intellectual movement from empiricism to transcendentalism (Cārvāka to Advaita), from pluralism to monism and from description to explanation (phonetics to philosophy of grammar in Bhartṛhari).

11

Concept of Pratibhā
In Grammar and Literary Theory

DISCUSSIONS in Western linguistics and literary theory refer to "Innate Ability" and "Genius" as the sources of creativity in language and literature. *Pratibhā* is a concept in an analogous inquiry into creativity in relation to comprehension and constitution of meaning. The concept has been given the first complete formulation in Bhaṛthari's *Vākyapadīya*: *Kāṇḍa* II. We propose here to reconstitute the concept of *pratibhā* as articulated by Bhartṛhari and then its adaptation and use by the literary theorists, particularly by Rājaśekhara, a ninth-century poetician-poet-dramatist, who partly redefines the concept to explain the sources of the literary creative process.

Bhartṛhari posits *pratibhā* as the ability to comprehend sentential meaning. The meaning of a sentence is more than the aggregate meaning of the constituting words (lexis) and the grammatical *particles* and inflections and this meaning, though unique to the experiencer is accepted as authoritative. How does this meaning arise? Or, in other words, how does a person understand this meaning of a sentence. It is clear in Bhartṛhari that *pratibhā* is a cognitive faculty of comprehending/constituting meaning in a communicative act. What is the content or nature and source of this power? To answer this question we have to examine Bhartṛhari's conception of sentential meaning, or the relationship between the meaning of a sentence and the meaning of words, and of the nature of meaning.

Giving the analogy of a painting which is understood/ explained in terms of its compositional colours, Bhartṛhari says that sentence-meaning is a unified cognition that is explained through individual words: ". . . one sentence, entirely self-sufficient and complete, is explained through individual words which require one another" (*Vākyapadīya*, II.9).* Sri Subramania Iyer explains Bhartṛhari's intention in his comment on *kārikā* 7: "The sentence is the *sphoṭa*, either external or internal. It is external when it is clearly uttered. Till then, it is internal. . . . It has two aspects: the sound aspect and the meaning aspect which are identified with one another (see *kārikā*s 30, 31). It is essentially in the nature of knowledge or consciousness because it illuminates an object. Because of articulation, it assumes the form of sound. Though indivisible, it appears to have divisions just as our complex cognition, though one, appears to have inner differentiation because of the objects in it. The picture is one but we seem to see different colours within it. This is what happens with the sentence and the sentence-meaning. Both are indivisible. . . ." (1977: 4) The sentence meaning is a single wholistic entity but it is perceived as having components and divisions. "This indivisible (sentence) is understood as having the capacity for sequence. . . . Hence its meaning, though devoid of all division (*bheda*) is perceived as having division" (II.27). Even when a sentence is looked upon as a collection of words and is differently articulated by different persons, when "sentence-universal" (*sphoṭa*) is postulated, "it is the one sentence which expresses an inalienable meaning (*ekasyaiyarthatā*)" (II.56). "According to the upholders of the (indivisible) sentence, unity precedes division. . . ." (II.57).

---

* All references in parentheses are to the *Vākyapadīya of Bhartṛhari*, K.A. Subramania Iyer, 1977.

What relationship holds between this unified, indivisible sentence meaning and the meanings of its constituting words? Bhārtṛhari asserts meaning is in *ukti,* statement. It is not denied that sentence-meaning is related to individual words both severally and collectively — "The one sentence-meaning is the common expressed meaning and it is related to each individual word. It is related to the collection and to each unit in the collection. . . ." (II.394) Again — ". . . the sentence and the sentence-meaning, indivisible and devoid of the sequence of the words, shine from words having a sequence" (II.415). So the sentence meaning is related to word-meanings. But how? Is the sentence meaning an aggregate of the separate meanings of words? Or is it that plus interconnections that arise when words are put together in one arrangement? Do the words in a sentence have the same meaning as in isolation? Or does the word in a sentence have its meaning determined uniquely by the sentence/utterance meaning? Bhartṛhari's position is clear — lexical denotation is itself a matter of speaker's *vivakṣā* and *tātparya* and is highly unstable (II.135). Also, in isolation a word has no referential content — it is only when a word is used in an utterance that it acquires a reference which then assigns a particular meaning to the word. In this sense though words have an "expressed sense," they acquire meaning only from the wholistic sentential meaning — ". . . The individual words though expressive of their own meaning, have no meaning at all if they are isolated from the sentence" (II.420). "The meaning in the nature of an interconnection is grasped when the things are connected together. . ." (II.421). The "meaning" of a word is determined by the "object" to which it refers — "Even knowledge (or consciousness) does not appear in its true (pure) state. It is formless but appears as coloured by the object" (II.422). To the extent that the meaning of a single word is expressed as "connected with existence or non-existence, it is the sentence which is used (for communication)" (II.423). So the word-meanings are inferred from the total meaning of an utterance — "From the sentence-meaning which is of the nature of cognition, a word meaning having or not having something external corresponding to it, but appearing to have it, is analysed. The analysis consists in abstracting the powers capable of conveying the word meanings" (II.440). What is inferred from sentence meaning are the "connections" between words and objects/concepts as conceived by the speaker. That the words acquire particular meanings through their use in a sentence is supported by the fact that sentential meaning is always more than (or different from) the aggregate of word-meaning and we have to understand where this additional meaning rests. Proof is offered to show that the meanings or individual words in a sentence are unreal. Often the sentence meaning is quite different from the aggregate of expressed (*abhidhārtha*) word meanings. The difference may be due to unintended associations or it may be intended. Thus, the sentence "one has to go look at the sun," though it expresses something about the sun, really says that time should be ascertained (II.310). So the words "look," "sun," "go" acquire a "meaning" other than their expressed meaning. Again, example is given of how in usage, particular may stand for the general — "when a boy is told: 'save the butter from the crows,' he does not refrain from protecting it from dogs, etc. . . . " (II.312). Again, concomitant meanings are invariably suggested even though no specific words are used to denote them — when a teacher tells his students "This should be done," he means "you do it," or "I expect you to do it". "(When an order for feeding somebody is given) the washing of dishes and plates, though not actually mentioned, is also understood" (II.313). Also — "An enlightened hearer knows that praise and blame, meant to promote action and abstention from action respectively, are really unreal." (II.319) Thus what meaning an individual word has in a sentence is determined by the sentence meaning as a whole. In fact, it is often dificult to clearly describe the meaning that a word has in a sentence; thus all the words together evoke the sentence meaning. "The meaning of all individual words has its source or basis in the meaning of the sentence." (II.325)

This is true though not so obviously, of simple, straightforward sentences as well, on account of the essentially subjective nature of denotation (*abhidhārtha*) of words. What words denote depends on what holistic meaning is desired (*vivakṣā*) and intended (*tātparya*) by the speaker. Meaning ". . . is something mental view but resting on an external object and is looked upon as the meaning of the word when it is externalised" (II.132). But the external object/forms denoted by words depend on subjective conceptions. Thus, a word like "pot" conveys, for both the speaker and the hearer, as part of its meaning a shape which is the residual trace of some actual experience of the corresponding external object and this "shape" differs from one person to another. Words like "god," "heaven," "righteousness" that refer to no actually visible entities, mean different things to different people (see II.133). Therefore "the meaning of words, intended by the speaker to be one thing, is understood by different listeners differently, according to their own background" (II.135). Not only that "the same person sees the same thing differently at different times" (II.136), and "To one and the same word are attributed many meanings by one and the same persons or by many persons, according to undefined circumstances" (II.137). We all perceive things with our senses and the mind and use words according to what figures in our mind. Thus — "The sky is perceived as a surface and the firefly as fire. There is no surface in the sky nor is the firefly fire" (II.140). In this way, great care and reasoning is needed to determine the nature of "even an object apprehended by direct perception" (II.141). And when the object is evoked by a word, the greater indeterminacy demands all the more care and reasoning to determine which meaning is primary, or even what primary meaning is actually intended. A number of factors enable us to decide this:

> The meanings of words are determined according to the sentence, situation, meaning, propriety, place and time and not according to mere external form.
>
> Connection, separation, association, opposition, meaning, context, indication, the presence of another word.
>
> Suitability, propriety, place, time, gender and accent, etc., these are the causes of our determining the meaning of a word.
>
> —II. 314-16

Once the individual words have been understood separately, "an understanding takes place which they call the meaning of the sentence brought about by the meanings of individual words" (II.143). This sentential meaning is a cognitive experience and cannot be described or explained to others — "It is experienced by everyone within himself and even the subject (of the sentence) is not able to render an account of it to himself" (II.144). It is something indefinable (*avicārita*). This indefinable understanding, as far as its status is concerned, is authoritative (II.147), and indispensable (II.146). How does this unique understanding of sentence-meaning arise? What ability is the source of this understanding? This understanding is intuitive, a cognitive experience that is experienced within and cannot be described to others (II.144). Bhartṛhari terms this transcendental meaning of a sentence as *pratibhā* (II.143), the cognition of a wholistic meaning immanent in the expressed meanings of words but not overtly marked by any element in the sentence. *Pratibhā* with Bhartṛhari is this cognition, or, to look at it from another point of view, the power that gives birth to this activity of understanding, the power to grasp signification/verbal symbolism.

Bhartṛhari characterizes this ability, first, as a product of *abhyāsa,* a practise, a predisposition, in opposition to *āgama* (II. 117), which suggests that *pratibhā* is an inborn faculty. It is a heightened awareness. Sri Subramania Iyer cites (1977: 62) Puṇyarāja's comparison of this intuition to the conscience of good people — their instinctive ability to discriminate right and wrong. Bhartṛhari suggests that these cognitions are born in those that possess them "without any special effort" (II. 148). This makes *pratibhā* a species — specific ability, one that explains and motivates the characteristic human activities. It is not taught — it comes naturally "just as some substances acquire the power to intoxicate and the like by mere maturity. . . ." (II.148)

Here then there is a seeming problem. Bhartṛhari goes on then to say that this intuition is the result of Āgama (tradition) accompanied by *bhāvanā.* How does this cohere with his statement in *kārikā*s II.117-18 that the *abhyāsa* is not a product of Āgama. A careful reading shows that Bhartṛhari is throughout making a distinction between the ability or faculty of moving from words to the transcendental meaning and the product of this ability, the understanding itself. This understanding is recognised as *pratibhā* because it is the result of *pratibhā* — the faculty becomes manifest only in the result or activity. This *pratibhā* is an active, creative principle; the *pratibhā* as sentence-meaning is the result of this faculty. This understanding, this knowledge is of six kinds (II.152) — (i) inborn or a natural endowment (a natural tendency such as to awake after sleep); (ii) born of learning in a tradition of scholarship (thus, for example, those who study poetry develop an intuition about poetic meaning); (iii) resulting from experience (as for example, the intuition of tea tasters); (iv) product of special training of the mind, through methods of *yoga,* for example; which enables *yogī*s to gain knowledge of the non-present; (v) or unknown origin, as for example some persons who are known to compute faster than the computing machines; (vi) developed through the intervention of specially qualified people, i.e., developed through learning. Sañjaya in *Mahābhārata*, for example, was blessed by Sri Kṛṣṇadvaipāyana with the power to observe far away and widely dispersed scenes.

This is the linguists' *pratibhā*, an inborn cognitive faculty that enables one to uniquely experience and understand the objects of knowledge.*

It is interesting to compare the concept of *pratibhā* in literary theory. The comparison is in order, as the literary theorists, particularly Rājaśekhara who makes a systematic statement on the poets' *pratibhā* in his *Kāvya Mīmāṁsā* (ninth century AD), has evidently adapted Bhartṛhari's construct of *pratibhā* to explain, literary creativity.*

In the hands of Rājaśekhara, and other theorists, the general cognitive faculty of Bhartṛhari becomes a specific poetic faculty. In the effort to understand literary creativity, the theorists posit *pratibhā* (natural endowment) in opposition to *śāstra* (learning), and *abhyāsa* (practice). In the process, Bhartṛhari's system of *pratibhā* is rearranged, the concept is restricted in its scope, and in Rājaśekhara, it is extended in the direction of the critical faculty as well.

It is pertinent to recall that in the tradition of literary thought, in the effort to define a literary composer's equipment and abilities, there is all through a stress on the Kavi's knowledge of Śāstra. Mīmāṁsā says that the knowledge of *śastras* is justified only in a Kavi — otherwise such knowledge is "like the pauper's charitableness . . ." (1.3). All learning

---

* Intuition in Chomsky an linguistics is also an ability to comprehend new utterances. The poeticians, even otherwise acknowledge their indebtness to the grammarians (see Bhāmaha, VI).

must subserve poetry — such is the Kavi's responsibility (V.4). Rājaśekhara said much later — Kāvya and Śāstra have a relationship of mutual instrumentality — Kāvya serves the ends of Śāstra and Śāstra serves Kāvya. The compositions of a *kavi* who is learned in *śāstras* are thoughtful, lucid and excellent . . ." (*Kāvya Mīmāṁsā*, Chapter 5). So, says Bhāmaha, "The desire to compose *kāvya* should be entertained (only) after learning grammar and the meanings of words and after having served the masters therein and after having studied other (*kāvyas*) works" (I.10). But knowledge of Śāstra alone is not enough. Poetry is an intelligent activity no doubt, but it is more than that — "poetry, however, is to him (*kavi*) who has a natural capacity and that too not invariably" (I.5).

What is this "natural capacity" in a *kavi* ? In other words what are the sources of creativity? Learning or knowledge, *vyutpatti*, is one factor. It is asserted that wide and varied knowledge (*bahujñātā* and *vividhajñāna*) is necessary for a *kavi* because in his compositions, "he has to describe any number of subjects" (*Kāvya Mīmāṁsā*, Ch. V). Two other factors have been suggested — *pratibhā* (innate ability) and *abhyāsa* (practice). And the fourth factor that has been mentioned in the tradition is *samādhi*, heightened consciousness attained through deep mental concentration, as a necesary cognitive creative process for literary creation.

Theorists differ about which factor is primary or indispensable — *pratibhā or vyutpatti* — and about the role, these factors have in the process of composition. Three positions are taken —

1. *Pratibhā* alone is the source of composition,
2. *Vyutpatti* and *abhyāsa* alone can be the source of poetry,
3. *Pratibhā, vyutpatti* and *abhyāsa,* all the three are *kāvya-kāraṇa* — the sources of composition.

Pratibhā is an innate faculty — a predisposition. This faculty may be a *saṁskāra* from previous birth (a genetic endowment) or is produced here and now by the example and guidance of others or by a study of Śāstras and Kāvyas. *(Kāvya Mīmāṁsā,* Ch. 4). Functionally, this ability is of two kinds — (i) *kārayitrī,* and (ii) *bhāvayitrī,* the ability to feel and understand experience, of composition (*bhāvayitrī*) and the ability to put/represent one's felt experience in apt words and devices of communicaion (*kārayitrī*).

Vāmana and Pt. Jagannātha believe that *pratibhā* alone is the source of compostions. Vāmana says in *pratibhā,* lies the very seed of poetry (*Kāvyālaṁkāra* I.3.16). Pt. Jagannātha says only *pratibhā* (and not *śakti, nipuṇatā* and *abhyāsa* as believed by earlier scholars such as Mammaṭa) is the cause of poetry (*Rasagaṅgādhara,* 1st *ānanam*), and *pratibhā,* for Pandit Jagannatha consists in the prompt recall/appearance of appropriate words and meanings for building up a composition. Also *pratibhā* is a kind of *buddhi,* mind, that keeps getting new insights and ideas — (*Rasagaṅgādhara,* 1st *ānanam*). Once you believe that *pratibhā* alone is the source of poetry, you are arguing that poets/writers/composers are born — not trained.

On the other hand, Daṇḍin seems to allow that some kind of poetry may be the product of *vyutpatti* and *abhyāsa,* though for excellent poetry, *pratibhā* is indispensable :

> An inborn genius, learning quite free from defects and no slight application,these constitute the one cause of the excellence in poetry.
>
> Even though there be not that extraordinary genius which depends upon the (specific) nature of the earlier latent impressions, yet speech, cultivated with study and effort, certainly grants her own rare favour.
>
> — *Kāvyādarśa,* I.103, 104

But the most widely agreed position is that all the three factors — *pratibhā, vyutpatti* and *abhyāsa* — together constitute the source of poetry:

> poetic genius, knowledge born of a study of the world, of sciences and of poems, and the practice of the teachings of those versed in writing poetry — these three together constitute the source of poetry.
>
> — Mammaṭa, *Kāvyaprakāśa*, I.3

Rājaśekhara, on the other hand, has a very complex theory of sources of creativity. He posits *ukti* as yet another entity, apart from *pratibhā, vyutpatti, samādhi* and *abhyāsa.* We notice that Rājaśekhara proposes as independent power *pratibhā,* and *vyutpatti, samādhi* and *abhyāsa* as dependent powers. In Bhartṛhari, *vyutpatti, abhyāsa,* and *samādhi* are sub-types of *pratibhā*. This redefines *pratibhā* narrowly as just the innate power. His conception is something like this. In literary creation, *samādhi* is the supreme instrument — *samādhi* is intense concentration/focussing of the mind (*ekāgratā*). When the *citta* (faculty of cognition) is in *samādhi,* it actually sees meanings (with the mind's eye?). This, says Rājaśekhara is the view of Śyāmadeva, an earlier thinker. On the other hand, we are told that Maṅgala, another theorist, asserts that *abhyāsa,* practice is the chief source of literary creation.

Rājaśekhara harmonizes these views — *samādhi* is the internal/mental effort, while *abhyāsa* is the external/physical effort. Together, they generate *śakti*, the power of literary creation. This *śakti* in turn triggers *pratibhā* and *vyutpatti*. *Pratibhā* is, as we have already recorded, of two kinds — (i) *kārayitrī*, the faculty of the poet to create, and (ii) *bhāvayitrī*, the ability to appreciate and enjoy literary compositions. *Kārayitrī pratibhā* is then of three kinds — (i) *sahaja* (genetic), (ii) *āhārya* (produced by knowledge of Śāstras and Kāvyas), and (iii) *aupadeśikī* (acquired by training). Rājaśekhara's theory looks like this:

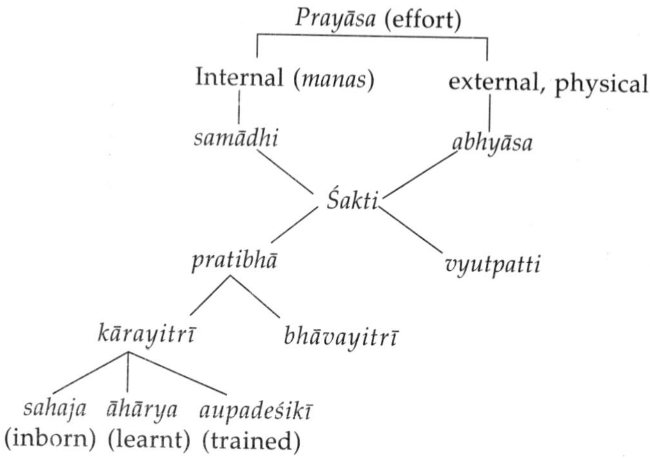

This is to be read from bottom to top.

This analysis enables Rājaśekhara to classify poets according to excellence. The finest *kavi, sārasvat,* has the inborn *saṁskāras*, and his compositions can be heard on the lips of ordinary people round the world.

Pratibhā is therefore a trans-disciplinary explanatory principle that seeks to account for not only the human faculty but also that of animals and birds.

12

Aṣṭādhyāyī
Computer Applications and Possibilities

GREAT deal of interest has been taken all these days, and there is considerable activity, in the use of computers in relation to natural language settings — language description, language analysis, language teaching, building language texts, including dictionaries. Much more than the earlier technological aids — the tape and cassette recorder, the audio-visual instruments, the language laboratory — the computer is seen as a powerful device with a more wide-ranging versatility and is expected to retain a more abiding interest on account of its two specific abilities — the ability to store, scan and analyse data at high speeds and its ability to interact with the user.

The computer, as far as languages are concerned, is at present, essentially, a tool for description, teaching and research in languages. Its two basic capacities are for storage and search for both of which the computer has to be prepared/ programmed. Developmental research has developed sophisticated programmes to enable the computer to store vast bodies of information in accessible formats, and to search that information to answer questions which may involve a number of operations such as classifying, sorting, relating, inferencing, generalizing, rejecting, accepting, summarizing, transferring, storing and recalling, etc. How to enable the computer to perform all such tasks is the subject-matter of artificial intelligence. The more the number of tasks a computer can perform, and the more quickly, the more intelligent it is supposed to be; but, it is important to remember that the computer has to be endowed with intelligence and that the computer cannot increase or sharpen its intelligence on its own. It can do only what it has been trained/programmed to do. It is important to have this very clear conception of the dependency of the machine on man. It can replicate but not create. The computer cannot do what the human beings cannot do and it can do what it has been taught to do though much faster. It performs prescribed operations on the stored data and supplies the results of these operations. It lacks Judgement — the ability to interpret. These two constitute genuine computer limitations.

The abilities and limitations define its relationship to language study :

It can —

(i) store texts;
(ii) permute texts;
(iii) sort and classify texts;
(iv) recognize visible patterns;
(v) identify patterned elements or behaviour;
(vi) allow repeated recall;
(vii) allow simultaneous recall, from different places, of all related data or information;
(viii) allow temporary/permanent storage; and
(ix) evaluate new data (accept/reject).

All these abilities are intimately involved in language learning and teaching and description.

It cannot —

(i) decide the order of description or learning;
(ii) determine the level of difficulty or complexity;

(iii) innovate.

(iv) judge actual learning/teaching needs.

Since visibility is an important condition of its functioning, the computer can do morphological analysis very well, syntactic analysis reasonably well, and semantic analysis/ interpretation with great difficulty. It cannot determine the meaning of texts, particularly creative texts — it cannot interpret.

In view of these possibilities, a whole new interactive discipline has developed over the years — Computational Linguistics (also called Natural Language Processing), which seeks to build computer models of natural language production, comprehension, acquisition in order to build intelligent computer systems, such as:

(i) machine translation

(ii) natural language interfaces

(iii) man-machine interfaces in general

(iv) speech understanding system

(v) text analysis and understanding systems

(vi) computer aided instruction systems

(vii) systems that read and understand printed or hand-written text

(viii) speech-synthesis.

This discipline leans on Computer Sciences and Systems, Linguistics, Psycho-linguistics, Physics etc.

Computational Linguists worldwide are taking great interest in Sanskrit language, texts and particularly in Sanskrit grammar.

First a look at the kind of research that is being done — in the VIIIth World Sanskrit Conference (Vienna, 1990), seven kinds of research was reported:

(i) Analysis and description of Sanskrit Structure, especially phonology and morphology (at the University of Helsinki, Finland and at Institute Kern, Leiden).

(ii) Textual Research (for example, the Berlin *Mahābhārata* research project under Prof. W. Morgenroth).

(iii) Compiling Lexicons and Dictionaries and computerizing classical dictionaries (proposed by Dr. P. Apte of Pune).

(iv) Computerizing and storing MSS (reported by Dr. S. Narayan, I.G. National Centre for Arts, Delhi).

(v) Preparing data banks as research tools (for example, the medical texts by R.E. Emmerick, University of Hamburg).

(vi) Inferring from *Aṣṭādhyāyī* universal features and properties for (a) language learning, understanding and production, and (b) cognitive methodology for language usage and knowledge representation (C-DAC, Pune proposal of Drs. Bhatkar and Bhavasar, and of E. Schredl, Aidurgen, Germany).

(vii) Research in developing learning/teaching systems within the Pāṇinian framework (at I.I.T. Kanpur, for example, Professors V. Chaitanya and Rajeev Sangal and Prof. G.V. Singh at J.N.U.).

In at least three of the above areas (1, 6, 7) the research is *Aṣṭādhyāyī*-centred. In this context, we may identify three questions about the interaction between Sanskrit grammar and the computer:

(i) What can be done with Sanskrit grammar on the computer?

(ii) What Sanskrit grammar can do for the computer systems?

(iii) What the computer technology and systems can do for Sanskrit grammar? ("Expert System").

The answers to these questions explain why the computational linguists and also the Artificial Intelligence Experts are so interested in *Aṣṭādhyāyī*.

For processing natural languages, the computational linguists —

(i) need to work with an adequate grammatical theory which should enable them to develop a successful computational grammar. *Aṣṭādhyāyī* exemplifies a rich theory of grammar.

(ii) are privileged if they have access to an actually worked out grammar (devloping one is a difficult task), *Aṣṭādhyāyī* is the only one, perhaps.

(iii) need a particular kind of grammar, a formalism, algorithmic/explicit, rule-bound, and exhaustive. *Aṣṭādhyāyī* comes very close to meeting these conditons — metalanguage, method, parts and organization, rule types and rules, operations enjoined, system of derivation, etc.

(iv) need access to an abstract analysis of what human beings knew about language/reality and to a statement of that knowledge. *Aṣṭādhyāyī* is a possible candidate for "a primary modelling device" for its universal interdisciplinary categories.

Aṣṭādhyāyī can be approached in several ways — one can approach it severally as —

(i) a Sanskritist

(ii) a Linguist

(iii) a language teacher

(iv) a computational scientist/linguist

So that one can (a) make *Aṣṭādhyāyī* itself the object of study, (b) learn/teach Sanskrit by using *Aṣṭādhyāyī*, (c) analyse and describe Sanskrit through *Aṣṭādhyāyī*, and very importantly, (d) use *Aṣṭādhyāyī* as a Core-Grammar/Proto-grammar for learning/teaching/describing Indian languages and for inter-translating between languages.

How it is done in Computational Linguistics?

NLP has several phases from Input to Output. The stages and format between and of the Output can vary depending on the Task one choses, but the Input is the analysis (separating a text into units and assigning the units to classes and categories so that a meaning can be constituted) of language which proceeds from sounds/characters to meaning in the following order —

Stage 1. Sounds or characters

Stage 2. Lexical Phase:

(a) Morphological analyser.

(b) Syntactic analyser.

(c) Non-linguistic analyser (punctuation and structural information such as paragraph breaks, stanzas, lines in poetry).

(d) Discourse/Textual Analyser (for markers such "as" "firstly," "the," "however," etc.).

Stage 3. Dictionary (for semantic information about the minimum units into which the text is separated).

All this language-analysis is fed into the system to be stored for processing. This is the static knowledge. Then programmes are developed to enable the computer to receive questions, search the databank for information, and represent the information recovered.

13

Norm and Variation

A Classical Indian Debate

INTELLECTUALLY and politically, our sub-continent has always seen a tension between centripetal and centrifugal forces. The age-old linguistic diversity, in itself both a reflex and an index of her ethnic and socio-cultural diversity, has motivated competing movements of transcendence and maintenance of this diversity, movements that have been built around theoretically interesting questions of (i) nature of linguistic change and variation, (ii) factors in such change and variation, (iii) need and arguments for a linguistic norm, (iv) grammar as the norm, and (v) the status of variants.

The central question of interest in linguistics has always been why people talk differently and what are the social consequences and causes of this. Change leads to diversity and diversity seen in relation to a norm is "variation." The emergence of a "standard," related to several non-linguistic factors-literary, social, cultural and political, is the pretext for the grammar's "norm," just as it is the societal "standard" that becomes the "norm" when a language is described by referring to its paradigm. The "norm" then is in existential tension with the "variants," and this opposition is the linguistic analogue of the centripetal and the centrifugal forces operating in a given society. India is traditionally seen as having three socio-cultural, linguistic units — *udīcya, prācya, dākṣiṇātya* and there is also evidence of linguistic diversity from the geographical variation noted in ninth century BC exegetist Yāska to stylistic variation noted in tenth century AD literary theorist Rājaśekhara.

Early in ninth century BC, Yāska, while enunciating his etymological/exegetical principles, draws attention to the processes of change leading to diversity in usage, a diversity that comes to mark historical, geographical and registeral "dialects." On account of the existence of an ancient body of texts — the world's oldest — held all through in high esteem as of great significance and consequently preserved intact, one of the important divergences in the Indian context is that between the language of the texts and the language of current use. Yāska cites two kinds of examples:

(i) the verb-root $\sqrt{\textit{dem}}$ is in current use both as a verb and as a nominal, while in the literary texts only its primary derived nominal formation is found employed, and conversely;

(ii) only the derived nominal form is in current use, while the verb-root has gone out of use, viz., *uṣā* and $\sqrt{\textit{uṣ}}$.

Yāska also cites instances of geographic variations:

(i) In the north west (Afghanistan) $\sqrt{\textit{śav}}$ is used only as a verb in the sense of *go*; while in the middle-land (northern Indian plains), *sev* is used as a noun in the sense of a "dead-body" (an extended meaning based on death as "a great journey").

(ii) *da* is used in eastern India in the general sense of "to cut," while in the north-west, it is used in the restricted sense of "cutting crops, harvesting."

Pāṇini's *Aṣṭādhyāyī* records extensive diversity. Pāṇini lived and worked in times of great intellectual and social ferment in the rising tide of the Nanda empire and records six different kinds of variation in a widespread area of usage spread from Assam to Afghanistan:

First, there is the usage restricted to the texts (*vaidikī*), c.f. 1.1.18. This includes a good deal of specific ritual enunciation, cf. 1.2.34 to 37, and ritual performances as well (8.2.88).

Second, there is the difference in usage between the *vaidika* language and *bhāṣā*, the contemporary language, cf. 3.2.107, 3.2.108, 4.1.62, 6.1.180, 6.1.181, 8.2.98.

Thirdly, there are specific instances of geographically distributed variation, cf. 2.4.20, 4.1.160, 6.3.10, 6.3.32.

Fourth, there is the "stylistic" variation, specific usages in uninterrupted flow of speech, cf. 6.3.115, 6.3.122.

Fifth, there is the "free variation," differences in usage not ordained by any rules of grammar but that occur in the usage of *śiṣṭa*s, the cultivated speakers.

Finally, and most importantly, the optionality in living usage, *loka-vyavahāra*, captured and described by rules that explicitly or by *anuvṛtti* include the term *vibhāṣa*, which even as a non-technical term conveys the meaning of "particular option in speech."

It is the sixth kind of variation that is of considerable interest. Pāṇini's optionality rules capture this variation in *Bhāṣā* and employ three different terms — for similar phenomena *bahulam* (viz., 6.4.75), *vibhāṣa* (6.3.106) and *anyatrasyām* (viz., 6.4.117). *Bahulam*, literally "variously, abundantly applicable," is used in rules that necessarily apply in some cases, optionally in a few others and not at all in still other cases (see 2.1.32; 2.3.62; 2.4.39; 3.1.34). *Anyatarāsyām*, literally "in another way," is also commonly employed to mean an optional or alternative form. It is generally used in the same sense as *vibhāṣa*. Of the three terms, only *vibhāṣa* is a "technical" term, in the sense that it covers both *bahulam* and *anyatarāsyām*, and hence is the only term of the three that Pāṇini lays down and defines in his *Saṁjñā-prakaraṇa,* the chapter that introduces technical terms. *Vibhāṣa* means optionally, alternatively, and is explained by Pāṇini as *na* "no, not," and *va* "or, else," "optionally, facultatively" in the rule 1.1.43 in consonance with its derivation from the root *bhāṣa* with *vi* (in different direction). Thus in some rules, *na* appears, in others *va* and in still others *vibhāṣa*. Patañjali in his discussion on *P,* 1.1.43 cites some *vibhāṣa* rules among which he has included some containing words *anyatarāsyām, va,* etc., instead of the word *vibhāṣa* thereby suggesting that all these optionality words are practically synonymous (see *Mahābhaṣya* on 1.1.44). As Prof. Devasthali pointed out: "In fact, he (Patañjali) has actually declared that Pāṇini used all these words to convey the idea of optionality, and that these words are nothing but the *prapañca* ('an explanation') of the same idea (namely a wide variey, perhaps not reducible to order)" (G.V. Devasthali 1981 p.18). Thus Prof. Kiparasky's opinion (vide his book *Pāṇini as a Variationist*) that the terms *va, vibhāṣa* and *anyatarāsyām* are not synonymous does not find acceptance with Indian scholars (see Yajanveer's review of Kiparasky's arguments in Yajanveer 1981: pp. 31-32).

The large number of optionality rules (339 *na, va, vibhāṣa* and *bahulam* — rules listed by Katre. See Katre 1968, pp. 326, 409, 507, 519) capture the whole range of phonological and morphological variation under different conditions in the language of Pāṇini's time (seventh century BC). This multiplicity of optionality terms and rules emanates from the need to describe and distinguish the "abundant variety of options . . . in the various *śākhas* of the Veda . . . and also the variety of usages in the various parts of the vast land. . ." (Devasthali 1981:18). Pāṇini's overwhelming regard for usage is evident so that even palpably indefensible constructions, current among the people of the north are approved (vide 3.4.19). He offers a number of illustrations where he holds that the *posodaradi* words as pronounced by the cultivated speakers, the *śiṣṭa*s, however, apparently wrong in formation, are to be accepted and the grammatically correct froms if used in their place would be unacceptable. The use of a term like *anyatarāsyām* in apposition with *bhāṣāyām* to show deviation from the *chanda*s language shows a clear awareness of the existence of dialectal varieties and could in fact refer to some of them.

Clearly Pāṇinian view of language is "polylectal" oriented as it is to incorporate more than one variety of the same language into a single grammar, a single internally multiple standard. This grammar does not concern itself with the gradation among options that are laid down or made available. There is no indication in this grammar whether any such gradation was assumed or intended by Pāṇini. As Prof. Devasthali has said, Kiparasky's hypothesis about the gradation of preferences among the optionality terms, has "no support in the background of grammatical science in India. Acceptance of such gradation would fall a prey to *śrutaparityāga* and *aśruta-kalpanā* which cannot be accepted" (1981, p. 19). That Pāṇini's goal was merely descriptive is also evident from the fact that, contrary to the Śāstra-*paddhati,* he does not describe the purpose, *prayojana,* of his grammatical science. This ties in with the fact that the Vyākaraṇa-*sampradāya* (the School of Grammarians) holds that the statement *atha śabdānuśāsanam* is Patañjali's statement (*vacana*) and not Pāṇini's.

Thus though Pāṇini's grammar, as a codification, a laying down of a single, albeit internally complex, standard historically correlates with the consolidation of a single central political authority (the Nanda-empire) and the predominance of a given intellectual belief system (monotheism) yet it is not intended to be a prescriptive norm. It is when the asymmetry developed, in course of time, between the language generated by the Grammar and the language of use — a fact that motivated Kātyāyana's exegesis — that the process of exclusion begins, and a systematization of the assumptions of grammar is undertaken by Patañjali in his *Mahābhāṣya*, and an important principle is then enunciated — what is not generated (*siddha*) by grammar is *apaśabda*. It is then that the valence or gradation begins, and the variation in usage is subordinated to the norm of grammar and grammar is raised to the status of Smṛti.

Patañjali's arguments of the norm are rich and interesting, though controversial. He addresses himself (*MB* 1.1.) directly to the question — what is the purpose of the science of grammar? And in answering the question, he sets up the options of (i) *sādhu-asādhu*, and (ii) *śabda-apaśabda*, and the guiding criterion of *dharma-niyama* in the context of the vast area and the immense variety of usage. He begins by mentioning six central purposes of grammar: three of them exegetical, two epistemological and one related to language-use. The science of grammar, says Patañjali, ought to be acquired for its own sake because a man of learning, or one whose profession is learning, must seek knowledge as an end in itself. Also, grammar is the best means of gaining knowledge of language being the most economical. Among exegetical goals, he includes: (i) understanding of the sacerdotal texts; (ii) correct reading or enunciation of these texts, and (iii) disambiguation or determination of the nature of specific use.

And, lastly, we must study this science so that the language we speak successfully communicates only the meaning we intend to communicate — use of inaccurate words would fail in communicating the intended meaning — and language after all is just communication of meanings. Later Bhartṛhari would claim that only *sādhu* words have *sphoṭa* (*Vākyapadīya* 1). It is in this frame that Patañjali sets up his heavily loaded construct of *apaśabda* — word that fails in the necessary purpose of communicating meaning. He employs the word *mleccha* as an alternative to *apaśabda*, thereby suggesting that the speech of certain communities (*anārya*) that are outside the main culture is to be classed as unacceptable because words that are mispronounced in their sound-substance, pitch or vocalicity (*duṣṭa-śabda* — due also sometimes to carelessness or incapacity) will necessarily fail to communicate the desired meaning. This is the hearer's point of view, and suggests a situation of contact or interaction between different communities of speakers. Hence Patañjali's injunction that the Brāhmaṇa, the man of learning, the speaker belonging to cultured community, must not do *apabhāṣaṇa*, must not allow his own speech to be influenced by the *anārya* modes. Just as there is benefit — fulfilment of purpose (*dharma*) in right knowledge, the knowledge of right words, there is disadvantage (*adharma)* in the knowledge of the *apaśabda*s or variant forms. In fact, says Patañjali, there is greater possibility of failing in communicative goals because *apaśabda*s are far more numerous than *śabda*s, i.e., there are innumerable dialectal variants. So what the grammar does is to lay down, generate *śabda*s such as *gau:*, cow, the right forms, and Patañjali, by implication excludes the dialectal variants such as *gavi,* very much as by specifying what is edible we exclude by implication everything else as inedible. The grammar could follow the other path and specify all the excluded variants but that would be uneconomical because the universe of variants is much larger than that of the norm each word such as *gau:*, cow, having several *apabhraṁśa*s — *gavi, goni, gota, gopatalika,* etc. So, the Grammar generates the right forms which, the grammar assumes, have given associated meanings. (It being not the function of grammar to assign meanings to words.) The "associated meanings" are known from *loka*, the use of language, wherein available words are used in given meanings. But then, even *apaśabda*s, the variant forms are similarly and widely employed effectively — to successfully denote associated meanings. And if both *śabdas* and *apaśabdas*, in actual use, equally effectively perform the function of communicating meaning, then in terms of which overriding principle does the grammar restrict itself to generating *sādhu śabdas* alone? Patañjali's answer is *dharma- niyama*, discipline, injunction of the desirable. He explains this by analogy — one can satisfy one's hunger with dog's flesh as well as with jungle fowl. So a *niyama* is laid down — the injunction of the desirable. "In the same way when it is possible to cognise meaning by both *śabda* and *apaśabda*, then the grammar enjoins "communicate meaning through *śabda*, not *apaśabda*" (*Mahābhāṣya* 1.1.). To be able to do this — to use *śabdas*, the right forms, one needs the knowledge of what is *apaśabda*, so as to be able, knowingly, to excise them from one's speech.

Thus does the normative, prescriptive argument built around the function of communicating meaning an argument that downgrades the variants by subordinating them ultimately to the norm of grammar that subordinates usage to grammar. The grammar becomes absolute. And this coincides in history with the rise of the Śuṅgas and the Kaṇvas, when the last great Mauryan emperor had been laid low and the central authority was beginning to be subjected to new centrifugal forces.

This linguistic absolutism came to be challenged during the Buddhist revival under the Kuṣāṇas and through the Gupta and the Harṣa periods when Hinduism and Buddhism both flourished side by side. This challenge is represented as the *Pūrva-Pakṣa* in *Adhikaraṇa* 9, of *Tantra-Vārttika* of Kumārila Bhaṭṭa (seventh century AD). The argument, a defence of the dialectal variety, becomes in the end a total argument against the science of grammar and its status as Vedāṅga. It is structured to show that "the science of grammar pointing out the correctness or incorrectness of words cannot be accepted to be more authoritative than ordinary usage; that is to say, the correctness or incorrectness of words can be ascertained only by ordinary usage;" specially as the variationists continue — "correctnesss and incorrectness are universally recognized as identical with expressiveness and inexpressiveness, respectively (i.e., the word that expresses some meaning is accepted as correct, and that which fails to as incorrect); and whether a certain word expresses a meaning or not can be ascertained only by ordinary usage" (*Tantra Vārttika* III.9.24 p. 260). Only indistinct sounds, single sounds or a conglomeration of sounds "without any reference to their signification" can be said to be *asādhu,* according to this point of view. "The vernacular words, *gavi,* and the like . . ." on the other hand "are found to be capable of denoting the cow, just as well as the Sanskrit word *go* in fact they are quicker . . . in their action . . . as they are used more commonly than the Sanskrit word. . . . Thus then, if the words *gavi,* etc., be declared to be *asādhu* on the ground of their inexpressiveness (which has been shown to be the only reason for incorrectness), then such declaration, being in direct opposition to a well-recognized fact of ordinary experience (that the words in question do actually denote the cow), cannot be accepted (as true)" (*Tantra-Vārttika* III.9.24, p. 263). Even if something like true denotation is assumed to be a property of only such and such words, and not of such and such words, which then can form the object of injunctions and prohibitions, it is not tenable, for no extensive enumeration of *sādhu* words is available or possible, and it is equally imposible to prohibit separately or singly the use of *asādhu* words whose number in any case is far greater than that of *sādhu* words.

Reacting to the claim that the science of grammar lays down *niyama* restriction, it is argued that the exercise is fallacious in that "it is only whose application is uncertain that is restricted in its application by the Smr̥ti; while the word has its application or use always certain and as such it can never be an object of restriction" (*TV* p. 264). Nor can it be forwarded that some transcendental result, viz., merit, flows from the use of *sādhu* (correct) words, for ". . . when the necessary explanation is found in the facts of ordinary experience, it is not right to have recourse to the transcendental . . . the sole purpose of these (declarations) is to persuade other people to such usage" (*TV* p. 265).

Further, it is argued that Grammar cannot have self-sufficient authority ". . . because in the case of all human assertions, what we conclude from such an assertion, is only that this person knows the matter thus, and not that such is the real state of things" (*TV* p. 266). Besides "there are endless contradictions among the assertions of the *Sūtra* (Pāṇini), the *Bhāṣya* (Patañjali), and the *Vārttika* (Kātyāyana); how then can one ascertain what the truth is?" (*TV* p. 266). Therefore, the synonymous terms *mlechcha* and *apaśabda* must be applied only to foreign language and not to variants such as *gavi* spoken in the Āryāvarta. Attention is then though drawn to usages that are at variance with what is challenged, variation is not tolerated. Buddhists spoke for usages that the science of grammar lays down as *apśabda* but which cannot be classed as *apśabda* or *mleccha*, and cite in support anomalies in the Vedas, usage of excellent writers such as Nārada and Jaimini, the language of Pāṇini's own rules, the forms employed by Kātyāyana and Patañjali himself (*TV* pp. 271-76).

The exegetical role of grammar is also rejected — Vedas are rather preserved, understood and analysed by the students and teachers with the help rather of the Prātiśākhyas which deal with "accent, conjunction of letters, hiatus, explanations, precedence and sequence, etc., all of which are directly connected with the study of the text of the Veda itself. And as such this fact distinctly points to the fact of the Prātiśākhyas, and not the grammar of Pāṇini, etc., being the real "subsidiary" of the Veda (Vedāṇga)" (*TV* p. 282).

Taking a material view of language, the variationists also reject the pedagogic role of grammar, for "the process employed is terribly complicated . . . extraordinary nomenclatures and postulates . . . only a few students . . . can rightly apply these processes to words other than those that are actually cited as examples" (*TV* p. 283).

And, the last major use of grammar mentioned in *Mahābhāṣya, asandeha* or *artha-nirdhāraṇa* determination of the meanings of the texts, is also rejected. First of all, many doubts regarding meanings "are set aside by the observation of the usage of experienced and learned people; and the few that are still left are cleared by the help of commentaries, etymological explanations . . . because all these later deal with the meanings (of words and sentences). On the other hand, Grammar takes no notice of the meanings of words, dealing with merely verbal forms . . ." (*TV* p. 283). In fact, when we have doubts about the meaning of the grammatical rules themselves, we have to take the help of the commentaries, which address themselves to specific problems and bring about specific ideas.

Rejecting further the central assumption of Pāṇinian grammar, *śabda-nityatā* which implies *sphoṭavāda*, and charging the *bhāṣyakāra* with "simply trying to hoodwink his disciples" (*TV* p. 294), the variationists conclude categorically . . ." we should make use of all words; they are all equally *sādhu* (correct)" (*TV* p. 298).

This brings us to the end of our present limited task — to highlight the parameters around which the norm-variation debate took place, and to sketch the context of the debate. Kumārila Bhaṭṭa's rejoinder to the *Pūrva-Pakṣa* lacks the strength of the attack, but must constitute the subject-matter of another discussion.

A pattern of correlation emerges between the consolidation of a central intellectual-political authority, challenge to this authority and re-establishment of the authority, on the other hand, and linguistic variation and absolutism, on the other. When the authority is strong, variation is allowed; when the authority is challenged, variation is not tolerated. Pāṇini and the Buddhists spoke for variation with the rising tide of one central authority; the absolutists — Patañjali and Kumārila Bhaṭṭa — spoke for a norm in times of threatened disintegration and upheavel. It is also evident that the whole debate from Yāska to Kumārila Bhaṭṭa arises from, and makes sense, only in the context of wide variation in spoken usage.

14

What is the Function of Grammar?
Patañjali, Buddhists and Kumarila Bhaṭṭa

A THEORY of grammar is implicit in Pāṇini's *Aṣṭādhyāyī*. This grammar has or had a function. But what is this function, or to put it more generally, what in any case is the function of grammar? A great controversy erupted in the Indian grammatical tradition, from Patañjali through Buddhists to Kumarila Bhaṭṭa, which bears directly on the discussion of the same question in contemporary linguistics. Pāṇini's *Aṣṭādhyāyī* is not a pedagogic grammar in the strict sense — it is a linguistic grammar that makes explicit the native speaker's knowledge of Sanskrit. But this knowledge, is the knowledge of *sādhu śabda* the acceptable, forms — the "rules" that embody this knowledge generate the acceptable variety of language, both written and spoken. Now this norm, if one may use this term, in Pāṇini is an internally complex norm — the language generated is not equal to any one actual dialect of Sanskrit. And yet it is a preferred form and a whole lot of dialectal variants are *asiddha*. On what justifiable grounds can we exclude those words that are widely employed and as successfully communicate their meaning as the *sādhu śabda*s? This is the crux of the controversy. The grammarians (Patañjali and Bhartṛhari) argue that this precisely is the function of grammar — to lay down restriction (*niyama*). What are excluded are *asādhu* forms and the *śiṣṭa*s do not use them. But the Buddhists disagree — "only an indistinct sound or single letters, or a conglomeration of letters without any reference to their signification . . . that can be said to be incorrect/unacceptable (*asādhu*), the vernacular words, *gavi* and the like are found to be capable of denoting the cow as well as the Sanskrit word *go* . . . in fact are quicker . . . in their action of denoting . . . are used more commonly, they cannot but be recognised as correct."

But if this position is accepted, how does one justify the discipline of grammar? It is interesting to chart the terms of this debate and to understand the grammarian's response which defines and extends the domain of grammar as a science — apart from the use of words, it articulates the abstract system that underlies the manifest language. And above all, argues Bhartṛhari, variation makes sense only because there is a self-evident, recognized and recognizable norm which constitutes the domain of grammar.

Pāṇini does not make any statement about his grammar. Buddhists as the *Pūrva-Pakṣa* in Kumārila Bhaṭṭa's *Tantra Vārttika* (1.3.9) foreground this fact — ". . . Pāṇini has not mentioned any purpose of the Science of Grammar." They fault Pāṇini on this account — "it still remains to be explained how he forgot to explain the purpose. . . . It is a general rule that whenever a work begins to be written, its aim is always stated . . . yet the author when composing the Śāstras has not stated either *dharma* (duty) or *artha* (wealth), or *kāma* (pleasure) to be the aim of science. Nor can it be held that the aim was too well-recognized to require a distinct mention" (Ganganatha Jha, tr., 1983, rpt. 266-67).

The Buddhist objection is not well taken. First, even the Ṣmṛtis do not expressly say that achievement of the four ends of life (*puruṣārthas*) is the purpose of inquiry. Rather, the fact that the purpose of all *darśanas* is *dukha nivṛtti*, freedom from suffering, has to be inferred. Each *darśana* begins with a statement of its field of inquiry. And Patañjali conforming to this, prefaced his Great Commentary with *atha śabdānuśāsanam*. Pāṇini's conscious economy of statement precludes this. Secondly, grammar strictly is a Vedāṅga (auxiliary science), along with astronomy, etymology, etc., a descriptive science and as such its purpose is description. The Vedāṅgas begin by describing what they are going to do and not what their ultimate purpose is (see, for example, *Nirukta*, 1.1) Bhartṛhari no doubt calls grammar a *Smṛti* (*Vākyapadīya* 1.145) but it is clear that he is using this term to characterize the nature of grammatical knowledge — unlike the Vedic knowledge it is variable and organized from time to time by different thinkers. Evidently, it has a tradition and as such it is well-known. It is Patañjali who expressly talks of the purposes of grammar, one of them being *dharma*, which as we shall see is a complex term in Patañjali. Bhartṛhari, too, later describes this discipline as a step towards *mokṣa* but it is clear that for Bhartṛhari all knowledge is a means of liberation of the self (from, following Sāṁkhya, three kinds of suffering — physical, spiritual, and accidental).

What is the purpose of *Aṣṭādhyāyī*? It has been noted that it is not designed to teach Sanskrit to non-native speakers (Jayanta Lele and Rajendra Singh, 1987) In fact, it is not really a learner's grammar (much later the *prakriyā* and *kaumudī vyākaraṇas* served this end). It is an explanatory description of the innate knowledge of the native speakers. Product of a thriving rationalist tradition (that systematized a number of intellectual fields), *Aṣṭādhyāyī* responded to the rampant linguistic diversity of its times (noted earlier by Yāska in *Nirukta* 1) by taking a "polylectal" view (Trudgill 1983) and sets up not a "monolectal" norm but an internally complex norm that does not prestige one variety or dialect over others. [It accounts for (a) the compositional language, e.g., 1.2.34-37, (b) the spoken language, e.g., 3.2.107, (c) stylistic variation, e.g., 6.3.115, (d) free variation or optionality in living speech, e.g., 6.4.75, and (e) geographic variation, e.g., 2.4.20.1. The level of acceptability, has been so fixed as to preclude a one dialect norm. We know on Patanjali's authority (*paśapaśa āhnika*) that *loka*, the universe of usage, is the authority of this "acceptability."

Patañjali accepts as norm the language generated by *Aṣṭādhyāyī* which he identifies as the *śiṣṭa vyavahāra*, the speech of the "educated", which is set up as the ideal for all speakers. What get excluded are the dialectal varieties that must have become quite recognizable by then. Now these variants are facts of usage, of *loka*. Thus though usage is authority, grammar decides what forms are to be used — there are *asādhu* words and there are *sādhu* words. This linguistic norm was set up when the Śuṅgas rose to power after the last great Mauryan emperor had been laid low and the central authority was beginning to be subjected to centrifugal forces. And this came to be challenged during the Buddhist revival under the Kuṣāṇas and during the Gupta and the Harṣa periods when Hinduism and Buddhism were locked in an intense intellectual debate. Buddhists are, understandably, variationists and they argue that *sādhutva* is determined by expressiveness — a word that conveys a meaning is *sādhu* and one that fails to is *asādhu*.

So, the Buddhists say : ". . . we should make use of all words they are all equally correct" (Ganganatha Jha 1983: 298). To support this, they counter the grammarian's standpoint by forwarding a number of arguments which can be paraphrased as: (1) the words *gāvi, goni,* are equally expressive of cow because they are used in that sense like the word *gauḥ*, etc.; (2) since they have a denotation, they are correct (*sādhu*); (3) because they are comprehensible, they are not corruptions ; (4) they are also given (*nitya*) in that their beginning is not known; (5) no transcendental result follows from the use of *sādhu* words — the result is exactly the same, denotation of an object; (6) grammar is not necessary for the use of words because usage precedes grammar (Ganganatha Jha 1983: 298). Besides, it is argued that because grammar does not have the form of the Veda; because it does not deal with the subjects that are treated of in the Veda, and because the Veda is found to express a meaning even without the help of grammar, grammar is not rooted in the Veda and therefore does not have the same authority. In fact, its status is no different from that of a drama or a story or the words of a human being (Ganganatha Jha 1983: 298-99). Therefore, it is concluded that the words *gauḥ, gavi, goni,* etc., being synonymous are all found to be used in ordinary speech, and that such usage cannot be prohibited particularly when we note that such forms are used by even the eminent grammarians (Ganganatha Jha 1983: 272), and many excellent writers and even the Veda are found to be using words at variance with the rules of grammar (Ganganatha Jha 1983: 271-72).

Patañjali distinguishes between the principal purpose and the ancillary purposes of the science of grammar. Apart from questioning the chief enterprise of separating acceptable and unacceptable forms, the Buddhists also deny the auxiliary purposes of *rakṣā* (defence), *uha* (interpretation), *lāghava* (economy), *asandeha* (removal of doubt), *āgama* (study of Veda), etc. We are here concerned only with the principal function of establishing the acceptable forms. If the Buddhist position is accepted, grammar ceases to have any function at the level of lexical usage. Patañjali had argued and subsequently Bhartṛhari had reinforced the position that when *loka* is authority and in the *loka* all kinds of variants are successfully employed, what the grammar does is to lay down *dharmaniyama. Niyama,* according to Mīmāṁsā, means "restriction" — restricting the choice to one of the available possibilities. It is a very powerful explanatory construct for both systems of ideas and practical life: thus furniture can be made of all kinds of wood but teak is to be preferred; hunger can be assuaged by eating the flesh of any animal but the flesh of only some animals is to be eaten; all water is water but only Gaṅgā water is auspicious; all colours are colourful but only some are soothing. In a speech situation, the intended meaning may be conveyed by (1) a "standard," form or (2) any of the dialectal variants or (3) an erroneously articulated or deviant (*apabhraṁśa*) form. In this situation, grammar lays down a restriction — the standard form is to be preferred. As stated by Bhartṛhari, while meaningfulness is common to all the three choices, *dharmajanakatva*, the property of "linguistic righteousness," being generative of *dharma* belongs only to the "norm." What is this *dharma*? Does this necessarily stand for the first of the four ends of life? There is reason to think that *dharma* here is to be taken in its sastraic sense of consisting in such actions as bring about a desired result. The "desired result" in language transaction is the successful transfer of meaning — this is the *dharma* of language and towards the attainment of this *dharma* it is the function of grammar to lay down *niyama* — this is *dharma-niyama*, restriction laid down for an efficacious transfer of meaning. As noted by Kumārila Bhaṭṭa in his rejoinder to the Buddhist arguments, discrepancies may arise in the use of variants.

This *sādhu* form, one can infer from Bhartṛhari's discussion, is an extant form, is widely in use, is historically older being one from which the *apabhraṁśa* forms can be shown to have developed (*Vākyapadīya* 1.23, 148). In keeping with the principle of *ekatva*, the many variants are manifestations of one. Three kinds of such variants, *apabhraṁśa*s, are noted (first by Patañjali) in the tradition: *mleccha*, *apaśabda* and *duṣṭa śabda*. There is some division of opinion about what they exactly stand for (see, Ganganatha Jha 1983: 270). There is no room here to present all the arguments but on the basis of the discussion in the cited texts of Patañjali, Bhartṛhari, and Kumārila Bhaṭṭa one may define these as follows:

(1) *mleccha prayoga* is the usage of the non-native speakers, the language of the foreign countries, of the lands that lie outside the limits of Āryāvarta and in this sense, we Indians are *mleccha* speakers of English;

(2) *apaśabda* is any of the dialectal variants; and

(3) *duṣṭa śabda* is an inaccurate or deviant usage caused either by physical infirmity or ignorance.

Grammar establishes *sādhu* words as *siddha* and *asādhu* words as *asiddha* for it is a learned discipline and as such it records the tradition of usage of the educated, the cultured, and the learned, that is the *śiṣṭa*s.* This is the *dharma* of grammar and of a good man. When one can achieve one's purpose by both *śabda* and *apaśabda*, the man of virtue employs *śabda*.

It remains to be reiterated that this debate about the function of grammar is strictly with reference to the product of the rules of grammar, that is the forms that are shown to be *siddha*. There is no dispute about the other function of grammar, namely to describe the structure of language. The rules of *Aṣṭādhyāyī* describe the structure of Sanskrit as a given system of affixation of *pratyaya* (inflectional and derivational) to *prakṛti*, bases (basic and derived) a process which first generates the nominal base and then the dependent verb base through rules of agreement etc.

---

* *Śiṣṭa* is defined by Patañjali as one whose worldly goods are constituted by a jar of grain, who without motive or purpose devote themselves to a branch of learning and excel in it are called *śiṣṭa*.

15

Programming
Pāṇini's Derivational System

PĀṆINI's grammar, *Aṣṭādhyāyī*, lends itself admirably to computational adaptation as a teaching/learning system for its following characteristics:

(a) it neatly organizes its description into two parts — (i) stores of information (memory), and (ii) a set of operational rules;

(b) its rules are in the form of explicit instructions;

(c) there is an access system for stored information; and

(d) the operational rules apply in conditions of visibility.

As the only exhaustive, rule bound and explicit grammar of a natural language, *Aṣṭādhyāyī* can be studied as a proto-grammar, a primary modelling device for organizing descriptions of languages and for use as core grammar in systems for machine translations among Indian languages.

As an example of its explicitness, that is, leaving nothing to the judgement of the users, consider the deletion rules 1.3.2 to 1.3.9:

'The nasalized vowels are *IT* in *upadeśa*' (1.3.2)

'In *upadeśa*, the final consonant of roots' etc., is *IT*' (1.3.3)

'The final dental consonants, and the final *s* and *m* are not IT in affixes called *vibhakti* (inflections)' (1.3.4)

'The initial *ni, tu,* and *du* are *IT*' (1.3.5)

'The initial *s* of an affix is *IT*' (1.3.6)

'The initial palatals (*cu*) and linguals (*ṭu*) of an affix are IT' (1.3.7)

'The initial, *l* and *ś,* and the gutturals (*ku*) of all affixes except *taddhita,* are *IT*' (1.3.8)

These rules 1.3.2-1.3.8 specify the different indicatory sounds *IT,* (the sound that signals the termination of a set or a form). Rule 1.3.9 then says — *tasya lopa* (of that elision). But what is *lopa*? Rule 1.1.60 says — *adarśanam lopa* that is "non-visibility is elision." It is not left to our judgement.

There are seven kinds of rules in *Aṣṭādhyāyī*: *tasya lopa* represents the most important kind, the injunctive rule called *vidhi*; *adarśanam lopa,* on the other hand, is a definitional rule. There are also metarule, topic rule, restriction rule, exception rule and extension rule (for examples, see 1.1.3, 3.1.1, 1.3.12, 1.1.10, 1.1.56). Unambiguous, verbless and nominalized language is employed in the rules. The operational rules are stated in the substitute-substituend order. "Substitution" is the operational principle of this grammar. (Not transformation, which is the case in Chomsky's grammar.)

This grammar analyses language as a system of affixation — one can see it as a system of adjoining an affix to a base, as in Chart 1 below or as an inflectional system as in Chart 2 below:

Chart 1 ADJOINING MODEL see p. 51

Chart 2 INFLECTING MODEL see p. 51

Language is seen as a structure, a hierarchy of inter- and intra-category relationships obtained among bases and inflections as shown in the chart of *Śabda-Rāśi* on p. 88.

The categories of this grammar (its metalanguage) are either defined in the grammar itself or are assumed from the tradition. All the information necessary for its grammatical operations is distributed into two sets:

(a) lists and lexicons (stores of data, memory), and

(b) rules (operational instructions). as shown below in Chart 3 :

Rules — STORED INFORMATION

STORED INFORMATION: Lexicons — Lists

	Lexicons: Referred to in Grammar	Lexicons: Not referred to in Grammar	Lists: Nominal Related	Lists: Verb-Root Related
1.	*Varṇasamuccaya*		*Sup*	*Tiṅ*
2.	*Gaṇapāṭha*	*Liṅgānuśāsana*	*Taddhita*	*Kṛtkṛtya*
3.	*Dhātupāṭha*		*Strī* (Fem.)	*Saṇ-Vikaraṇa*

Rules access the stored data through their metalanguage : that is, the categorial terms trigger the ensuing operations such as search/scanning/deletion/modification/substitution, etc. [categorial terms = terms referring to classes or sets of elements such as *pratyāhāra* (sigla), *dhātu* (verb root), *pratipādika* (nominal stem), *nipāta* (indeclinable), *upasarga* (prefix)]. In the case of injunctive rules that enjoin substitution or any other such operation; metarules decide which member of the class is to replace the class term (for example, the principle of *savarṇa* correspondence in the replacement enjoined by the rule *jhalām jaśa jhaśi* (8.4.53)).

The whole derivational process is organized as a sequential order as the list of rules involved in the derivation of the verb *paṭhati* (see, essay 8, p. 115-17) shows:

1.3.1	3.1.2	1.3.9	1.4.108	3.1.67-68
1.3.2	3.4.69	3.4.77	1.4.101	1.3.3
1.3.9	3.4.67	3.4.78	1.4.22	1.3.8
1.1.8	3.1.91	1.4.98	3.4.113	1.3.9
1.1.60	1.3.3	1.3.78	3.1.1-2	1.1.60
3.1.1	1.3.2	1.4.100	3.1.91	

The order is intrinsic (*artha/vidhi krama*) and not the order of statement (*pāṭha krama*). [Intrinsic ordering is the necessary feature of an oral text (a text of the oral tradition) which is by definition simultaneous.]

The system lends itself to computational programming. Such a programme, itself based on the grammar's explicit system, will in fact in turn explicate the principles implicit in the operational system.

We will illustrate the nature of programming that this grammatical system requires by specifying each of the steps involved in the first three stages in the derivation of the third person singular present tense form (*paṭhati*) of the verb root *paṭh*. For a sentence like *rāma aḥ paṭhati; rāma aḥ* would be generated first and then *paṭhati* (because the verb has to agree with one of the co-occurring nouns in number and person).

In the derivation of *paṭhati* one can isolate, on the basis of category replacement, seven main stages or cycles in the application of rules:

1. *paṭh + upadeśa*
2. *paṭh + laṭ*
3. *paṭh + laṭ => paṭh + l*
4. *paṭh + l => paṭh + tip*
5. *paṭh + tip => paṭh + śap + tip*
6. *paṭh + śap + tip => paṭh + a + tip*
7. *paṭh + a + tip => paṭh + a + ti => paṭhati*

On the basis of our knowledge of the grammar we can develop an automatic generation system. We propose to present here now just an example of such a system with reference to just the first three stages. It is being presented in three columns:

Operation	Programme	Rewriting grammar

Under OPERATION, we give the external input by the learner/researcher and receive the screen output. Under PROGRAMME, we describe what operations the computer is programmed to carry out — the operations inside the machine. Under REWRITING GRAMMAR, we indicate the small explicatory additions that are required by this programme of ours. This is only a tentative programme — the purpose is to understand the kind of rewriting that would be needed in any such effort to develop an automatic derivation system based on Pāṇini's rules. No claim is intended to either exactness or completeness. But even this tentative proposal shows the built-in explicitness of Pāṇini's grammar. As we said above, there are stores of information, a body of rules and in the metalanguage an access system. In developing the following sample programme, all we have tried to do is to externalize the implicit mechanism which a *paṇḍit* in the tradition in any case exploits to show how a particular form is made *siddha,* that is how it is derived by Pāṇini's system of rules. It is a very *provisional* attempt scholars of *Aṣṭādhāyī* and computational Programming need to work together to develop such a programme.

PROGRAMMING

Operations	Programme	Rewriting grammar
Stage I		
Step 1: ↳ *paṭh*	(look for it even as a *segment*)	
2. ⟹ Searches/scans	(scans lists/lexicons in the order *upasarga nipātā dhātupāṭha*)*	

3. Found in *Dhātupāṭha*

4. | *PĀṬHA - Dhātu* 1/222 |

5. ? (asks) O.K.?

6. ↳ Yes

7. | PĀṬHÃ - + UPADEṢA | (if found in a list make it as *upadeśa*)

8. | UPADEŚA | ⟹ (triggers) search in rules

9. Found 1.3.2 (upadeśe anunāsika ac IT)

10. (What is found in relation A - X, add on to A)

11. | PĀṬHA + [UPADEŚA + ANUNĀSIKA + AC = IT] | [Rewrite/ add '='/ IT]

12. ⟹ Search ANUNĀSIKA (follow left to right order for identification)

13. Found 1.1.8 [Modify and add visible ~]

14. (mark any element with ~ in the string as ANUNĀSIKA)

15. | PATH A - ANUNASIKA | + | | UPADEŚA | + | a C | = | IT | |

16. ⟹ Search a C

17. Found 1.1.71 [add introduction : go to Prātyāhara Sūtra]

18. Searches Pratyāhāra Sūtra

19. | a | . . . . | c |

20. enumerates | a, i, u . . . = a C |

21. (mark element in the string, if available)

22. | PATH | Ã | - ANUNASIKA ac | + | | UPADEŚA | = IT |

23. (replace 'X=' by = IT)

24. | PATH | Ã | - IT | + UPADEŚA

25. (Delete UPADEŚA)

26. | PATH | Ã | - IT |

27. IT ⟶ <1.3.3 - 1.3.9>
28. [Delete$_{\times}$IT] (by 1.3.9)
29. Make IT non-visible (1.1.18)

Stage 2 :

30. | PAṬH - |
31. ? Want forms (*lakāra*) of *pāṭha*
32. ↳ Yes
33. | - LAṬ | [choose in order from 10 forms]
34. ? Proceed or skip
35. ⟶ proceed
36. Searches rules
37. Found (3.1.91) 3.2.123 [Rewrite, incorporate अनुवृत्ति anuvṛtti]
38. | (dhato) vartmāṇe laṭ |
39. *pāṭha* ~ *- dhātu* ?
40. (scan derivation)
41. | PAṬHA Dhātu 1/222 | (repeat step 4)
42. Add on *-Laṭ* to *Paṭha*
43. '-Affix' -Laṭ? (*pratyaya*)
44. Scan?
45. Yes
46. Search for '*pratyaya*'
47. Found 3.1.1., 3.1.2
48. (Follow instructions)
49. PAṬH-, -LAṬ
50. (Delete 2nd occurrence of [-]
51. | PAṬH - LAṬ | delete IT by 1.33; 1.3.9; 1.1.8
52. | PAṬH - LA [Ṭ] |

53. Paṭh - *Lah*
54. Ṡearch *Lah*
55. Found (3.4.67) (3.4.69)
56. [(kartṛ) - karmṇi - bhāva] [Reproduce rules FEED CONDITIONS]
57. Kartṛ
58. ? Proceed or Skip
59. ↳ proceed
60. PATH - LAH^{Kartṛ}

and so on

Notes on Operations

1. 'x-,' in 'Paṭha-,' tiggers scanning of three lists, of *upasarga, nipālā, dhātupāṭha*
2. '-x' as instruction may search lists of affixes in the grammar.
3. 'a C,' a sign a ending in capital letter will trigger search of *pratyāhāra sūtra* and enumerate the members of the set.
4. Instruction such as 'x' will search the body of rules.

Other Conventions of this Chart

[box] = The display on the screen; ( ) = programming;

[ ] = re-organise grammar information.

16

The Colour of Sounds

Phonetics in Prātiśākhyas and Upaniṣads

It is known from Yāska (*Nirukta* 1.18,19) that the phoneticists in the Indian tradition were the intellectual opponents of the Nairukta, the etymologists. What is less well known is that they were also the opponents of the grammarians. The two differ fundamentally in their concern — the phoneticists are concerned with the substance of speech, with *śabda-tattva,* while the grammarians are concerned with the form of speech, *śabda-rūpa.*

If we keep in mind the dominant Indian conception of the three levels of reality — *pāramārthika, tattvārthika* and *prātibhāṣika* (the apparent, the essential and the ultimate real) *sattā* — we can understand the phoneticists' claim that ontologically, the grammarians' concern is superficial as compared with theirs because *rūpa,* or form, exists at the level of appearance which is a level of constant change and transience and the grammarians are therefore analysing the changing forms in which the substance manifests itself. The phoneticists say that they on the other hand analyse the sound substance, the being of speech. For them, sound is an ontological entity, a *tattva.* For the Vaiśeṣikas too, *ākāśa* (space or ether), the *dravya* (substance) of sound (*dhvani*) is a *tattva* while *rūpa* is a quality. For the modern physicists, sound is not a substance because it has no mass — the particles, of sound are only audible. But according to the Indian phoneticists the sound "particle" is the ultimate constituent of the material universe.

The philosophical concept of *Brahman* stands for both *puruṣa*, the principle of energy, and for *prakṛti*, matter. The two, matter and energy are separately enumerated as two ontological entities in Sāṁkhya but are understood as immanent in each other. What the philosophers call *prakṛti* or *svabhāva* is the *śabda tattva* or *ākāśa tattva* of the phoneticists. In the order of creation and destruction, this *ākāśa*, the vast "emptiness" or space, is the dividing point from which everything originates and into which everything dissolves. It is the *paramāṇvika*, literally the ultimate sub-atomic particle, the vast "silence," the *śūnya* in which *dhvani* (sound) originates, setting in motion a given cycle of creation. This is *kham-brahman* or *śabda-brahman*, the *akṣara* of Vedas called *praṇava*, *AUṀ*, which is an abbreviatory symbol of all the primary sounds, manifest as well as non-manifest, composed as it is of *a* (first vowel) + *u* (last vowel that involves the whole vocal tract) + *m* (last, of the consonants). Its three divisions symbolize (i) the three-fold *prakṛti* (*sattva, rajas, tamas* of Sāṁkhya) (ii) the three divisions of time: past, present and future, (iii) the three states of consciousness: wakeful, sleep, dream. As the unified fourth entity, it stands for the matter beyond qualities, time beyond divisions, and the fourth state of consciousness, *turīya*. A whole Upaniṣad, *Māṇḍūkya*, is devoted to its signification.

This *mūla, prākṛta dhvani* (primal or ontological sound) is the *ŚABDA BRAHMAN* — the "words," of the grammarians are not the *śabda-brahman*. Bhartṛhari himself uses for *śabda-brahman*, the term *akṣara-brahman* to refer to *samvṛta a*, (*Vākyapadīya* 1.1). This *śabda-brahman* is also Veda —

> *śabdasya pariṇāma ayam iti amnayavidovidu* ।
> *chāndobhya eva pratharnarn etad viśvam vyāvartata* ॥
> — *Vākyapadīya* 1.12.1

From *mūla dhvani* (primal sound) to sounds of language to language to knowledge to all this enumerable universe, *ayam iti āmnāya* — this is the order of evolution, *vyāvartata*, the expanse or manifestation (of individual consciousness and consciousness of the universe).

Śabda-Brahman is *dhvani* not "words" or language, because words or language are forms cognizable in terms of sequential, discrete elements. This sequence, *krama*, which implies discreteness, is assymetrical with reality which is *a-krama*, that is, without sequence and discreteness (*Vākyapadīya* 1.86). It is *dhvani tattva*, sequenceless and without parts, which is *Brahman*. It may be said that the *dhvani tattva* like its evolutes; the sounds (*varṇas*) of language, is itself an aggregate of so many phonetic features such as aspiration (*mahāprāṇa*), voicing (*ghoṣa*), resonance (*nāda*), etc. Isn't it itself a form a *rūpa*? No. The features of *dhvani* are not discrete and, therefore, not sequential — one cannot be separated or marked off from the other. They are not relative to each other. So, a *dhvani* has *ākāra/ākṛti* but not *rūpa*.

Sphoṭa also is sound-impression (*dhvani citra*) in the mind, the sound picture evoked by a sound or by the last of a sound aggregate. By "sound-aggregate," the phoneticists (for example Auḍumbarāyaṇa as quoted by Yāska) mean "the sound aggregate of a sentence/utterance." This concept is then appropriated by the grammarians (beginning with Yāska) to postulate *pada-sphoṭa*, the *sphoṭa* of a grammatical form (as against that of a unit of utterance). This is to move away from the *tattva* to *ābhāṣa*.

Ontological primacy of the sound substance is argued, the phoneticists have noted, by several common-sense facts: (i) sound invariably co-occurs with the beginning of all actions, events, movements. processes, efforts; (ii) sound is never absent when we sit silent, our breathing and our heartbeat are there; (iii) in the external world, the wind always blows and everywhere; (iv) no river, ocean, human habitation, forest or field is silent; (v) when even a small gear which rotates produces sound, how about the cosmic sound of the earth and millions of heavenly bodies rotating around their axes and around other astronomical bodies in a cosmic dance the universe indeed is *śabdamaya*, permeated by sound; (vi) sound/space is invariably present in the primary forms of matter — air, water, earth and fire/energy; (vii) what is named as knowledge or science or meaning or being or language is only sound in its essence; (viii) someone is alive or not, has intelligence or not is decided by the presence or absence of sound.

The phoneticists therefore, made this substance the object of their study, of sound as the substance of language. There is a very long tradition of this study. In-fact, phonetics is the first "science," in India and phonetic observations and analysis are found in both linguistic and non-linguistic texts, the Śikṣās, the Prātiśākhyas, the Vedas and *Brāhmaṇa*s and the Upaniṣads. 108 texts of phonetics isolate and enumerate the sounds of Sanskrit. The term used for a sound complex is *varṇa*, a term also used for caste-group and colour and so is denotative of class and a spectrum in which it is not possible to say where one kind of identifiable sound ends and another begins, the whole being a continuum of shades. The sounds enumerated for a language are names given to potential complexes of (phonetic) features referred to in two ways : X-*akṣara* and X-*iti*, with *iti* indicating a more than one member set and *akṣara* indicating the sound-type, the "structure" of the sound-complex. The *halanta* convention transfers consonantal sounds into syllables, the *svara*s being in themselves *akṣara*s. There are two well-known *smāmnāya*s — Kātyāyana's *Varṇamālā* which is the basis of the "alphabets" of all modern Indian languages and Pāṇini's *Pratyāhāra Sūtras*. As the term *smāmnāya* means true knowledge (*veda*) because *āmanāya* is noted in *Amarakoṣa*

(1-6-3) as a synonym of Veda, it follows that knowledge is equated with the totality of speech sounds.

There are (vide *Ṛk-Prātiśākhya* 13-13,14,15) just seventeen root-sounds, *maulika dhvani*s: four primary root vowels *a, ri, i, u* four root sibilants *ha, ṣ, ś*; four root semi-vowels *y, r, l, v* and five consonants *k, c, ṭ, t, p*. These are the seventeen "given" sounds, the *mūla akṣara*s. The concept of "colour" is merely an indicator of difference (*bhedaka*) potentially inherent in each *akṣara*. Each *akṣara* has : (i) three places (*sthāna*) of articulation, *mandra, madhyama, uttama*; (ii) each of these has three paces (*vṛttis*), *vilambita, madhyama, druta*; (iii) and then each is of three kinds according to pitch *udātta, anudātta, svarita*; (iv) then three according to length, *hrasva, dīrgha, pluta* (not applicable to lenghthened vowels). This makes 72 varieties of each. Add 37 variants according to semi-vowel, sibilant, five "stops" and *anusvāra, anunāsika* to make a total of 109. The one root sound is made *sumeru* and then the 108 constitute the string of sounds, the *mala* of *japa*. This *smāmnāya* is the music of the self (*ātmā*) and the human vocal apparatus the *Aitareyopniṣad* sees as the *vīṇā*, the divine lute.

Another text establishes 2835 variants for each vowel — 3 lengths × 5 weights (*bhāra*) × 3 pitch × 3 paces (*vṛttis*) × 7 tones (*ṣaḍaja, madhyama, dhaivata, niṣada, niṣābha, gandhāra, kokila*) × 3 places (*grama*) = 2835. The *Taittirīya Prātiśākhya* (13-13, 232) says that any sound can assume infinite (*ananta*) variation on account of the desire of the speaker, the quality of the vocal organs, more or less degree of aspiration in a series of sibilants (*anupradāna*), degrees of nasalization (*saṁsarga*), varying degrees of contact, different measures of length, pitch and place, and other causes such as the specificities of efforts of the articulators (*pratiśrutaka*). It sounds speculative because our available instruments are not able to quantify or measure these variations.

This is the indefinably continuous spectrum of sounds. Segments recognized and named are mere constructs. The only reality is the *śabda-tattva*, the sound substance ṭhe *mūla dhvani*. This, when it is located in breath, *prāṇa* (inhaled air), and in the mind, *mana*, it becomes VĀK, (speech). The *Aitareyopaniṣad* points out the intimate relation of breath/speech and mind *vagve mata prāṇa putra* (*AP* 3-1-6). When one is engaged in speech, breath is dissolved in the mind and when one is in deep sleep, the mind is dissolved in breath. This mutual absorption of one by the other, points to a higher common source and the *R̥gveda* (X.119.4) notes this — ". . . the mother absorbs him and he the mother." This Vāk comprising of (*parā*), *paśyanti, madhyamā, vaikharī* covers almost the entire gamut of the mind ("almost" as *Chāndogya Upaniṣad* says, 7.3.1, ". . . mind is greater than speech") and the self — "Of the entire self, *ātman, prāṇa* is the sibilants, the bones the mutes, the marrow the vowels . . . the eye, the ear, the mind, the speech, the senses, and the whole self depend on *prāṇa*." (*AP* 3-2-1) The sage Kauntharava sets up another symbolism visualizing the self as consisting of syllables — *catvāra . . . śarīra puruṣa, chanda puruṣa, veda puruṣa, mahā puruṣa iti*. There are four persons — of the body, of the metres, of the Veda, and the great self — the corporeal self, the speaking self, the knowing self and the Self different from body and mind, who is not heard not seen not classified, not thought, not subdued, not reached, not understood but who hears, sees, classifies, thinks, sounds, understands, and knows. . . ." And then the secret doctrine of the whole speech . . . earth, fire, *R̥gveda*, eye and *prāṇa* are the stops; air, *Yajurveda*, ear and *apāna* (exhaled air) are sibilants; sky, sun *Sāmaveda*, mind, and *vyāna* (retained air) are vowels. This aggregate meditation on the garland of sounds is followed by a very poetic passage in which the human body is likened to a lute, a divine lute . . . "the human lute is an imitation of the divine lute. Just as the human lute has a head, so that has a head; just as this has a stomach, so that has a cavity; just as this has a tongue, so that has a tongue; just as this has fingers so that has strings; just as this has vowels, so that has tones; just as this has consonants so that has tones; just as this produces sound and is firmly strung so does that produces sound and is firmly strung ; just as this is covered with a hairy skin, so that is covered with a hairy skin. He who knows this divine lute is listened to when he speaks, the earth is filled with his fame, and wherever the learned speak in assemblies there he will be known. The meditation closes with a significant question — "To what end shall we study the Vedas? To what end shall we make effort?" For we sacrifice *prāṇa* in *vāk* and *vāk* in *prāṇa*. For what is this beginning that is the end? Śruti de̱clares — "May my speech rest in my mind and my mind rest in truth. ***Oṁ śāntiḥ, śāntiḥ, śāntiḥ.***"

17

Nature of the Linguistic Sign

Bhartṛhari's Sphoṭavāda

THE word *sphoṭa* is derived from the *bhavādi* root √*Sphuṭ* and means literally "that which becomes manifest" or "that which blossoms or develops." *Sphoṭa* is used by the grammarians to name "the essential word or language" (*śabda-tattva*) which is instrumental in communicating meaning to the hearers and is thus distinguished from the articulated word, realized as a structure of sound. According to the Indian grammarians the manifest language, which is discrete and sequential, is only a realization in heard sound of the essential language, which is non-discrete (*akhaṇḍa*) and universally unchanging (*nitya*) in a speech-community. It is this *śabda-tattva, sphoṭa,* non-partitive and invariant, which makes successful linguistic communication possible in spite of infinite phonetic variation, transitoriness of sounds (spoken words) and the mismatch between the spoken language's segmented and sequential organization of meaning and the integral wholistic meaning in reality. As Prof. K.A. Subramania Iyer explains —

> . . . the *sphoṭa* doctrine arose as a solution to the problem of the understanding of meaning. The problem was how to explain the understanding of meaning from the sounds which are uttered in a temporal sequence. As they are not simultaneous and cannot co-exist, they cannot co-operate in order to convey the meaning. The doctrine of *sphoṭa* is the grammarian's solution of the problem.
>
> — K.A. Subramania Iyer, *Bhartṛhari*, 1969, p. 160

Underlying infinite variety of forms, the grammarians posit an indivisible, invariant unit which is the signifier of meaning. It is *sphoṭa*. It is manifested in articulate speech where several units like sound, inflected word and sentence are visible as discrete and ordered units. However, segmentation, sequence and structuration are properties only of that part of language which is identical with articulated speech. At the level of *sphoṭa*, language is non-partitive and non-sequential. This is explained by Bhartṛhari with the help of an analogy — just as all parts of a peacock are present as an indivisible whole in the peacock's egg but appear as separate parts in a given sequence as the process of hatching proceeds, in the same manner, meaning is present as an indivisible whole before it takes the segmented, sequential form of manifest speech.

Sphoṭa concept may be understood as the following:

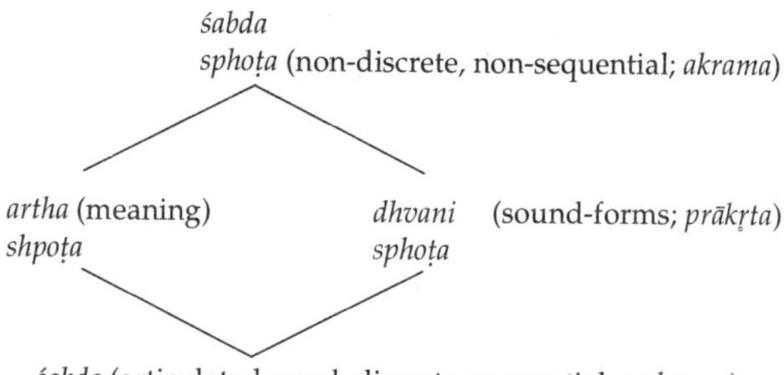

Patañjali is credited to be the first to set-up the construct of *sphoṭa*. In his famous definition of *śabda*, he says, "that which when made manifest in articulated sounds brings to reader's mind the cognition of an object, is called the *śabda* (*Mahābhāṣya*, I.1.). This is a close approximation of the concept of *sphoṭa*, though the word *sphoṭa* is not explicitly employed. However, Pāṇini's rule, 6.1.123 cites an early grammarian Sphoṭayānā, on a morphophonemic rule, and according to the commentator Haradatta (eleventh century AD), Sphoṭayāna was the originator of the *sphoṭavāda* although no work of Sphoṭayanā-cārya is now available. Pāṇini himself does not use the word *sphoṭa*, but the order of his rules strongly suggests that he was aware of, and accepted the concept of *sphoṭa*. In fact, Patañjali has described and discussed the *sphoṭa*-principle only in his commentary on *Pāṇini-Sūtras* beginning with *taparastatkālasya* (1.1.70). But it is the grammarians headed by Bhartṛhari who have discussed in depth and introduced by way of deduction from Pāṇini's grammar, the theory "that *śabda* which communicates the meaning is different from the sound which is produced and heard and which is merely instrumental in the manifestation of an internal voice which is called *sphoṭa*" (K.V. Abhyankar, *A Dictionary of Sanskrit Grammar*, Baroda, 1977, p. 436).

Bhartṛhari's exposition of the *sphoṭa*-theory begins with *kārikā* 44 of the 1st kāṇḍa (Chapter) of *Vākyapadīya*. Defining the scope of grammar, Bhartṛhari says it is concerned with that *śabda* which in one form (*rūpa*) is the *nimitta* (formal cause) of the manifest word produced and heard by the organs of speech and shearing, and in the other form (*rūpa*) is the abstract meaning-signifying unit. Both these forms explains Kaiyaṭa (twelfth century AD), are *sphoṭa*, that enables the hearer to recognize the articulate word and the other that enables the hearer to recognize the meaning being signified. Thus, it is *sphoṭa* which is realized both as the suggester (*vyañjaka*) and the suggested (*vyañjya*) (*VP* I.44). Between *sphoṭa* and manifest word a cause and effect relationship is said to hold (*VP* I.45), according to the point of view accepted by Bhartṛhari. Just as fire which is inherent in the wood becoming manifest after rubbing becomes a source of light and burning, in the same way the *sphoṭa* that inheres in the intellect of the speaker becomes manifest in a sequence in the form of produced and heard words (*VP* I.46). There is oneness, a correspondence, between the meaning-*sphoṭa* and word-*sphoṭa*. The speaker having made up his mind about the meaning-*sphoṭa*, makes effort then to make manifest, articulate the corresponding word-*sphoṭa* (*VP* I.47). And because the sounds that realize the *sphoṭa* are articulated in a given sequence, the sequence *appears* to be a property of the *sphoṭa* as well, which is in fact non-sequential (*VP* I.48) just as the same moon reflected in different bodies of water appears to be trembling while in fact it is only the reflecting water which is moving (*VP* I.49). But just as reflection is different from water and yet exists only in terms of the reflecting water, meaning is different from the articulated word, but comes into existence only when the word is produced (*VP* I.50). So non-sequential, non-partitive entity *sphoṭa* becomes manifest in discrete, sequential form (spoken word), which is again transformed into one, indivisible whole in the hearer's mind. Just as a painter decides to paint the picture of *one* individual, and then in actuality paints the picture part by part which is then again viewed whole as the picture of *one* individual by the viewer, the same three-fold process is to be observed in language (*VP* I.52). Just as the lamp-light reveals the lamp as well as the other objects, *sphoṭa* reveals — makes possible the expression and the cognition of — both the *śabda* (word), and *artha* (the meaning). Thus, the *word* is both the revealer and the revealed (*VP* I.55), like the word *agni* (fire), in the *Pāṇini-Sūtra* (4.2.33) which is pronounced in so many different ways by different individuals, stands for its essential phonological shape (*agniś-abdatva*), as well as for the real life object, fire, it denotes (*VP* I.60).

Does the *sphoṭa* stand for the particular or the universal, the individual or the class? According to Bhartṛhari, there is no difference in the two positions. The same *sphoṭa* communicates both the idea of class is not independent of the individual and the idea of the individual is not independent of the class (*VP* I.69). The difference, in fact, arises from the ontological assumption — there are the variationists who believe in the separate identity of all individual instances, and there are the normativists (like the Mīmāṁsā philosophers) who believe that behind multiplicity and variation, there is the same single entity. Thus, even when *d* has different phonetic realizations in different contexts, the hearers still cognize all instances as *d* (*VP* I.70, 71). The same holds true of the word (*pada*, the fully inflected form) and the sentence. So there is *varṇa-sphoṭa, pada-sphoṭa* and *vākya-sphoṭa* (*VP* I.72). But then *vākya-sphoṭa* is the only reality — the idea exists as an undifferentiated whole and the divisions like word and sound are facts of segmentation and sequences peculiar to *dhvani*, the manifest speech, and exist only in terms of the *vākya*, the whole utterance (*VP* I.73). The ultimate, indivisible, sequenceless *sphoṭa* is unaffected by these partititive units, just as it is unaffected by the phonetic variations such as length in *dhvani* (*VP* I.77).

What is the relationship between *dhvani* and *sphoṭa*? Or, how does *dhvani* manifest *sphoṭa*? Bhartṛhari cites three views (i) the spoken word creates an impression (*saṁskāra*) in the ear of the hearer; (ii) the spoken word creates an impression of its *sphoṭa* in the hearer's intellect (*antaḥkaraṇa*); (iii) the spoken word creates the impression both of the sound-structure, and the *sphoṭa* (*VP* I.80). Bhartṛhari appears to support the third view which implies that the knowledge of the sound-structure of the word and of the *sphoṭa* is interdependent and simultaneous and both are cognized in association with each other, and are integral. The *dhvani* leaves a super- or trans-sensory impression of both. Also a series of sounds constitute the structure of a word, and all of them have a role to play in the cognition of *sphoṭa*; each sound separately is not a revealer of *sphoṭa*, but all succeeding sounds build up a cognition of a word which is fully established when the last sound is uttered and heard, and then the *sphoṭa* is clearly cognized (*VP* I.83).

The cognition of *sphoṭa* therefore, is made possible by the structure of the word — the given number of sounds in a fixed sequence closed by a particular sound. Though it is the last sound that finally reveals the *sphoṭa*, the preceding sounds are equally necessary in that, in the order they appear, they enable the hearer to conceptually grasp or imagine a possible word, with the possibilities getting narrowed down with every successive sound, till the last sound restricts the certainty of realization to particular word (*VP* I.84). The cognitive process, therefore, is one of proceeding from ignorance through progressive elimination of error (the awareness of parts such as sounds, *pada*, etc.) to certain knowledge (*VP* I.85).

So although *sphoṭa* is *abheda*, non-paratitive, it cannot be cognized except through parts (*VP* I.86). If the sounds and *pada* are seen and understood separately, we cannot get any meaning; it is only when they are seen as one, that the *sphoṭa*, the wholistic conception can emerge (*VP* I.88). The awareness of parts and sequence is a cognitive error or illusion which has to be transcended to gain true knowledge (*VP* I.89). Through the two analogies of milk turning into curd and the seed becoming a full grown tree that involve successive transformations (*vikāra*) in a fixed order, Bhartṛhari demonstrates how *sphoṭa* is cognized by passing through several cognitive stages in a fixed sequence (*VP* I.90, 91). But these stages are simply *means* to final true knowledge, and nothing more (*VP* I.92).

A subtle distinction then is made between an invariant, universal abstract *sphoṭa* and *śabda* manifested by *dhvani*, sound-structure, which in itself is transitory. Then how can the transitory manifest the constant? (*VP* I.93). Bhartṛhari says it does so, the transitory particular individual suggests the constant universal/class (*VP* I.84). Also the argument that the substrata of *dhvani* and *sphoṭa* being distinct from each other (the ear and the intellect respectively), logically, one cannot be the suggester (*vayañjaka*) of the other (*VP* I.96) also does not hold, as the fitness of one (*dhvani*) for the other (*sphoṭa*) is established in the same way as the fitness of the eye to grasp forms, and of the nose to grasp smell (*VP* I.97). Bhartṛhari at this point uses the term *nāda* for the physical speech sound produced by the articulatory organs, reserving by implication the term *dhvani* for the sound-structure, the phonological shape, of words. He says that appropriateness, fitness, of *sphoṭa-nāda* to be involved in the suggested-suggester relationship is established by the fact that it is the sound produced in the speech-tract that stands for or suggests *ū-kāra*, etc., *varṇa-sphoṭas*, i.e., what modern linguistics calls functional sound-types.

Any phonetic difference (*vaikṛta-dhvani*) in the manifesting sounds would show in the *sphoṭa* also, for the properties or attributes of the medium are also seen as attributes of the product (*VP* I.99). But the temporality which is the determinant of phonetic differences (*vaikṛta-dhvani*) is not a dimension of the *sphoṭa*, the invariant constant, and therefore, the variations generated by temporality have to be transcended by the hearer to correlate only the *prākṛta-dhvani*, the phonological shape, with *sphoṭa* (*VP* I.102), for *sphoṭa* being *amūrat* (formless), does not change with time given to the manifestation (*VP* I.103).

And this brings Bhartṛhari to the important philosophical consequence of his *sphoṭa*-theory — what is the essential substance of the word, *śabda*? Bhartṛhari reports three positions: (i) it is air that takes the form of words, (ii) it is atoms that take the form of words, and (iii) it is knowledge that takes the form of words (*VP* I.108). The phoneticists took the first position, the Jaina thinkers the second (*VP* I.109-11). But the grammarians led by Patañjali hold that the intellect (*antaḥkaraṇa*) is knowledge, and there is in the human mind the power to communicate this knowledge in the form of meaning; therefore, word (*śabda*), is but the result (*pariṇāma*) of knowledge (*jñāna*) (*VP* I.112, 117). The process is described as this: the substratum of knowledge, the intellect (*antaḥkaraṇa*), with the birth of desire to communicate meaning, becomes the mind (*mana*) and associating itself with energy (*jaṭhrāgni*) pushes the life-breath (*prāṇa-visphoṭa-vāyu*), i.e., the same air which is the breath, upwards, and the air dividing itself into speech sounds such as *ka, kha*, manifests itself as a *śabda*, word, and then subsequently dissolves itself into the speech itself (*VP* I.113, 115). Thus both the life-breath and the mind have an inherent power (*śakti*) to express meanings and it is this power that manifests itself as segments of sequential speech which enable us to cognize the reality as made up of so many different objects or forms (*VP* I.118). Therefore all meaning and all difference (*bheda*) is the product of language (*VP* I.119). Hence the sages have said: "all this world (*jagat*) is the result (*pariṇāma*) of language" (*VP* I.120).

Thus, *śabda* is knowledge and is in the learning self and the linguistic sign quite appropriately is a mental construct like other theories in the Indian tradition the *sphoṭa* theory begins by accounting for and explaining a given physical, perceptible phenomenon that of the speech act and ends up by building an explanatory theory. However, the *sphoṭa*-thoey, is not accepted by all the philosophical systems. The Jains, the Mīmāṁsakas, the Naiyāyikas and even Vedānta disagreed with its formulations. The construct of *sphoṭa* is rejected outright as illogical by Mīmāṁsa, Nyāya and Cārvāka systems, and as unnecesary by Vedānta as represented by Ādi Śaṅkara. The Mīmāṁsakas reject the "constancy" (*nityatā*) of *sphoṭa*, reject in fact, along with Cārvākas, the principle of oneness (*ekatva*) behind multiplicity and argue that it is the *sounds* themselves that communicate meaning. The Naiyāyikas reject *sphoṭa* on epistemological grounds, cite *Mahābhāṣya*, in support of their contention and assert that the word (*śabda*), is merely a structure of sounds. The Sāṁkhyas do not accept the existence of any subjective knowledge indpendent of external reality and agrue that the grammarian's intellect (*antaḥkaraṇa*) merely reflects images of external reality and that there is nothing like abstract meaning (*baudhārtha*). The Jaina thinkers similarly reject the grammarians' nexus between knowledge and language and argue that words are products of atom of air (*paudagalik*).

But the grammarians upheld the doctrine of *sphoṭa* by offering a variety of reasoned arguments against each of their contenders. Apart from Bhartṛhari, a number of grammarians either wrote specific treatises on *sphoṭa* or also argued *sphoṭa-vāda* in their commentaries on the *Aṣṭādhyāyī* of Pāṇini and the *Mahābhāṣya* of Patañjali.

18

Concept of Padārtha in Language and Philosophy

WHEN I say "I know *X*" what do I mean in the Indian tradition? This question involves the concept of *padārtha* (*X*) and its four aspects — as an object, its name, knowledge of the object and how this knowledge is acquired. Patañjali in *Paspaśāhnika* uses the term *padārtha* for denotation, i.e., meaning of words. In the context of his stated assumption of grammar, *nitya śabdārtha sambandha* (the relationship between word and meaning is given), it is pointed out that both *ākṛti* (form or particular) and *dravya* (substance) are accepted as *padārtha* in this assumption — *pada-artha*, i.e., the meaning of fully inflected forms. Now *padārtha* quite significantly also means "object" denoted, and in this sense it is an important concept in all the major Indian philosophical systems. The purpose of this paper is to investigate the concepts of *padārtha* in language and in philosophy and the interrelation that holds between them.

In language, *padārtha* is a *name* for something, while in philosophy it is the object that is named by language. The grammarians look at it in this way — it is language that, by its process of naming, marks out, i.e., identifies objects which would otherwise not be cognized separately as such. In what is an ancient conception reality is assumed to be a continuous, non-discrete, non-sequential entity — the difference (*bheda*) that we recognize between one thing and another, between one object and the next, is a *pariṇāma* (result) of language. The *Ṛgveda* first makes the original observation to this effect —

> Language cuts forms in the ocean of reality. . . .
>
> — I.164.41

The school of grammarians has evidently built up its system of ideas on this key insight. Language, in this manner, in fact, virtually *constructs* the extraordinarily multiple and manifold reality that is this *jagat*, which exists only as a form of *pratibhā*, the individual consciousness or understanding (*Vākyapadīya*, I.118) that alone is real, as it alone persists in all states (*VP* III.17-18). Since all knowledge is essentially linguistic (*VP* I.123), our knowledge of ontological reality is of the nature of *vikalpa* (*VP* I.119), *vikalpa* in the sense of Yoga philosophy (*Yoga-Sūtra*, I.6, 9) — there being virtually no difference in the cognition of a non-existing entity such as "rabbit-horns" and of the actually existing entities such as "pitcher" and "curtain" (*VP* I.129-30). While recognizing three forms of reality (*sattā*) — the ultimate reality (*pāramārthika*), the manifest reality (*vyāvahārika*) and the reality as evoked by language and experienced in the individual consciousness (*prātibhāsika*), the grammarians argue that our *knowledge of reality* is limited to the third form of reality, the *prātibhāsika* — all cognition is determinate and no direct apprehension of objects is, therefore, possible.

Other philosophical systems, however, make a distinction between a direct cognition of objects (*anubhava*) and the *bodha* (cognition) of objects as expressed or designated by words. The Yoga system in fact makes a three-fold distinction (*Yoga-Sūtra*, 3.17) between *śabda* (language), *artha* (denotation or object denoted) and *jñāna* (knowledge of the object) arguing that the three are completely different from each other. The Buddhists took a position radically different from the grammarians in arguing that the linguistic knowledge of reality is illusory, that *jñāna* (knowledge of objects), is not of objects but of the mental conceptions of momentarily frozen objects and that, to achieve valid knowledge of the ultimate reality, it is necessary to apprehend the reality directly by transcending language, by eliminating the filter (or "curtain") of words so that the objects impress themselves as they are on consciousness. Even some theistic (*āstika*) systems, Vedānta for example, consider the linguistically generated knowledge of *bheda* (difference) as a form of *avidyā*, ignorance, and argue for the need to go beyond *bheda*, the fragmented reality, and realize *abheda* (non-difference/non-discreteness), as the essential attribute of reality.

This debate revolves round a set of questions —

(1) What is the concept of *padārtha* in philosophy?

(2) What are the *padārtha*s posited in different systems?

(3) What constitutes the totality or structure of a *padārtha*?

(4) What is the structure and nature of verbal denotation of objects (*padārtha*) and its relationship to the "total" reality of an object?

(5) What constitutes the knowledge of an object and what is the role of language in the knowledge of an object?

What is at stake in this debate is the status of the visible world — the materiality of the universe, the "ultimate" and the "total" reality of discrete and diverse objects that crowd and constitute the cognizable world, and the relationship of these visible forms to the transcendental, "invisible" structures underlying them. What is an "object" (*padārtha*)? How many objects are there? How do they relate to each other in a system? What is the reality, or the *total* reality of an object? And what is the relationship between the particular reality of a specific object (*padārtha*) and the one ultimate reality (*sattā*) underlying all the objects?

What is the context of this crucial investigation? The context is — The goal of knowledge. Each system claims that a vaild knowledge of objects is the efficacious means of achieving the ultimate goal of *mokṣa*, liberation, which, in final terms, amounts to freedom from suffering (*duḥkha*). The Mīmāṁsā system asserts that this *mokṣa* is the result of proper performance of enjoined acts of sacrifice and duty (*karma-kāṇḍa*). This proper performance grants positive happiness (*sukha*) in its purest form (and not just elimination of sorrow). But we can have the right performance only if we have a right knowledge of objects involved in all the activities. Mimāṁsā believes in the reality of the external world (*bāhya sattā*) — reality of the physical world is a fact of perception (*pratyakṣa*), and the objects of this world are constituted by the diverse physical primordial elements. In the Vedānta system, valid knowledge is the instrument of liberation (*Vedānta-Sūtra* 3.4.1) and this knowledge consists in the awareness that all the visible, diverse, multiple forms, objects, both with and without life, are reflexes of the same one undifferentiated, non-discrete being (*sattā*) that pervades the entire universe. This knowledge of the infinite is the source of endless joy, it is asserted. The Sāṁkhya system explicitly addresses itself to the problem of suffering and beings by stating (1.1) its central concern — explanation of the effort (object of man's effort) that leads to freedom from three kinds of *duḥkha* (sorrow), physical, spiritual and accidental. The effort must be directed at achieving a discriminating intellect (*viveka-jñāna*) which tells us that this entire visible creation is a product of *prakṛti* (matter) and *puruṣa* (spirit or life principle) interaction. *Prakṛti*, a modulation of 25 primordial elements, is characterized by three attributes (*guṇa*) which are in balance in the original state but are modulated in interaction with the life-principle (*puruṣa*) so that one or the other attribute dominates and becomes the cause of suffering or happiness, as the case may be. A proper knowledge of *puruṣa*, the essential self, enables one to see all suffering as unrelated to the essential self. But the discriminating intellect alone is not sufficient to free us of suffering — we need to meditate on the primordial elements, the objects of our discriminating intellect, and make constant effort (*abhyāsa*) to dissociate our essential self from them. The Yoga system attributes our sorrows to the distractions of our *citta* and advocates, as the means of joy (*ānanda*), a disciplining of the *citta*, a disciplining of its potential to attach itself to objects of cognition. This disciplining depends on an understanding of the true nature of objects, on the ability to discriminate between *nāma* (designating word), *rūpa* (the form in which the object appears to the senses or is recalled in) and *jñāna* (knowledge, including experience of the object). Progressively more evolved cognizing consciousness, achieved through different froms of *yogic* meditation, enables one to achieve the discriminating intellect (*viveka-jñāna*) that frees us from the bondage of the word that filters indiscriminately into our self. Like other Indian systems of thought, Nyāya also seeks to liberate the self (*ātmā*) from the body, senses and the worldly objects that constitute the objects of senses. The objects are either grasped by senses, in which case they are physically perceptiable or they are cognized by our mind in which case they are "mentally perceptible" but yet products of perception. This creation (*sṛṣṭi*) is a permutation of atoms (*paramāṇu*) and each object represents a particular permutation. Only a proper knowledge of the true nature of object (*tattva-artha*) enables one to decide what is to be acquired or grasped and what is to be rejected or renounced. With the rise of such proper knowledge of the world, and of the self, one's self is no longer subordinate to one's consciousness and, therefore, does not experience either joy or sorrow, i.e., transcends the dichotomies (*dvandvātīta*). The Vaiśeṣika system also seeks to show the path to *mukti*, cessation of sorrow, through *tattva-jñāna*, knowledge of the essential reality of this world. "Let us now explain *dharma*. *Dharma* leads to *tattva-jñāna* (prior knowledge of the primordial elements). *Tattva-jñāna* leads to the highest good" (*Vaiśeṣika-Sūtra* 1, 2, 4). It divides all the worldly objects of knowledge into seven classes (and their sub-classes) and analyses the structure of these objects — their nature, properties and stages. The Jaina system says that *samyagdarśana*, proper and valid knowledge of the self, is the means of salvation (*mokṣa*) which in the case of Jaina thought is the achievement of the natural pure self through a final cessation of *karma*, i.e., mental, verbal and bodily acts (*Tattvārtha-Sūtra* 10.2). The Buddhists attribute all sorrows to "ignorance" (*avidyā*) — the sorrows are "real" but it is possible to be unaffected by them by attaining or practising *nirvāṇa mārga*, which includes proper or valid knowledge as the first of its eight paths.

Therefore in all the major Indian systems of thought, investigation into the nature and totality of objects is a part of the central quest for peace and happiness which is attained only when we comprehend the true nature and totality of the objects that constitute the world around us and the substance of our cognitions. There are five distinctions in the means of liberation — in Mīmāṁsā, *mokṣa* is the result of rightly performing the enjoined acts; in Vedānta it comes from a knowledge of the one ultimate principle that transcends all difference; in Sāṁkhya, it is achieved through a discriminative intellect that appreciates the true reality of the visible world: in Yoga, it comes from disciplining and controlling the *citta* (receptive and creative consciousness); in Nyāya, it is achieved through an authoritative knowledge of what is to be grasped/acquired and what is to be rejected/renounced; in the Vaiśeṣika system, it is attained through a knowledge of what constitutes the highest good; in the Jaina thought it is achieved through a comprehensive and objective knowledge of the self and the non-self and in the Buddhist thought it comes from following the eightfold middle path in one's day-to-day life. Thus the systems alternate between knowledge and action, and often the two are closely related. But all these different means, in one way or the other, depend on a knowledge of the objects, of the cognizable world, for it is the proper knowledge of the cognizable world, both physical and mental which in turn enables us to perform the right acts, reject the undesirable, discover a unity between the self and the non-self, and, finally, become aware of the fundamental unity of the material and the conceptual worlds.

This cognizable world, what we call the world (*jagat*), is an aggregate of particular objects which are uniquely recognized by us as such and as different from the other objects. At the same time all the objects so cognized are seen to be parts of a larger construct, a system. Further the objects while differing from each other, may also resemble some others in given ways, and may also share some properties with some other objects. Thus "water" and "fire" differ from each other but are non-different in their function of purification. Again the peacock-feather resembles the plant *mora-paṅkha* in its shape and colour but the two are actually different. It is to be noted that the difference (*bheda*), the similarity (*sādṛśyatā*) and the non-difference (*abheda*) are not always apparent or perceptible, and the one can discover these only when one has complete knowledge of the true nature and totality of objects in question. To account for this fact of specific diverse particularity (*bheda*) and universal common properties (*abheda*), a distinction is most often maintained, and is maintainable, between what we cognize and refer to (*padārtha*) and what all exists as primordial elements (*tattva*). In other words, the word around us is basically conceptualized as a construct of a few finite primordial elements (*tattva*). We may cognize these elements individually and refer to them as specific objects (*padārtha*) or we may cognize specific objects (*padārtha*) as given permutations of these elements (*tattva*). Thus the ontological constituents of this world (*tattva*) are one thing, and what we talk about as existing and as cognizable (*padārtha*) are quite separate, though the two are inextricably related, in that each *padārtha* is either a *tattva* or a complex or permutation of *tattva*s.

The different enumeration of *tattva*s in each system such as Vaiśeṣika or Nyāya represents that system's specific conceptual analysis of the cognizable reality. Scuh enumerations claim multiple or "pluralistic" reality and support the *bheda* thesis of reality being an aggregate of discrete and diverse objects referred to as *padārtha*. But *bheda* (in the general ethos of the Indian intellectual tradition) is seen as a form of *avidyā*, i.e., incomplete or inadequate knowledge. So long as we do not have *pūrṇa-jñāna* (complete knowledge), objects are cognized as distinct and different from each other. With the rise of complete knowledge, we understand that objects being complexes of *tattva*s are in fact, reflexes of the same one principle (*sattā*). This is the Vedānta claim of a remarkable monism that goes beyond the Sāṁkhya duality of *prakṛti* and *puruṣa* and roots itself in the inseparability of *matter* and *energy*. Such complete knowledge results, says the Yoga system, not from senses and language by themselves but through deep concentration of mind, *samādhi*, which enables one to transcend the trichotomy of knower, known and knowledge and by establishing complete identity of the three leads to illumination, that is, complete experiential knowledge. The Yoga Darśana in this manner mediates between the *padārthavādī* system such as Nyāya-Vaiśeṣika and the *sattā-vādi* philosophy of Vedānta.

Only the Vaiśeṣika system uses the term *padārtha* (*Vaiśeṣika-Sūtra* 1.4) for what the other systems designate as *tattva*s, implying thereby its agnostic standpoint about the objective reality which in the Vaiśeṣika systems becomes the equivalent of cognizable and nameable reality. The *Sāṁkhya-Sūtra* uses the term only when it refutes the Vaiśeṣika doctrine (*Sāṁkhya-*

Sūtra, 5.85) — it uses otherwise, like all other systems, the term *tattva* for the primordial elements. The concept of *tattva* stands for the pre-existing reality as against that which is designated by words, language (see, *Sāṁkhya-Sūtra,* 1.58). As we said, the systems offer different enumerations of *tattvas* — up to eleven in different articulations of Mīmāṁsā,[1] seven in Vaiśeṣika,[2] seven in Jaina thought,[3] twelve in Nyāya,[4] twenty-five in Sāṁkhya.[5] Each system sets up a structure of

---

1. See Table 1.

2. *Vaiśeṣika padārtha* : *dravya* (substance), *guṇa* (attribute), *karma* (action, activity), *sāmānya* (generality or class-character), *viśeṣa* (particularity or individual), *samavāya* (inherence). — *Vaiśeṣika-Sūtra* 1.4.

   For sub-types of each, see *VS,* I.5-7, and for their properties and interrelations, see *VS,* I.8-31.

3. Jaina *tattva* : *jīva, ajīva, āsrava* (sources of action), *bandha* (emerger of self, substance and action), *saṁvara* (blocking of *bandha*), *nirjarā* (slow detachment from actions), and *mokṣa* (complete separation of self from action). — *Tattvārtha-Sūtra* 1.4.

   The two, *jīva* and *ajīva,* are the basic *tattva* — the subsequent five are modifiers of our sub-types of these two.

4. Nyāya *tattva* : *ātmā* (self), *śarīra* (body), *indriya* (of senses), *indriyārtha* (objects of senses), *buddhi* (intellect), *mana* (mind), *pravṛtti* (verbal, bodily and mental actions), *doṣa* (faults), *pretyabhāva* (rebirth), *phala* (fruits/consequences), *duḥkha* (sorrows), *apvaraga* (liberation) (12) — *Nyāya-Sūtra* 1.1.9.

   For definitions and characteristics of each, see *Nyāya-Sūtra,* 1.10-22.

5. *Sāṁkhya tattva* : (a) *prakṛti* (1); (b) *vikṛti* (16) of cognitive senses — *cakṣu, ghrāṇa rasanā, tvak, śrotra* (eyes, ears, taste, touch, hearing) of sense of action — *vāk, pāṇi, pāda, pāyu, upastha* (speech, foot, hand, reproductive organ, excretory organ) *mind,* five elements (earth, water, fire, air, ether/space); (c) *prakṛti-vikṛti* (7) *mahātattva, ahaṁkāra, tammātra* (*śabda, sparśa, rūpa, rasa, gandha*); (d) neither *prakṛti* nor *vikṛti* (1) *puruṣa.*

Table 1: The Mimāṁsā *tattva* (categories)

	1 *dravya* (substance)	2 *guṇa* (attribute)	3 *karma* (action)	4 *śāmānya* (general)	5 *abhāva* (absence)	6 *para-* (dependence)	7 *śakti* (power)	8 *sādṛśya* (similarity)	9 *saṁkhyā* (number)	10 kāla (time)	11 *Deśa* (space)
Kumārila	✓	✓	✓	✓	✓						
Prabhākara	✓	✓	✓	✓		✓	✓	✓	✓		
Murāri	✓ *dharmi*	✓ *dharma*								*ādhāra*	*pradeśa*

these *tattvas* in different hierarchies in accordance with its specific conceptual system. Thus, to take an example, in Nyāya, senses (*indriya*) are a sub-type of the third of the twelve objects of knowledge (*prameya*) and *earth*, etc., the five elements (*bhūta*) are the causes (*kāraṇa*) of senses, and the *smell, taste, form, touch* and *sound* are the five attributes (*guṇa*) of these elements:

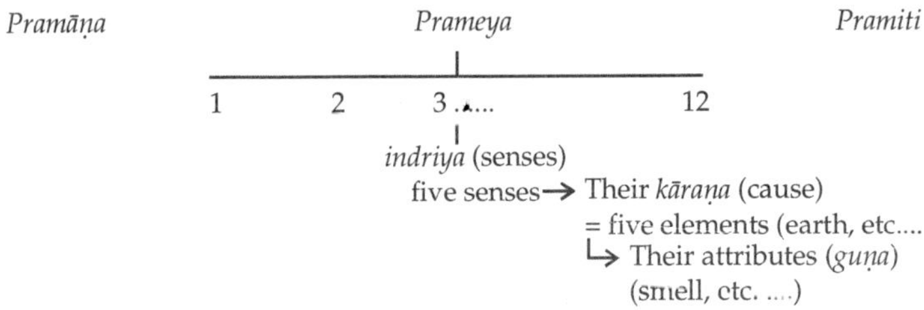

(See *Nyāya-sūtra* 1.1.9-14)

In the Vaiśeṣika system, the hierarchy is different:

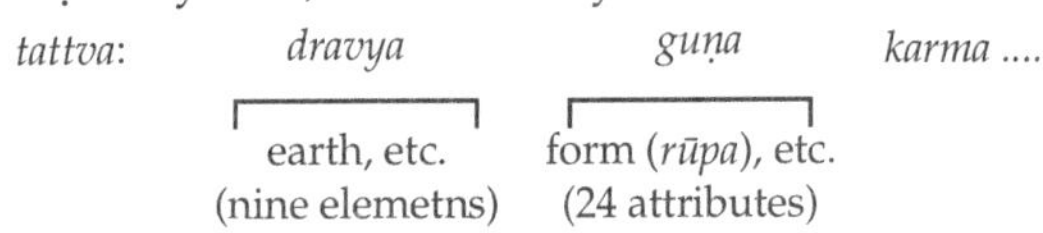

The Nyāya structure represents a more complex conceptual system in which a class of objects of knowledge is identified as that pertaining to the senses, and the elements are identified as "causes," and "smell," etc., are identified as attributes of these "causes" in a dependency hierarchy. But in the Vaiśeṣika system, the elements *earth, etc.,* and *smell, etc.,* are independently posited as primary elements. In this way even the allied systems, such as Nyāya and Vaiśeṣika make different conceptual analysis of the cognizable reality.[6]

We need to carefully desynonymize *padārtha* and *tattva*. *Padārtha* is *artha* of *pada*. *Pada* is a fully inflected word form and *artha* is "that which is intended by the senses."[7] So *padārtha*

6. See Table 2.

7. See *Tattvārtha-Sūtra* (I.17) (with the commentary *Svārthasiddhi*). *Nyāya-Sūtra* also defines *artha* as "objects of sense" (*NS* 1.1.14).

Table 2: *Tattvas in* Indian Philosophical Thought

Mīmāṁsā	1 *dravya* (substance)	2 *guṇa* (attribute)	3 *karma* (action)	4 *śāmānya* (general)	5 *viśeṣa* (particular)	6 *samavāya* (inherence)	7 *abhāva* (absence)	8 *paratantra* (dependence)	9 *śakti* (power)	10 *sādṛśya* (similarity)	11 *saṁkhyā* (number)	12 *kāla* (time)	13 *deśa* (space)
Vaiśeṣika	✓	✓	✓	✓	✓	✓	✓						
Nyāya	covered by *indriya, indriyārtha, pravṛtti*		14 *+duḥkha* (sorrow)	15 *sukha* happiness		16 *apavarga* (liberation)	17 *ātmā* (self)	18 *śarīra* (body)					
Sāṁkhya	Objects of *jñane-nidriya* and *Karmendriya* = *viṣaya and mahābhūta*		19 *+ mana* (mind)	20 *mahat* (infinity)	21 *ahaṁkāra* (pride)	22 *tanmātra* (subtle quality)		23 *puruṣa* (energy)	24 *prakṛti* (metler)	*Mokṣa*[16] (liberation)			
Vedānta	all these as *vivarta of sattā*												
Yoga	All the 25 Sāṁkhya categories												
Jaina	*jīva* *ajīva* cover these with eye eyeless		25 *+ āsrava* (source of righteous and unrighteous conduct)		26 *bandha* (attachment of self to substance)	27 *saṁvāra* (blocking of *āsrava*[(25)])	28 *nirajarā* (gradual non-attachemnt of actions)		*Mokṣa*[16] (liberation)				

is "that which is intended to be referred to or designated by an inflected word." That which can be given a name (designation) is *padārtha*. Designation depends on knowability and; therefore, that which has the capacity to be the object of knowledge is *padārtha*. It has been pointed out[8] that "nameability" and "knowability" are the two characteristics of *padārtha*. Anything that falls within the ken/domain of cognition is *padārtha*. It may be a *tattva*, or it may be a *vastu* (thing). The Yoga system uses this term *vastu* (4.14-17) for the cognizable elements of *dṛśya*, the world amenable to all the three kinds of senses *jñānendriya* (cognitive senses), *karmendriya* (senses that act) and *mana* (mind). These elements are *grāhya* — those that are to be grasped by our cognitive apparatus. The Jaina *Tattvārtha-Sūtra* also uses the term *vastu* for objects that people this world (*TS* 5-38). Bhartṛhari in *Vākyapadīya* also uses the term *vastu* in three *sūtra*s (*VP* II.435, III.4.3, III.3.5) to refer to objects. Bhartṛhari also sometimes uses the term *dravya* for *vastu* (see 3.8.11-12). The *Tattvārtha-Sūtra* explains, there is a *dravyatva* (substancehood) to what are strictly the three primary *tattvas* — *dravya*, *guṇa* and *karma*. *Tattvārtha-Sūtra* clearly says that both basic *tattvas*, *jīva* and *ajīva* are also *darvya* (*TS* 5.3.28-29).

Padārtha is a purely cognitive category, while *tattva* is an existential category and *vastu* is a perceptive category. *Padārtha* is the *vastu* intended to be denoted by it — "independent realities experienced in percception and expressed in language"

Level 1	*tattva*,	Primordial element (*dravya sometime*)	all are *padārthas* linguistically designated and denoted.
Level 2	*vastu*,	discrete objects cognized as such, (*tattvas* or complexes of *tattvas*)	

8. *Pramitiviṣayāḥ padārthaḥ (sapta padārthī); abhidheyatvaṁ padārthasya sāmānyalakṣanaṁ — Tarkadīpikā.*

(S.N. Dasgupta, *A History of Indian Philosophy*, vol. 1, p. 319). These four terms represent this conceptual structure, then:

In this world, there is an extraordinary multiplicity of objects that are variously classifiable as —

1. *mūrta* and *amūrta* (with perceptible form and without form),
2. *parokṣa* and *pratyakṣa* (non-present for the ego and present; remembered versus perceptible),
3. *laukika* and *alaukika* (worldly/sensuous versus supersensuous or divine/cosmic).

This extraordinary multiplicity is made sense of by the *tattva-vastu-padārtha* analysis which arranges objects in an expanding hierarchy that moves from the autonomously existing entities (*tattvas*) to the cognitive constructs (*padārthas*). And when certain philosophical systems, such as Vedānta. postulate the superordinate category of *sattā* (universal being), they seek to reduce the bewildering difference or multiplicity of the cognizable reality to a single principle :

sattā	-	*avyakta* (unmanifest, non-differential) *abhedātmaka*
tattva	-	*anubhūta* (experiential, existential) *bhāvātamaka*
vastu	-	*vyakta* (manifest, differential) *bhedātmaka*
padārtha	-	*vikalpa* (cognitive construct, differential) *bhedātmaka*

We express or designate objects linguistically. Each object that the word refers to each *padārtha*, ontologically, is a structured object, a complex reality. But what is the totality of an object? What is its complete reality? And what is the relationship or proportion that holds between the totality of an object and what is expressed by its linguistic designation/ denotation? That there is an asymmetry between the two, between the existential *padārtha* and the *pada-artha*, is argued at length by Bhartṛhari.

What is the totality of an object? The Yoga system distinguishes three dimensions of an object — (i) *nāma*, its designation, (ii) *rūpa* (its form or appearance), and (iii) *jñāna*, knowledge that arises from its verbal designation. The object *ghaṭa* (pitcher), is different from all the three — the word *ghaṭa* is different from the earthen object it denotes; its form (*rūpa*), that we perceive is only a small part of the reality of *ghaṭa* and not separable from its substance;[9] the object which is cognized when we hear the word *ghaṭa* is a conception of our *citta*, individual consciousness and, therefore, different from the object *ghaṭa* and is asymmetrcial with the existential reality of the object.

It has been pointed out, that when our senses just come into contact with an object, our knowledge of the object is limited to perception — *nirvikalpa*. Subsequently we acquire the *savikalpa jñāna* — class, name, form, colour and properties of the object (*Ślokavārttika*, Perception, 112, 120). The Jaina system points out that an object is *anantadharmātmaka* — has endless properties. For example, to know a human being, we must know his country, birth, class, caste, society, profession, income and name. These are the positive properties (*svaparyāya*) and are necessarily finite. But we also need to know its negations — what the person is not. For example, it is not an elephant, not a leaf, not a meteor. These are the negative properties (*para-paryāya*) and are endless. To that extent, complete knowledge of an object, at least in Jaina thought,

9. If you say "I am not the form, you thereby will understand I am not endowed with form, I do not dwell in form, the form does not dwell in me, . . ." (Nāgārjuna, *Suhṛllekha*, stanza 49).

may not be possible, because an object is an aggregate of all its positive and endless negative properties.

> All things (*vastu*) thus possess an infinite number of qualities (*anantadharmātmakam vastu*), each of which can be only affirmed in a particular sense. Such an ordinary thing as a *jug* will be found to be the object of an infinite number of affirmations and the possessor of an infinite number of qualities from infinite points of view, which are all true in certain restricted senses and not absolutely.
>
> — S.N. Dasgupta, *A History of Indian Philosophy*, vol. 1, p. 176

We propose to take a non-dogmatic view (not restrict ourselves to one school of thought) and build now an outline of "the total reality of an object" (in terms of properties which can be affirmed both positively and negatively):

1. *utpāda, vyaya, dhrauvya* (mutuability, immutability)
2. *pariṇati* (change).
3. *avasthā* (state of the substance, *dravya*)
4. *guṇa* (attributes)
5. *kriyā* (action or tendencies)
6. *svarūpa* (its native self)
7. *jāti* (class)
8. *lakṣaṇa* (marker; distinguishing characteristic)
9. *deśa* (physical location or substratum)
10. *kliṣṭa-akliṣṭa* (cause of sorrow or happiness)
11. *abhāva* (non-existence; negation).

Any given object is both mutable (*anitya*) and immutable (*nitya*) at the same time (see, *TS* 5.30). An object is produced (*utpāda*), expends itself (*vyaya*) and yet its substance remains the same (*drauvya*). This involves a particular conception of stability (*nityatā*), which in Jaina thought means "not giving up its *jāti*." So even when an object undergoes change, its essential substance remains unaffected, as for example when gold earrings are transformed into a gold bangle. This point of view allows for stability and unity in the midst of multiplicity and transformation of this word. This two-fold nature (transformation and stability) of an object implies the birth or coming into being of an object. It is believed by most systems that an object is an effect (*kārya*) of some cause (*kāraṇa*), and exists in an unmanifest form in its source (*kāraṇa*). The Sāṁkhya-Yoga systems, which expound this doctrine, then say that the ultimate source (*mūla tattva*) is *prakṛti* (matter), whose *guṇa*s (attributes) in interaction with *puruṣa* (the life principle), lead to different "effects," the objects. One recognizes in this process of production and transformation, the Buddhist concept of flux — ". . . the unstable, evermoving objects of the six senses" (Nāgārjuna, *Suhṛllekha*, stanza 24).

Change leading to a new effect is thus predicated of all worldly objects. A *ghaṭa* that we see in its present moment has had an origin and before its present *pariṇāma* (*ghaṭatva*) had an unmanifest existence in its *kāraṇa*, clay, and when it undergoes another change and is destroyed, shall persist as a substance, may be, in another form, the form of potsherds. An object, therefore, has a past, a present and a future, marked by three kinds of *pariṇāma* — the object, the form, and the condition or state. One object (pot) may be transformed into another (sherds) and this change takes place in the substance (*dharmī*). Again, a characteristic or marker may change or disappear and be replaced by another, so that there is a change in the form of the object (viz., a green and fresh brinjal dries up into something indefinable), and this change (*pariṇāma*) takes place in the object (*dharma*). Thirdly, the form of the object and the object apparently may remain unchanged but a subtle change takes place in its substance and its attributes, namely, curd growing sour. No *triguṇātmaka vastu* (object characterized by the three primary characteristics of *prakṛti* — *sattva, rajas, tamas*) remains the same even for one second. This *avasthā-pariṇāma* is constantly underway and can be grasped only through intellection and not by observation or experience. In these three kinds of *pariṇāma*, transformations, each subsequent one is more subtle than the preceding one. With reference to any one object, we have to cognize its past, present and future in terms of constant change as all worldly objects are afflicted by *pariṇāma*, effect resulting from either a real or an apparent change in the three-fold *prakṛti*.[10]

But in this flux, there is a core of constancy — the *dharmī* (substance). Its latent powers become manifest as the different objects and one can conceptualize three kinds of powers — those that are potentially present (future), those that have been realized at a given moment (present) and those that have been realized and expended (past).

Consider next the *avasthā* (state or condition) or the five primary elements. Each material element has five aspects and an object is evaluated or defined, among other things, by these and such aspects. Consider for example *vāyu* (air). It has (i) its gross experiential reality — we see the leaves and trees moving, paper and hair flying and inhale it and exhale it. This is its *gross reality*. It has then (ii) its specific *reality* (*svarūpa*) — flow and vibration of pitch. Next it has (iii) a subtle reality (*sūkṣma avasthā*) — the sense of touch (*sparśa tanmātra*) whereby we become aware of its existence. Fourth, what is (iv) its *svabhāva* or dominant mode? Just as it is light (*prakāśa*) for fire, it is movement (*kriyā*) for air in its *anvaya avasthā*. Finally, how it relates to us human beings — it is for our *bhoga* (consumption)

10. Real change in *dravya-guṇa* according to Sāṁkhya and *only* apparent change of form in Advaita-Vedānta.

and also for *mokṣa* (liberation) (through control of breath, *prāṇa vāyu* through *yogic* practices). This is its fifth (v) *arthavatva avasthā*.

Each object has, therfore, (i) its gross reality, (ii) its *svarūpa*, specific reality, (iii) its subtle reality, (iv) its dominant function, and (v) some nexus with human beings. A *ghaṭa*, for example, has its *gross reality* as a metal or clay object that we can see or touch. A round or oblong cylindrical shape with cavity inside and a narrow mouth is its *specific reality*. "Ability to preserve" is its *subtle reality*. To hold something (enclosed within its body) is its dominant *kriyā*. Its use as storage bin, as a musical instrument, as a symbol of life is its *arthavatva avasthā*.

The *fourth* element in the totality of an object is *guṇa*, the attributes. Each object has its *guṇa*s either in the Sāṁkhya sense, a given balance of the three primary elements (given two pitchers, *one* is very pleasing and pure in its appearance — *sāttvika* — while the other is stronger — *rājasika*; and third, *tāmasika*, we do not like the "look" of it, we do not want to touch it) or in the Vaiśeṣika sense, a structure or a complex of various pertinent attributes.[11] For example, in the Vaiśeṣika sense, an auspicious *ghaṭa* may be a complex of at least ten attributes; it is one (*guṇa* 5), bright brown (*guṇa* 1), with a lovely earthy smell (*guṇa* 3), rightly abrasive to the touch (*guṇa*

11. This is the Vaiśeṣika enumeration of *guṇa* : 1. *rūpa* (appearance or colour), 2. *rasa* (taste), 3. *gandha* (smell), 4. *sparśa* (touch), 5. *saṁkhyā* (number), 6. *parimāṇa* (extension), 7. *pṛthaktva* (separateness, individuality), 8. *saṁyoga* (conjunction), 9. *vibhāga* (disjunction), 10. *paratva* (priority), 11. *aparatva* (posteriority), 12. *buddhi* (intellection) 13. *sukha* (pleasure), 14. *duḥkha* (pain), 15. *icchā* (desire), 16. *dveṣa* (aversion), 17. *prayatna* (volitions, efforts). — *VS* 1.1.6.

    To this list, commentators add seven more — 18. *gurutva* (gravity or mass), 19. *dravatva* (fluidity), 20. *sneha* (viscosity), 21. *saṁskāra* (trace or self-restitution), 22. *dharma* (merit), 23. *adharma* (demerit), 24. *śabda* (sound).

4), small (*guṇa* 6), very different from others (*guṇa* 7), is preferable to all other pitchers (*guṇa* 10), a source of happiness (*guṇa* 13), auspicious (*guṇa* 15), and shall bring merit (*guṇa* 22). A *guṇa* is not an absolute — it is realized in each object as a token or modulation of its self.

Consider next *kriyā* — each object has a basic or derived/ extended function, like "holding" or "cooling" for a pitcher. These are the basic functions (*kriyā*). It may be used as a symbol of property and well-being in a marriage, or of death in a cremation. These are its secondary functions.

The specific complex of attributes (*guṇa*) and properties as they are realized in an object, constitutes the *svarūpa* of an object. The same combination of attributes may constitute another complex depending on the degree and proportion of the individual attributes. (For example, any two objects may, while possessing size and/or colour, vary in the size and the colour.) *Svarūpa* is the specificity of the object — its appearance: *svarūpa* is a *kārya* (resultant) of its *guṇas* (attributes). It is the *svarūpa* that separates two objects of the same class (say, two apples) from each other.

There are two senses of *jāti* in relation to objects — (i) universal, and (ii) class in the typology of objects. An object represents a universal apart from its specific *svarūpa* (the individual substance). As Bhartṛhari points out, in the concept/ object *kṛṣṇa tila*, there is substance that expresses itself as a universal *tilatva* and as a quality, *kṛṣṇa* (black) (*VP* III.14.9-10). So every object has these two aspects, the universal and the particular. "Ocean" and "drop" both share the universal substance *water*, and differ in *ākṛti* (form), *ākāra*, which is the shape a *dravya* (substance) takes and therefore, according to Advaita, is no different from *dravya*. Again an object can be placed in the following general typology.

A *ghaṭa* (pitcher) is a *bāhya, laukika, pratyakṣa vastu*. A "remembered *ghaṭa*" a *bāhya, laukika, parokṣa* (non-present in terms) *vastu*. That *one* attribute which separates the intended object from other objects is its *lakṣaṇa* (marker, characteristic feature). Such *lakṣaṇa*s are of two kinds — inherent (such as "heat" in fire) and external (such as the staff carried by a mendicant). The birth-mark in a human being or a scratch on the pitcher is an external *lakṣaṇa* because of its removability.

Physical location or relation (*deśa*) may also constitute a property of some objects and may be of one of the two kinds — *samvāya* (inherence) and *saṁyoga* (conjunction). One of the properties of any "oil" is that it inheres in seed — "inherence in seeds" is its *deśa* (physical location).

Again each object being a particular, attained balance and conglomerate of the three primary *guṇa*s, it is productive of *sukha* (happiness), *duḥkha* (sorrow) and *moha* (attachment). Accordingly, to use Yoga terminology, an object (knowledge of an object) may be *kliṣṭa* (productive of *kleśa*, pain) or *akliṣṭa*. This is how the object may relate to us and may be an instrument of our enslavement or liberation.

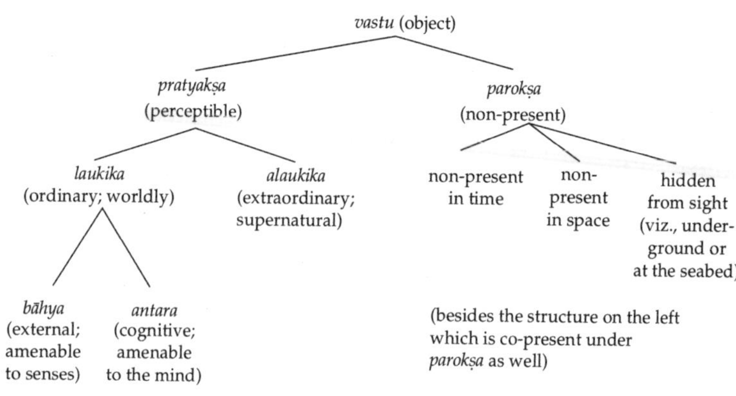

Finally we come to the all important question of nature of existence of objects. The Vaiśeṣika system postulates five kinds of existence of objects (*bhāva* or *sat*):

(1)	existent	*ghaṭa* (pitcher)
(2)	existent that becomes non-existent	broken *ghaṭa* (no longer a pitcher)
(3)	existent non-existent	*ghaṭa* (= *not* -jug)
(4)	non-existent	*ghaṭa-nāsti* (there is no *ghaṭa*)
(5)	absolutely non-existent	horned rabbit

In this projection, existence (*bhāva*) and non-existence (*abhāva*) are intimately interlinked, for non-existence is implicit in existence (as in 3 above), and existence is implicit in non-existence (as in 4 above) where the perception of *ghaṭa* depends on a preception of its existence elsewhere or at another time. In the same way non-existence is inferred from perception of existence (namely, "It wasn't like this then"). Only absolute non-existence (5) is unrelated to existence. Existence and non-existence are, however, different from each other, for no *guṇa* (attribute) or *kriyā* (action) is ascribed or ascribable to non-existent objects.

According to the Yoga system, one cannot predicate non-existence of an object at all as all objects are transformations of *sat* (*Yoga-Sūtras* 4.12, 13), and an object exists as *guṇasvarūpa* either in manifest form when it is seen as such, or as subtle presence or potential in its *kāraṇa-guṇa*s so that the past and the future of an object are as real as its present and constitute an integral part of its total reality.

The total reality of an object is in this manner a complicated matrix of at least eleven categories, varying realizations of which in different objects make for the diversity and multiplicity of objects. We present here in abstract, the "total reality" of *ghaṭa*, a pitcher :

ghaṭa :

- its *mūla tattva*, source material (what is it?)
- is a product (how, who, when, where produced?)
- has an immutable core (what is it?)
- is mutable (how?)
- is subject to three-fold *pariṇati*, transformations (what are these?)
- the states of its physical elements (*avasthā*) are inbuilt into it (what are they?)
- is a complex of *guṇa*s (attributes) (which ones?)
- has given and derived functions (*kriyā*)
- has a *svarūpa* (what is it?)
- has a *jāti* (what is its typology? its universal?)
- has a *lakṣaṇa* (what is it?)
- has a *deśa* (physical context) (what is it?)
- is either *kliṣṭa* or *akliṣṭa*? (which one? in what way?)
- its nature of existence (its past, present and future?)

A complete knowledge of this object involves knowledge of how each of these categories is realized in *ghaṭa* and in what way. Thus, for example, the category *mūla tattva* (source material or substance) may be realized as "clay" or as any one of the metals or wood or plastic, etc. Attributes (*guṇa*s) depend on the *mūla tattva*, are the defining properties of the source material, and therefore what attributes a given object actually has is determined by its *dravya* (material). The specific manifestations of each category constitute the total reality of the object, and these specific manifestations have to be grasped in order to acquire complete knowledge of the object. Besides, in each realization, in the realization of each category, the *ghaṭa*, enters into a series of oppositions to what it is not (*para paryāya*), and these negative properties also constitute its reality.

How is this knowledge attained? This knowledge is expressed in the *nāma* we give to the object. How much of this total reality does the *nāma*, the linguistic designation capture? How much of the reality of *ghaṭa* is communicated by the word *ghaṭa*? Is the *pada-artha* an equivalent or a near equivalent of the *padārtha*? What is the relationship between *pada-artha* and *padārtha*? In other words, when I say I know *X*, I mean I have this complete knowledge of *X*. But what is this complete knowledge and how much of this total reality is coded or communicated by the name *X*? We address ourselves to this question now.

Our exposition, henceforth, is based on Bhartṛhari who, in *Vākyapadīya*, among other things, analyses the relationship between linguistic categories and categories of reality. Our exposition covers the following grounds:

1. Nature of word meaning
2. Relation between word and object
3. How meaning is understood differently
4. Verbal cognition versus direct experience
5. The speaker's *vivakṣā* and the associated meanings
6. Mental imaging as the process or basis of word use
7. What is not expressed
8. What is expressed
9. Object as —
   (a) universal
   (b) substance.

Bhartṛhari notes that words communicate very general meanings — "All words have a meaning amounting to 'something exists' (*asti artha : sarvaśabdānāma iti . . . . VP* II.119). This meaning is the characteristic of the thing denoted by each word . . . ."[12] Particular forms of particular properties do not form a part of the meaning of words. Each word is used to convey a particular object but also has unintended meanings — "a word, when a particular meaning is meant to be conveyed, denotes, by association an unintended meaning also" (*VP* II.301). However, there is always a primary meaning — "Even when the unintended meanings are present and they are conveyed, it is still the meaning which led to the use of the word that is the acepted one" (*VP* II.303). Again, the meaning of word is in its use — without establishing a contact with the object, a word does not convey its meaning. "That is why it has been declared that the relation between a meaning (object referred to) and the word is through *ukti*," that is, application (in utterance) (*VP* II.399).

Three points emerge from the above statement — (i) meaning of reference is basically general and not particular; (ii) besides the primary, intended meaning, there are unintended, associated meanings, and (iii) meaning is established in the utterance that relates the word and its intended object. Therefore, *pada-artha* is neither unitary, nor particular, though there is always a primary meaning.[13]

---

12. The English renderings of Bhartṛhari *kārikās* are being quoted from K.A. Subramania Iyer (tr., ed., exegete) *The Vākyapadīya of Bhartṛhari*, Kāṇḍas II, III, Motilal Banarsidass, Delhi 1977, 1974 and the original Sanskrit extracts are Roman transliterations of the text in K.V. Abhyankar, V.P. Limaye (eds.) *Vākyapadīya of Bhartṛhari*, University of Poona, Sanskrit and Prakrit Series, vol. II, Poona 1965.

13. *na tadasti na tannasti na tadekam na tata pṛthaka* ı *na sansṛṣtam ca vibhaktam ca vikṛtam tattadanyathā* ıı — *VP* III, 2. 12.

What is the nature and status of this primary meaning? Bhartṛhari points out — "Just as it is when the eye is directed towards an object that it preceives it, in the same way, a word denotes an object when deliberately applied to it" (*VP* II.400), ". . . the relation of expression (*abhidhāna*) and expressed (*abhidheya*) is through the function called *abhidhā*" (*VP* II.401). The word through its power of denotation, denotes an object. In the process the word is imposed on the object — in the form "that is this" (*VP* II.128) — "*That* is a *cow*." It is not the object that identifies the word — the object is in fact defined in terms of the word. The word "cow" has an associated image in the speaker's mind which is mapped on to the object, and the hearer also has a mental image of "cow" which is matched with the object. This becomes very clear when the actual object is not present, in which case the object is reconstructed from the mental image. That is, an object is associated with the word through an image — "Others declare that the meaning/ object is something mental," says Bhartṛhari — *buddhiviṣaya* — "but resting on an external object and is looked upon as meaning when it is externalized" (*VP* II.132). So the object is not directly denoted by or cognized through words. This makes verbal cognition of object highly problematic.

Even otherwise we do not get complete or valid knowledge of the object even by perception. Bhartṛhari devotes two *kārikās* to show how perception may produce illusory knowledge. An object is not necessarily as we see it — The sky, he says, is perceived as a surface and the firefly as fire, yet —

> *na caivāsti tala vyomin na khadyote hutāṣanā.*
> There is no surface in the sky nor is the firefly fire.
> — *VP* II. 140

Again —

> Water and mirage are alike in perception (*darśaṇam tulya*).

> But in spite of the similarity of perception, mirage is not water. — *VP* II.287

Therefore,

> the wise man should examine by reasoning even an object apprehended by direct perception. He should not form his idea of the object on the authority of the perception itself.
> — *VP* II.141

So mental mediation, intellection (*yuktitāḥ*) is necessary to gain complete knowledge of even a perceived object; it is far more so in the case of verbal cognition of objects. The two modes in any case are very different, leading to qualitatively different comprehension —

> One who gets burnt experiences the burn through contact with fire in one way and one experiences it in another way through the word burn (*daha*). — *VP* II.418

It is recognized however that just as perception is partial — "It difficult for anyone to see all the parts of an object" (*VP*, II.161) — the knowledge obtained through words is also only partial —

> It is well known that the word expresses what is understood through the senses. It was said before that it expresses the universal and not the things which may accompany it. In other words it does not denote the whole object. Similarly, perception also does not cover the whole object.
> — S.A. Subramania Iyer 1977 : 67

In the verbal expression of an object, the speaker's intention (*vivakṣā*) brings about a focus on some one aspect of the object. Consequently there is great relativism in the way in which objects are presented by words. The same object may be presented differently by different speakers or even by the same speaker on two different occasions —

> . . . an object is presented as rendering whatever service the speakers think of. — *VP* II.430

Thus different "powers" of the object may be brought into focus —

(a) (i) The *arrow* killed the warrior (*kartā,* agent)

(ii) The warrior was killed by an *arrow* (*karaṇa,* instrument)

(b) (i) The child drowned in the lake (*adhikaraṇa.* locative)

(ii) The lake drowned the child (*kartā,* agent)

Also —

> Sometimes objects which are far from one another are presented as being connected and those which are near one another are presentd as being apart. — *VP* II.431

> Separation of what is united and union of what is separated; what are many are presented as one and what is one as many. — *VP* II.432

For this reason and since the word represents, diversely, only a part of the object, Bhartṛhari considers the word as

> . . . only an adventitious mark of an object (*vastupalakṣaṇam*) . . . it is not capable of touching (that is, of expressing) the powers of the object. — *VP* II.434

Prof. K.A. Subramania Iyer explains this *kārikā* thus —

> The point here is that a word really does not touch the essence of an object. It stands far from it and does no more than somehow bring it to the mind . . . it cannot express the powers of the object. — 1977: 186

Partial, intended and relative representation of objects is one aspect of verbal cognition. Another equally distracting aspect

— from the point of view of representation of objects — is the evocation of associated, extended and figurative meanings in addition to primary denotation. So, while on one hand the verbal *denotation* is partial, on the other, there is an excess of *denotation* through extension to resembling objects.

Consider first the associated meanings. The names of flowers are examples — *rajanīgandhā* and *rose* — "one understands those qualities which accompany and are always associated with the smell (of these two flowers)" (*VP* II.162). But such qualities are not invariably present or inherent in the designated object. Consider now secondary or extended usage (for example, use of the word "mountain" for a reflection of the mountain in water, or for the representation of a mountain in a map). Prof. K.A. Subramania Iyer notes :

> To call an earthenware image of a horse *aśvaka* is secondary usage based on similarity of shape. To call a reflection of a mountain *parvataka* is also secondary usage based on resemblance but resemblance due to the relation of original and reflection. — 1977: 294

Bhartṛhari expounds the foundation of secondary usage in a series of *kārikās* —

> Just as a lamp reveals, in an object like a jar, through association (or proximity) other things than that of the illumination of which it was employed.
>
> In the same way, a word conveys, from among the things which are connected together those that are different from the one to convey which it was used. — *VP* II.298, 299

In a brilliant analogy, he explicates the inevitability of associated denotation —

> Though the churning of the ignition sticks (*araṇi*) is done for producing fire, it also produces the unintended smoke in the same process.

> In the same way, a word also, when a particular meaning is meant to be conveyed, denotes by association, an unintended meaning also.
>
> Just as one cannot abandon (while taking a thing) something which is very closely connected with it, in the same way a word cannot but denote what is intimately connected with its primary emaning. — *VP* II.300, 301, 302

Finally consider the figurative meanings that a word acquires and evokes. It often happens in wordly usage, in whole utterances, that the object referred to stands for another, more general concept. "When a boy is told: 'save the butter from the *crows*,' he does not refrain from protecting it from dogs, etc., knowing that the order refers to destructive agents in general" (*VP* II.312). The learned editor and exegete, Prof. Subramania Iyer cites the *Vṛtti* to show that here "crow" stands for "destructive agents in general." Again (vide *VP* II.310) in *gantavayam dṛśyatāma sūrya iti kālasya lakṣaṇe* (*go look at the sun* is an indicator of time) Bhartṛhari shows that "sun" stands for "time." After a number of such examples from popular usage, Bhartṛhari notes that what the words refer to or mean depends not on the word alone but on a number of factors of internal context and external context such as the sentence, situation, meaning, propriety, place and time (vide *VP* II.314) and "connections, separation, association, opposition, the presence of another word" (*VP* II.315) and "suitability, propriety, place, time, gender and accent" (*VP* II.316). He concludes by saying —

> An enlightened hearer knows that praise and blame, meant to promote action and abstention from action respectively, are really unreal.
>
> Even if sometimes, the truth is told in connection with praise or blame, the object is always to teach action or abstention from action. — *VP* II.319, 324

This being so, that the words carry a penumbra of associated extended and secondary meanings, it is clear that there is no bare, absolute or unambiguous denotation of words and the identification and comprehension of the object referred to depends largely on the intellection (reasoning) of the hearer. Therefore, we notice in daily wordly usage, that listeners understand the object differently from the word (*VP* II.135). Thus the expression, "The sun has set" as spoken by a worshipper, a lover and a thief will have different meanings. Prof. Iyer comments:

> Puṇyarāja points out that everybody, in using and understanding a word, is influenced by his own background. A Vaiśeṣika may use the word *ghaṭa* to convey a whole but the Sāṁkhya will understand from it a mere combination of qualities and the Jaina and the Buddha a collection of atoms.
> — 1977: 58-59

In fact, the same person may see "the same thing differently at different times" (*VP* II.136) or

> To one and the same word are attributed many meanings by one and the same person or by many persons according to undefined circumstances. — *VP* II.137

Bhartṛhari in this manner demonstrates at length the extreme relativism in the representation and comprehension of objects in verbal usage and cognition. This relativism is accounted for by the very basis of word use — the images that are constituted in the intellect (*citta*):

> That which is projected on the insentient (*acetana*) forms of the Intellect (*citta*) as a reflection (*pratibimba*), it is that which is the basis of the use of words. — *VP* III.14.325

A particular theory of cognition underlies this statement. We use the word "jar" for a "jar" we have, say, actually observed because we *know* that it is a "jar." So knowledge of the object, of *universal* of the object, exists in our own self (*antaḥkaraṇa*). When we observe an object ("jar" in this case), our pre-existing knowledge is brought up to our consciousness — it is only a reflection because the knowledge continues to exist in our self even after it is brought up and impressed on our consciousness by the external object. This reflection of our knowledge interacts with the image of the external object in our consciousness — we say *image* of the external object because the total reality of the external object is not grasped and projected on to our consciousness but only *our* particular perception of the object. This interaction produces an understanding, in the mind, a mental image and this object "figuring in the mind" is the basis of word usage. The self, and knowledge in the self, is a non-discrete, sequenceless unity but when it comes in contact with different external objects, it takes the form of those objects and we have a fragmented consciousness as a result —

> That is how the form and the time of the consciousness of the experiences is diversified. It has no diversity of form of its own. — *VP* III.14.324

> The distinction between consciousness and objects has to be made and maintained, between "This is *X*" (where *X* is an object) and "This is *X* as *I know it*."

But the *X* in both is a mental construct —

> All wordly usage is carried out with objects created by mental construction as with primary objects.
> — *VP* III.3.82

Again —

> The primary thing has no form till it is determined by the mind. — *VP* III.14.350

Since the mental image is determined by the experiencer's necessarily limited knowledge (*see* again *VP* II.161), "verbal communication relates only to a part of an aspect of reality . . ." (*VP* III.3.52). Words are based on cognitions which do not reveal the full reality and so present things in another form, not determined by their real form" (*VP* III.3.54).

This being the case, we turn finally to what is expressed and what is not expressed by the verbal denotation of objects — the asymmetry between the *pada-artha* and the *padārtha*. It is already clear that words express only a part of the total reality of an object. If we recall here the eleven categories enumerated as constituting the total reality of an object, and the articulations or specific manifestation of those categories, it is now easy to see what the words do not express.

It has already been noted that a word characterizes an object (a) generally (*VP* II.119) and (b) partially (*VP* II.161). So no particular property of feature of an object is part of the meaning of the word used to designate that object. The source material, of which the object is constituted, is not part of the meaning of a word, Similarly, the qualities (*guṇa*) — whose specificity, permutation and proportion the object in any case is — are not part of the meaning of the word (though some of them may be necessarily understood). Everything that exists in an object is not expressed by words — what is expressed depends on the desire of the speaker to speak about it. So some quality may be expressly mentioned in a separate word to constitute a complex object — "white cloth." Otherwise — "just as qualities like *white*, though present (in the rice) are not meant to be conveyed by the word *rice* . . . ." (*VP* II.69). Again no particular form (*ākāra*) is part of the meaning —

> The perception of a particular form which takes place as a result of our seeing a word used constantly for a particular object does not come within the range of a word.
>
> — *VP* II.120

Again —

> An expressive word (like *ghaṭa* = a jar) does not denote the shapes and forms of a jar as it rests only on the general idea (that is common to all the jars). — *VP* II.123

Kriyā or functions of an object — basic or derived — are also not denoted. Nor does the word denote *avasthā, lakṣaṇa deśa, kliṣṭa-akliṣṭa* or class typology (*jāti*). Knowledge of all these has to be acquired by other means.

As for the last category, *bhāva-abhāva*, the *being* (existence) of every object is predicated by words — in fact this is the general meaning of words. Even the "non-existent" or negated objects are assumed to have a positive reality (see *VP* III.3. 59-69). We are already teling of what is actually expressed by words. Words express whole complexes of universal qualities and action. Since substance (*dravya*) in which the universal (*ākṛti/jāti*) inheres is the meaning of a word and a substance cannot be devoid of action and quality, associated qualities and actions also come within the range of words:

> In the cognitions, all the helpful things are connected with one another and so the word is expressive of all of them such as they figure in the cognition. — *VP* III.14.473

So

> words like brāhmaṇa stand for that which manifests the universal (*brāhmaṇatva*) which is invariably associated with certain acts, which is understood, through established convention, to possess certain qualities, irrespective of whether it is a combination of them or only a part. . . .
> — *VP* III.14.481-2

No one part is referred to nor is any excluded. In certain usages, the associated qualities become manifest and get independently expressed —

"In scholarship, he is a brāhmaṇa" ("scholarship" is an attribute of brāhmaṇas). In the same way "there are some actions invariably associated with the word and accepted in the world like the meaning of the word itself" (*VP* III.14.508). For example, the word *putra* (son) is associated with the action of obeying the parents, etc.

But the core denotation of a word is the expression of *Being* — *sattā* — of an object. It is granted by the Grammarians, that with reference to objects, words express both (a) universal (*ghaṭatva*) and (b) substance (individual) *dravya,* as it is through the particular forms as the limiting factors (*dravya*) that the ultimate reality (*sattā*) is expressed. If all objects are transformations of one ultimate reality (*prakṛti* and *puruṣa* of Sāṁkhya, or *sattā* of Advaita) then each object has a universal aspect and a particular aspect, and both are denoted by words. The Grammarians, Bhartṛhari, in particular, seem to take the Advaita position in their conceptualization of the reality of objects, and in their epistemology — of how valid knowledge of objects and of reality in the final analysis is to be gained. Their position has affinities with the Yoga system (see *Yoga-Sūtras* 3.14-20, 3.49-54, 4.18-23). Consider, for example, Bhartṛhari's view that all reality exists as a form of consciousness, and that reality is essentially non-discrete and non-sequential and that the "difference" we experience, the *bheda,* in the "forms" of objects is a form of *avidyā* impurity (*VP* III.3.57) and that knowledge of forms is also a tainted knowledge. For valid knowledge, one has to go beyond forms of external objects, beyond words/language. Verbal knowledge is only one kind of knowledge (see, *TS* 1.9) — and is essentially only indicatory and limited (see, *Vaiśeṣika-Sūtra* 7.2.20). Therefore, to repeat Bhartṛhari's injunction — since one cannot form an idea of the object on the basis of perception or words, one should examine each object of knowledge by "reasoning" (*VP* II.141). The Yoga system talks of *pūrṇa jñāna* (3.17), complete knowledge, *viveka jñāna* (3.49) (discriminating knowledge) and *kaivalya jñāna* (4.34) (knowledge of original unity). The Jaina system talks of *samyagdṛṣṭi* or *samyag jñāna* (*TS* 1.2). How is this complete knowledge of objects to be acquired? This is important because whole areas of the total reality of an object are not part of the meaning of words. We need a means of knowledge other than language. The Yoga theory of knowledge is devoted to this problem. It sets up several intermediate kinds of knowledge between *sāmānya jñāna* (ordinary knowledge) and *pūrṇa jñāna* (complete knowledge) which is defined as knowledge strictly of the object (*dhyeyamātra*) such that one loses awareness even of the self, so intensely does one meditate on the object (*Yoga-Sūtras* 3.11). Such knowledge is possible of acquisition only when the *citta* (consciousness) is rid of all other distractions and is made one-pointed (*ekāgra*) in its focus on the object. All the faculties of the mind, in that state, are applied to the object of knowledge. The consciousness thus seeks to grasp object in its totality: (i) the constant *pariṇati*, change, it is undergoing of three kinds — in form, in its *lakṣaṇa*, the distinguishing characteristic, and in its state: (ii) the three *dharma*s — powers of the substance (*dravya*) — those that exist as potential powers, those that are manifest, and those that have been fulfilled and expanded. In this manner, the knower grasps the past, the present and the future of the object; (iii) *karma*, the sequence in which change or changes have taken place in the object as a change in sequence can lead to a change in the object; (iv) the state of the attributes of the five primordial elements (earth, etc.) in the given object; (v) the non-difference of existence and non-existence of the object in terms of the continued existence of its *prakṛti* — the source material, and; (vi) the potential of the object for happiness and sorrow to those who come in contact with it.

As our discussion of what is not expressed in words shows, these are exactly the opaque areas in verbal denotation which render the verbal knowledge incomplete. In the Yoga theory of cognition, these become the focal points for grasping the reality of objects. How is their knowledge gained? The *draṣṭā*, the seeker or knower does *saṁyama* in these aspects; he follows the course of *yogic* meditation — *dhāraṇā, dhyāna* and *samādhi* as a result of which — he actually visualizes (*sākṣātkāra*) these aspects of the object and gains knowledge of the past and of the future of the object. It is the heightened consciousness, completely focussed on the object that becomes the instrument of meditation, and the knower, losing awareness of his self and of everything else merges with the object transcending the trichotomy of the knower, the known and the instrument of knowledge. As a result of this process, he acquires three kinds of knowledge of the object — (i) subtle knowledge that is not apparent to the senses; (ii) knowledge free of the temporality, and (iii) knowledge free of the spatial constraints. He acquires extraordinary powers of cognition and perception.

Citta (consciousness) is the prime instrument of knowledge in this process. When objects come into contact with it, they leave impressions (reflections) on the *citta*. When the reflection of an external object appears in the *citta*, an awareness of its existence also takes place. Its function is to record and show the true form of the external objects to the *draṣṭā*. The form of the *citta* that results from the reflection of an external object as *experienced by the draṣṭā* (the self) is its *vṛtti*. It is these forms of consciousness that filter into, and shape, the self. The *vṛtti*s come and go, but the *citta* or consciousness abides. It is possible, says the Yoga system, to rid the *citta* of all its *vṛtti*s and restore the pure, original consciousness which then becomes a pristine instrument of knowledge.

This proper knowledge, howsoever defined in different

systems, once attained, liberates man from the sorrows and sufferings of this world — as all sorrows and sufferings arise from *bheda buddhi*, the mind that perceives "difference" (between *here* and *there*, *now* and *then*, *I* and *you*, etc.) in terms of an extraordinary multiplicity of objects. Proper knowledge, *abheda buddhi*, of the oneness of ultimate reality (*sattā*) helps one transcend the difference and realize the unity of all beings, at this level of reality.

This knowledge enables us to see that all objects are ultimately reflexes of one (*sattā*). The conceptual argument runs thus —

> Soem consider the universal to be merely something which figures as a common characteristic in our mind and the particular (*dravya*) to be that which figures as differentia.
>
> . . . This diversity in objects arises only when they are united in some way.
>
> Neither identity nor difference, neither existence nor non-existence of objects is possible if they are not linked with one another. — *VP* III.1.19, 20, 21, 22
>
> The ultimate view is that it is one which has all the powers. — *VP* III.1.19-22

This one is the universal in all objects and expressed by words that denote objects. This universal is manifested in individual objects —

> Just as a face, reflected in water, etc., is only called as such (that is a face without any connection with water), in the same way a word expresses only the universal manifested by the individuals. — *VP* III.1.29

This universal is the Being (*sattā*) :

> It is Being which, being differentiated according to the object in which it is present, is called the universal. All words are based on that. — *VP*, III.1.33

This theory should not be mistaken as a mystic conception — it is an expression of the nature of the physical as well as the linguistic reality. The socurce and substance of all creation is the interaction of matter (*prakṛti*) and energy (*puruṣa*) and this single principle (*sattā*) takes diverse, multiple forms we recognize as different from each other. This is modern physics and also Sāṁkhya system of thought. Again the same one word, "apple," a common noun, is applied to all the millions of apples, not two of which are identical in terms of the emprical reality. There is, therefore, some universal, "appleness," that is common to all and enables the application of the same one word to all the individual objects.

Bhartṛhari in accordance with the Sāṁkhya and Advaita conception says; that everything is a transformation, *pariṇāma* and *vivarta*, and that there is no absolute difference between cause and effect, *sāmānya* (general) and *viśeṣa* (particular), *sattā* (universal) and *dravya* (individual substance) :

> When abandoing all distinctions, the essence of the individuals is perceived as one, then a single conception comes into existence. — *VP* III.1.96

But if the words only denote the universal in objects where is the need for so many words and how is the apparently differential reality cognized. Or does it amount to a rejection of the empirical reality? No. Bhartṛhari says the difference is as real as the non-difference and that the universal, as qualified by the individual is the denotation of words —

> Just as the word cradle (*mañca*) while continuing to denote that object, expresses by identification, what is on it, so does a word expressive of the universal, denote the substance (individual). — *VP* III.14.347

Dravya (substance) then is also the denotation of words. That is words denote the individual objects as much as they denote the universal present in all such objects. In fact, words cannot express the ultimate reality directly, that ultimate reality which is the invariant substance in all the objects. It expresses the ultimate reality through the limiting factors (*upādhi*) that these individual objects are (*VP* III.2.2) — it is as if the unmanifest one becomes perceptible only as many. It has been pointed out that the word *dravya* has as its synonyms such key concepts as *ātmā, vastu, svabhāva, tattva* and *prakṛti* (*VP* III.2.1). It is the grammarian's standpoint that the words express *prakṛti* through *vastus* (objects). These objects, these forms are transient and impermanent, while *prakṛtis* is without beginning (*anādi*) and without end (*ananta*). The object is like a *saṅketa*, an indicator of the primary, universal substance. The word thus conveys both the impermanent form and the eternal (*VP* III.2.6).

Therefore, it is through word use that the undifferentiated reality appears differentiated —

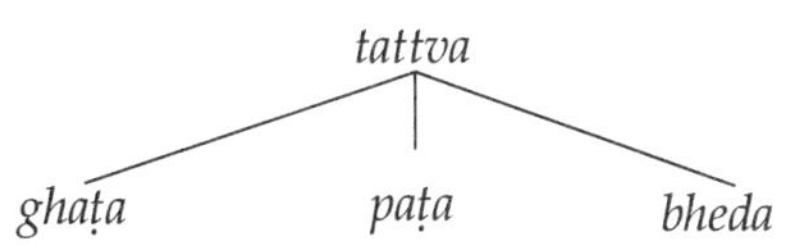

It is this sense that the *Ṛgveda* asserts, as we noted in the beginning, that "Language cuts forms in the ocean of reality" (I.164.41). These forms do not all belong to the Reality and yet they appear as one with it just as "attributes (*guṇa*) of the object cannot belong to cognition at all and yet . . . appear one with it" (III.2.8, 9).

What is this Reality? What is real? "That is real which persists. . . . when all the forms disappear. . . ." Prof. Iyer cites the *Mahābhāṣya* and reports "that is eternal whose *tattva* is not destroyed." The forms of the different ornaments vary and are impermanent, but the gold persists in all of them : . . .

compared to the different individual cows, *cow*-ness is *nitya* (without known beginning and end). Compared to cow-ness, horse-ness, etc., *pṛthvī*-ness is eternal. Compared to that, the fact of being just a thing is eternal, an idea which can be conveyed by the pronoun *tat*. This Reality is different from all appearances — we cannot say it has this particular form or that. It is beyond assertions, beyond human judgements —

> It does not exist and it does; it is one and it is many; it is connected and it is separted; it is transformed and it is not.
> — *VP* III.2.13

This Reality does not, cannot, undergo any change, yet the universe is manifested as change (*vivarta*). It is all encompassing and it holds everything within itself — *kāraṇa* (cause) and *kārya* (effect); *dṛśya* (the visible, material world), *darśana* (perception), *draṣṭā* (the seer, observer); knower, knowledge and known word, meaning and its relation. Nothing abides outside this Reality.

> Just as, when forms (*vikāra*) disappear, it is gold which is the truth (*satya*) in the earrings, etc., in the same way, when transformations (*vikāra*) (like earth, etc.) disappear the primordial substance (*prakṛti*) remains. — *VP* III.2.15

> All words express *Brahman* (universal), differentiated on the basis of limiting factors (*dravya*, substance). Even words like *ātmā, Brahman, tattva* express that *prakṛti* through some limiting factor or other. Because that which is beyond all limiting factors (*nirupādhi*) is also beyond the range of words. — 1971: 74

The differentiated, often contradictory and sequential reality we experience is like our dream experience — *svapne-rūpāṇicetasaḥ* —

> Just as, in a dream, one mind appears in contradictory forms, as the self and the non-self, friend and foe, the speaker and the spoken and the purpose, in the same way, while the ultimate reality (*sattā*) is unborn (*anādi*), eternal (*ananta*) and devoid of inner sequence (*a-krama*), we see it as having birth and other contradictory attributes.

The dream creation is impermanent; the wakeful state is only relatively more permanent. Both are unreal — the only persisting reality is the consciousness which creates these worlds out of itself. So is the *mūla tattva* (permanent), the *prakṛti*, recognized as manifold forms cognized as such by our consciousness.

Conclusion

Pada-artha, verbal denotation, creates for us the highly differentiated word around us, the *ghaṭa-paṭa-bheda*. However, *padārtha*s (objects), such as *ghaṭa* and *paṭa* are far more complex realities than what the *pada-artha* would indicate. A complete knowledge of these external objects would establish them as transient manifestations of a non-sequential, non-discrete *prakṛti* which persists (*nitya*) in all *vikāra* (specific forms assumed). It is our recognition of this structure of all existence that imparts a seeming order to this extraordinary transience, diversity and multiplicity. When I say "I know *X*," therefore, in the Indian tradition of thought I may mean "This is *X*" or that "I know this *X* to be a *sattā-vivarta*." That is, our knowledge of *X* can range from *sāmānya jñāna* (common knowledge born of perception or verbal denotation) though several intermediate stages of knowing to *pūrna jñāna* which can be grasped only by a single-minded concentration (*ekāgratā*) of the *citta*, and when attained this knowledge will release the knowing self from the bondage of joys and sorrows that flow form its attachment to object.

Bibliography

THIS is a classified listing of, mostly, modern writings on Sanskrit grammar, poetics and theory of meaning. It is arranged in four sections:

From among the classical Sanskrit works, only the major ones used in the book are included here. Other Sanskrit works, including those referred to in the text of this study, have been published off and on by the following oriental publishers, and generally available with them:

1. Chaukhamba Sanskrit Sansthan, Varanasi, India.
2. Chaukhamba Orientalia, Varanasi, India.
3. Chaukhamba Sanskrit Pratishthan, Delhi, India.
4. Gita Press, Gorakhpur, India (for Ādi Śaṅkara's exegetical works).

A. Grammar and Theories of Meaning

Abhyankar, K., 1955, "A Short Note on the Paribhāṣā works in Sanskrit Grammar," *Annals of Baroda Oriental Research Institute* (ABORI), 36: 157-62.

———, 1969, "Dramatic, Pictorial and Verbal Representation of Past Events at the time of Patañjali," *Festschrift Gopinath Kaviraja*, Lucknow: Akhil Bharatiya Parishad.

———, 1977, *A Dictionary of Sanskrit Grammar*, Baroda: Oriental Institute.

Agarwala, V.S., 1937, "Yāska and Pāṇini," in the *Cultural Heritage of India*, vol. I., Calcutta: The Ramakrishna Mission, Institute of Culture, 2nd rev. edn., 1958, pp. 293-310.

———, 1953, *India as Known to Pāṇini*, Lucknow: University of Lucknow 2nd edn., 1963, Varanasi: Prithvi Prakashan.

Aklujkar, Ashok N., 1970, "Ancient Indian Semantics," *Annals of Bhandarker Oriental Research Institute*, 51: 11-29.

Allen, W.S., 1953, *Phonetics in Ancient India*, London: Oxford University Press (Reprint 1963).

Apte, V.M., 1937, *The Vedāṅgas*, in *Cultural Heritage of India*, vol. I., Calcutta: Ramakrishna Mission Institute of Culture, 2nd rev. edn., 1958, pp. 264-92.

Barlingay, S.S., 1964, "Theories of Language in Indian Logic," New York: *International Philosophical Quarterly*, 4: 94-109.

Bhandarkar, R.G., 1877, "Dr. Goldstücker's Theory about Pāṇini's Technical; Terms," *Indian Antiquary*, 6.107-13.

Bhartṛhari, *Vākyapadīya*, K.A. Subramania Iyer, tr. & ed., 1977, Chapter I, Deccan College Poona, 1965. Chapter II, Chapter III, Part I, 1973 and Chapter III Part II, 1974, Delhi: Motial Banarsidass.

Bhaṭṭa, Nagesh, *Mahābhāṣya Pradīpodyota*, 1901-21 (Bibliotheca Indica, 142), 4 vols.

———, *Parama Laughumañjūṣa* (tr., exegete) Acharya Lokamani Dahal, 1991, Varanasi: Chowkhamba Surbharati Prakashan.

———, (18th century) *Paribhāṣendu Śekhara*, see under Kielhorn and Vishvanatha Mishra.

———, *Vyākaraṇa-Siddhānta Mañjūṣā*, ed. Dr. Kalika Prasada Shukla, 1977, Varanasi: Sampurnanand Sanskrit Vishwavidyalaya.

Bhattacharya, Bishnupada, 1956, "Constitution of Words: Sphoṭa Theory and its Opponents," *Our Heritage: Bulletin of the Sanskrit College*, Calcutta.

———, 1957, "Connotation of words" (A Comparative Study of the Viewpoints of Grammarians, Mīmāṁsakas, and Naiyāyikas), *Our Heritage: Bulletin of the Sanskrit College*, 5: 147-67.

———, 1958, *Yāska's Nirukta and the Science of Etymology: An Historical and Critical Survey*, Calcutta: Mukhopadhyaya.

———, 1962, *A Study in Language and Meaning: A Critical Examination of some Aspects of Indian Semantics*, Calcutta: Progressive Publishers.

Bhattacharya, G.N., 1937, "A Study in the Dialectics of Sphoṭa," *Journal of the Dept. of Letters*, University of Calcutta.

Bhattacharya, Ram Shankar, 1950-52, "Pāṇinian Principles of Determining the Desired Import of Words," *Journal of Andhra Historical Research Society*, 21: 133-141.

———, 1952-53, "Significance of the Examples in the Mahābhāṣya," *Journal of Ganganatha Jha Research Institute*, 10: 39-48.

———, 1953, "Kinds of Agents (Kartā) as Depicted by Pāṇini," *Vāk*, 3: 129-33.

———, 1954-55, "On the Original Reading of a Pāṇinian Sūtra," Baroda: *Journal of Oriental Institute*, 4: 268-29-69 (on the rule 6.1.115).

———, 1956, "Some Objections on the Textual Order of the Aṣṭādhyāyī and their Refutation," Allahabad: *Journal of Ganganatha Jha Research Institute*.

Bhawe, Shrikrishna Sakharam, 1953, "Pāṇini's Rules and Vedic Interpretation," Ahmedabad, *Proceedings of the All India Oriental Conference*, 17: 231-40.

Bloomfield, L., 1933, *Language*, New York, Holt, Rinehard Winston, 1965.

Botha, Rudolph P., *The Conduct of Linguistic Inquiry*, Mouton: 1980.

Brough, J., 1952, "Audumbarāyana's Theory of Language," London: *Transsactions of the Philosophical Society*, 73-77.

———, 1953, "Some Indian Theories of Meaning," London: *Transsactions of the Philosophical Society*, 161-76.

Buddha, Prakash, 1969, "On Pāṇini's Sūtra V.3.99," *Festschrift Adityanath Jha*, 3: 394-404.

Burnell, A.C., 1875 (1976), *On the Aindra School of Sanskrit Grammarians*, Varanasi: Bharat-Bharati.

Burrow, T., 1936, "Indian Theories on the Nature of Meaning," London: *Transsactions of the Philosophical Society*, 93-93 (summary of paper).

Cāndra-Vyākaraṇa, See under Kshitish Chandra Chatterji.

Cardona, George, 1967, "Pāṇini's Syntactic Categorism," Baroda: *Journal of the Oriental Institute*, 16: 201-15.

———, 1970, "Some Principles of Pāṇini's Grammar," Dordrecht: *Journal of Indian Philosophy*, 1: 40-74.

———, 1971, "Cause and Causal Agent: the Pāṇinian View, Baroda: *Journal of the Oriental Institute*, 21: 22-40.

———, "Indian Grammarians on Adverbs," *Festschrift Kahane*, Urbana, University of Illinois, pp. 85-98.

———, 1974, "On Pāṇini's Metalinguistic Use of Cases," *Festschrift Charudeva Shastri*, Delhi : The Charudeva Shastri Felicitation Volume Committee, pp. 305-26.

———, 1974, "Pāṇini's Kārakas: Agency, Animation and Identity," Dordrecht: *Journal of Indian Philosophy*, 2. 231-306.

———, 1976, *Pāṇini — A Survey of Research*, The Hague: Mouton Co. (Rpt. Motilal Banarsidass, Delhi, 1980).

———, 1976 (Indian reprint 1980), *Pāṇini: His work and its Traditions*, vol. I., Motilal Banarasidas, Delhi.

Chakravarti, P.C., 1933, *The Linguistic Speculations of the Hindus*, Calcutta: University of Calcutta.

Chatterji, Kshitish Chandra (ed.), 1953-61, *Cāndra Vyākaraṇa* of *Candragomin* 2 vols., Poona: Deccan College.

———, 1964, *Technical Terms and Technique of Sanskrit Grammar*, Kolkata : University of Calcutta.

Chomsky, N., *Aspects of the Theory of Syntax*, Mass: MIT Press, 1965.

Comrie, Bernard, 1981, *Language Universals and Linguistic Typology*, Basil Blackwell.

Devasthali, G.V., *Apropos of Vibhāṣa*, in International Seminar on Pāṇini — Summaries of Papers (*ISP-SP*), University of Poona. 1981.

Dīkṣita, Bhaṭṭojī, *Siddhānta Kaumudī*, see under S.C. Vasu.

Ducrot, Oswald and Tzvetan Todorov, 1981, *Encyclopaedic Dictionary of the Sciences of Language*, Latherine Porter (tr.), Oxford.

Ghatge, Amrit Madhav, 1968, "Pāṇini 1.4.32.," *Festschrift S.M. Katre, S.M. Katre Felicitation*, Vol. 2, pp. 150-54.

Gonda, Jan, 1974, "Nimitta," *Festschrift Charudeva Shastri*, pp. 233-40.

Gopala Sastri, Darsana Kesari, *Pāṇinīyaprabodha*, Saraswati Bhawan Granthamala, Varanasi.

Haradatta, 1892-9, *Padamañjarī*, Banaras: Pandit Series.

Heimann, Betty, 1941, "Sphoṭa and Artha," *A Volume of Studies in Indology*, presented to Prof. P.V. Kane, pp. 221-27, Poona: Oriental Book Agency.

Jaini, Padmanabh S., 1959, "The Vaibhaṣika Theory of Words and Meanings," London: *Bulletin of the School of Oriental and African Studies*, 22 : 95-107.

Jigyasu, Pt. Brahma Dutt, *Sanskrit Paṭhan-pāṭhana ki Saralatama Vidhi* (2 vols.), Bahalgarh (Haryana): Ram Lal Kapur Trust, 1982.

Joshi, S.D., 1966, "Patañjali's Definition of a Word — An Interpretation," *Bulletin of the Deccan College Research Institute*, 25: 65-70.

Joshi, S.D. and Roodbergen, 1971-73, J.A.F., *Patañjali Vyākaraṇa-Mahābhāṣya*, Poona: University of Poona.

Kapoor, K., 1992, "Norm and Variation: Pāṇini to Kumārila Bhaṭṭa — A Classical Indian Debate" in R.N. Srivastava, ed., *Text and Language, Papers in Honour of A. Kelkar.*

———, 1994, *Language, Linguistics and Literature — The Indian Perspective*, Academic Foundation, Delhi.

———, 1994, "Pāṇini's Vyākaraṇa: Questions of Theory and Order" in *S.M. Katre Felicitat*, Poona: Deccan College.

Katre, S.L., 1938, "Kautsa Vyākaraṇa: A Detailed Notice," *New Indian Antiquary*, Bombay, 383-96.

Katre, S.M., *Dictionary of Pāṇini*, Parts I-III, Deccan College, Poona, 1968.

Kielhorn, F. (ed.), 1960, "The Paribhāṣenduśekhara of Nāgoji Bhaṭṭa," Part II, 2nd edn., K.V. Abhyankar, Poona: Bhandarkar Oriental Research Institute.

———, 1882, 1883, 1885, *Mahābhāṣya of Patañjali*, vols. I, II, III, Bombay Sanskrit and Prakrit Series.

———, 1887, "Some Devices of Indian Grammarians," *Indian Antiquary*, 16: 244-52 (Rpt. Stall, 1972: 123-34).

———, 1898, "The Jātakas and Sanskrit Grammarians," London: *Journal of the Royal Asiatic Society of Great Britain and Ireland*, 1898: 17-21.

———, 1962 (ed.), *The Paribhāṣenduśekhara of Nāgoji Bhaṭṭa*, Part I, New edition with an Introduction by K.V. Abhyankar, Poona: Bhandarkar Oriental Research Institute.

Kiparsky, Paul and J.F. Staal, 1969, "Syntactic and Semantic Relations in Pāṇini," *Foundations of Language*, 5 : 83-117.

Kiparsky, Paul, 1980, *Pāṇini as a Variationist*, University of Poona, Poona.

Kishore, Nanda, 1990, *Aṣṭādhyāyī Sūtra Pāṭha* (*Vārttika-Gaṇapāṭha-Sahita*), Panipat: Anita Arya Prakashan.

Kunjunni Raja, K., 1954, "The Theory of Meaning According to the Buddhist Logicians," *Adyar Library Bulletin*, 18 : 178-95.

———, 1955, "Indian Theories on Homophones and Homonyms," *Adyar Library Bulletin*, 19: 193-222.

———, 1957, "Ākāṇkṣā: The Main Basis of Syntactic Unity," *Adyar Library Bulletin*, 20: 282-95.

———, 1957, "Yāska's Definition of the 'Verb' and the 'Noun' in the Light of Bhartṛhari's Explanation," *Annals of Oriental Research*, Madras.

———, 1958, "The Elliptic Sentence — Indian Theories," *Adyar Library Bulletin*, 22: 25-31.

———, 1958, "The Indian Influence on Linguistics," *Journal of the Madras University*, 30: 93-111.

———, 1962, "Prārthayanti — A Ghost Word Discussed by the Grammarians," *Adyar Library Bulletin*, 26 : 26-28.

———, 1963, "Indian Theories of Meaning," Madras: *The Adyar Library Bulletin*.

———, 1964, "Bhartṛhari's List of Sentence Definitions," *Adyar Library Bulletin*, 28: 206-10.

———, 1965, "Pāṇini's Attitude Towards Lakṣaṇa," *Adyar Library Bulletin*, 29 : 177-87.

———1956, "Transfer of Meaning — A Buddhist View," *Adyar Library Bulletin*, 20: 345-348.

Laddu, Suresh Chandra Dhyaneshwar, 1971, "Ancient Sanskrit Grammarians and the Literary Records," *Hoshiarpur: Vishveshvarananda Institute Journal*, 9: 315-22.

Lele, Jayant and Rajendra Singh, 1987, "Pāṇini, Language Theories and the Dialectics of Grammar" in Hans Aarsleff *et al.* (eds.), Papers in the History of Linguistics, Amsterdam/ Philadelphia: John Benjamins Publishing Co.

Mahulkar, D.D., 1981, *The Prātiśākhyan Tradition and Modern Linguistics*, Baroda: M.S. University of Baroda.

Mehendale, M.A., 1965, Nirukta Notes, Series I, Poona: Deccan College.

Mishra, Narayan (ed., tr., exegete) 1972, *Kāśikā* (of Vāmana and Jayāditya), Varanasi: Chaukhamba Sanskrit Sansthan (Sanskrit text with Hindi explanation).

Mishra, Prabhakara, Bṛhati, unpublished (only incomplete manuscript in the Library of the Asiatic Society), Calcutta.

Mishra, Ramakant, 1966, *Vyākaraṇa Śāstra Ka Sankṣipta Itihāsa*, Varanasi: Chaukhamba (Hindi).

Mishra, Vidyaniwas, 1964, *Pāṇini's Grammar as a Mathematical Model*, Festschrift Baburam Saksena, pp. 157-78.

———, 1970, "Structural Meaning: An Indian Standpoint," *Actes du ... Congress International des Linguists*, 10.2: 555-59.

Mishra, Viśvanātha (tr. and commnt.), 1985, *Paribhāṣenduśekhara*, Varanasi: Chaukhamba Surabharati Prakashan.

Moghe, S.G., 1971, "Paribhāṣās of Vyākaraṇa and the Mīmāṁsā Rules of Interpretation," *Festschrift Rajeswar Shastri Dravid*, Allahabad: Bharati Parisad, English Section, pp. 90-100.

Narayana, Murli, M.S., 1973, *Sanskrit Compounds, A Philosophical Study*, Varanasi: Chaukhamba.

Narayana Murti, M.S., 1973, "Philosophy of Grammar," Proceedings of the Seminar on Andhra's Contribution to Indian Culture, Tirupati, *Sri Venkateswara University Oriental Journal*, Tirupati, 37-54.

Narendra, Chandra Nath, 1969, *Pāṇinian Interpretation of the Sanskrit Language*, Varanasi: Banaras Hindu University.

Palsule, Gajanan Balakrishnan, 1961, *The Sanskrit Dhatupāṭhas — A Critical Study*, Poona : University of Poona.

———, 1970, *Some Views of Pāṇini and his Followers on Object-language and Meta-language*, University of Poona: Publications of the Centre of Advanced Studies in Sanskrit, A36.

Pandey, Kanti Chandra, 1963, *Abhinavagupta, an Historical and Philosophical Study*, Varanasi: Chaukhamba.

Pandey, Pt. Ramanarayanadatta Sastri, 1955, *Mahābhārata*, 6 vols., Gorakpur: Gita Press (Sanskrit text with Hindi translation).

Pandey, Ram Chandra Sharma, 1962, "Zero in Pāṇini," *Journal of the Maharaja Sayaji Rao University*, Baroda, 11.1 : 53-66.

———, 1963, *The Problem of Meaning in Indian Philosophy*, Delhi: Motilal Banarsidass.

———, 1971, *Pāṇini and the Vedic Interpretation*, *Festschrift Rajeshwar Shasri Dravid*, Allahabad: Bharati Parishad, English section, pp. 49-53.

Pāṇini, *Dhātupāṭha*, see under J.L. Shastri.

———, *Aṣṭādhyāyī*, S.C. Vasu (ed. & tr.). Motilal Banarsidass, vol. I and II, 3rd Reprint, 1980.

Patañjali, *Mahābhāṣya*, Y. Mīmāṁsaka (Commentator), Part I, Ram Lal Kapur Trust, Bahgarh, 1979 (S.K. Text with Hindi commentary).

———, *Mahābhāṣya*, see under (i) Y. Mimamsaka, (ii) S.D. Joshi and J.A.F. Roodbergan, (iii) Vedavrata Varnin.

———, *Mahābhāṣyam*, Part 1, Yudhiṣṭhira Mīmāṁsaka (tr. & explanator), 1979, Bahalgarh: Ram Lal Kapur Trust Press, (Sanskrit Text with Sanskrit/Hindi explanation).

Patanjal, Deo Prakash Shastri, 1963, *A Critical Study of Ṛgveda* (1.137-163) particularly from the point of Pāṇinian Grammar, New Delhi, Patanjal Publications.

Pathak, C., 1976, "Brahma-Jijñāsā as a Fundamental Hermeneutics," in *Bharata Manisha Quarterly*, I. No. 4, 13-27.

Pathak, Kashinath Bapuji, 1912, Danḍin, Nyāsakāra and Bhāmaha, *Indian Antiquary*, 41 : 232-36.

———, 1932, "On the Text and Interpretation of some Passages in the Mahābhāṣya of Patañjali," *Annals of Bhandarkar Oriental Research Institute*, 13: 17-24.

Saraswati, Dayananda, *Aṣṭādhyāyībhāṣyam*, Ajmer, Vedic Pustakalaya, 1961.

Sarma, K. Madhava Krishna, 1962, *Pāṇini, Kātyāyana and Patañjali*, Delhi: Shri Lal Bahadur Shastri Rashtriya Sanskrit Vidyapeeth.

Sarup, L. (tr. and introduction) 1927, *The Nighaṇṭu and the Nirukta*, Lahore: University of the Panjab (Rpt. Delhi: Motilal Banarsidass, 1967).

Scharfe, Hartmut, 1971, *Pāṇini's Metalanguage*, Philadelphia: American Philosophical Society.

Sebeok, Thomas A., 1987/1988 *The Semiotic Web 1987*, Berlin: Mouton de Gruyter.

Shastri, Charudeva, 1957-58, "Paniniya Dhātu Paṭhārtha-Nirdeśaḥ (The Statement of Meanings in Pāṇini's Dhātupāṭha)," Madras: *Journal of Oriental Research*, 27: 79-84 (in Sanskrit).

———, 1962, *Vyākaraṇa-Mahābhāṣya*, Prathama Āhnika, Delhi: Motilal Banarsidass (text with Hindi commentary).

Shastri, Gaurinath, 1959, *The Philosophy of Word and Meaning*, Calcutta: Sanskrit College Research Series 5.

———, 1968 (tr.), *The Mahābhāṣya of Patañjali*, tr. into Hindi with comments: first nine *āhnikas*, Delhi: Motilal Banarsidass.

Shastri, J.L. (ed., tr.), 1984, *Dhātupāṭhah*, Delhi: Motilal Banarsidass.

Sastri, S. Suryanarayana, 1932, "Vācaspati's Criticism of the Sphoṭa Theory," *Journal of Oriental Research*, 6 : 311-321.

Shastri, Satyavrat, 1978, "Sanskrit Grammar," in *Cultural Heritage of India*, vol. V., Calcutta: Sri Ramakrishna Mission Institute of Culture.

———, 1981, "Pāṇini's Regard for Usage" in International Seminar on Pāṇini — Summaries of Papers (*ISP-SP*), University of Poona.

Shastri, V.A. Ramaswami, 1932-33, "The Doctrine of Sphoṭa," *Annamalai University Journal*, 1: 233-40, 2: 109-20.

———, 1952, "Mukhya and Gauṇa Words in Language," *Bulletin of the Deccan College Research Institute*, Poona 14 : 183-94.

Singh, Jagdev, 1972, "Pāṇini's Theory of Language," *International Journal of Dravidian Linguistics*, 1 : 80-96.

———, 1974, "Pāṇini's Theory of Kārakas," *International Journal of Dravidian Linguistics*, 3: 287-320.

Sreekrishna, Sharma, 1959, "Syntactic Meaning — Two Theories," *Adyar Library Bulletin*, 23: 41-64.

Staal, Johan Frederick, 1966, "Indian Semantics," *International Journal of the American Oriental Society*, 86: 304-11.

———, 1966, "Analyticity," *Foundations of Language*, 2: 67-93

———, 1969, "Sanskrit Philosophy of Language," *Current Trends in Linguistics*, vol. 5 (ed. Sebeok); pp. 449-531.

———, 1972 (ed.), *A Reader on the Sanskrit Grammarians*, Cambridge, Mass: The MIT Press.

Subramania Iyer K.A., 1935, "Who are the Anitya Sphoṭavādinaḥ?" *Proceedings of the All India Oriental Conference*, no. 8, Mysore, 258-63.

———, 1941, "Pratibhā as the Meaning of a Sentence," *Proceedings of the All India Oriental Conference*, no. 10, Tirupati : 326-32.

———, 1947, "The Doctrine of Sphoṭa," Allahabad: *Journal of Ganganatha Jha Research Institute*, vol. 5, pt. 2, 121-47.

———, 1965, *The Vākyapadīya of Bhartṛhari with the Vṛtti*, Chapter I, tr., Poona : Deccan College.

———, 1968, "Bhartṛhari on the Primary and Secondary Meaning of Words," *Festschrift S.M. Katre* I, pp. 97-112.

———, 1969, *Bhartṛhari : A study of the Vākyapadīya in the Light of Ancient Commentaries*, Poona: Deccan College.

———, 1971, *The Vākyapadīya of Bhartṛhari*, Chapter III, Part I, English tr., Poona : Deccan College.

———, 1973, *Vākyapadīya of Bhartṛhari (with the Prakīrna Prakāśa of Helarāja)*; Kāṇḍa III, Part II, Poona: Deccan College.

———, 1977, *The Vākyapadīya of Bhartṛhari*, Kāṇḍa II, Delhi: Motilal Banarsidass.

Tewary, B.N., 1972, *Bhāratīya Bhāṣā Vijñāna ki Bhūmikā*, Delhi, Shaitya Sahkar.

Tiwari, Kapil Muni, 1971, "Asiddham Bahiraṅgam Antaraṅge: A Metarule of Rule-ordering in Pāṇini," *Indian Linguistics*, 32: 241-57.

Vajpeyi, Kishoridas, *Hindi Sabdanuśāsana*, Prayag: Nagari Pracarani Sabha.

Vākyapadīya of Bhartṛhari, K.V. Abhyankar and V.P. Limaye (eds.), 1965, Sanskrit and Prakrit Series, (Sanskrit), Poona: University of Poona.

The Vākyapadīya of Bhartṛhari, Kāṇḍa II, III.2. R.A. Subramania Iyer (ed., exegete) 1977, 1974, Delhi: Motilal Banarsidass.

The Vākyapadīya of Bhartṛhari, Kāṇḍa III, 1, R.A. Subramania Iyer (ed., exegete), 1971, Poona, University of Poona.

Vāmana and Jayāditya, *Kāṣikā-vṛtti*, see under Narayana Mishra.

Varma, Siddheshwara, 1925, "Analysis of Meaning in the Indian Philosophy of Language," *Journal of the Royal Asiatic Society*, London: 21-35.

———, 1929, *Critical Studies in the Phonetic Studies of Indian Grammarians*, London: Royal Asiatic Society.

———, 1953, *The Etymologies of Yāska*, Hoshiarpur: Vishveshvarananda Vedic Research Institute.

———, 1963, "Scientific and Technical Presentation of Patañjali as Reflected in the Mahābhāṣya," *Vishveshvarananda Ontological Journal*, Hoshiarpur, 1: 1-36.

———, 1972, "The Concept of 'Agent' — Philosophical and Grammatical in Sanskrit," *Festschrift K.C. Chattopadhyaya*, pp. 713-21.

Varnin, Vedavrata (ed.), 1962-63, *Mahābhāṣya*, 5 vols., Jhajjar, Gurukul.

Vasu, Srisa Chandra (ed., tr.), 1891, *The Aṣṭādhyāyī of Pāṇini*, ed. and tr. into English rpt. 1962, Delhi : Motilal Banarsidass.

———, 1905-07, *The Siddhānta-Kaumudī of Bhaṭṭoji Dīkṣita*, ed. and tr. into English Allahabad : The Panini Office, Reprint, Delhi: Motilal Banarsidass, 1962.

Yajan Veer, "An Examination of P. Kiparasky's book" in International Seminar on Pāṇini — Summaries of Papers (*ISP-SP*), University of Poona, 1981.

Yāska, *Nirukta*, Lakshman Sarup (ed. & tr.), 1967, Delhi: Motilal Banarasidass, 2nd Reprint, 1967.

Yudhisthira Mimamsaka, 1973, *Saṁskṛta Vyākaraṇa-Śāstra Kā Itihāsa* (complete in Three parts) Sonepat: Rama Lal Kapur Trust

B. Interpretation

Bhandarkar, R.G., 1873, "On the Interpretation of Patañjali," *Indian Antiquary*, 2.94-96.

Cardona, George, 1973, "On the Interpretation of Pāṇini," 1.4.105-8. *Adyar Library Bulletin*, 37: 1-47.

Chatterji, Kshitish Chandra, 1955, "On the Interpretation of a Rule of Pāṇini," *Festschrift S.K. Chatterji*, (Indian Linguistics. 16), pp. 194-95 (Rule 1.1.36).

Devasthali, Govind Vinayak, 1965, "Pāṇini as an Aid to R̥gvedic Interpretation," *Festschrift H.D. Velankar*, Bombay : Prof. H.D. Velankar Commemoration Committee, pp. 20-26.

Devasthali, Govind Vinayak, 1967, "Pāṇini and R̥gvedic Exegesis," *Indian Antiquary*, 2.3 : 1-8.

Joshi, S.D., 1966, "Two Methods of Interpreting Pāṇini," Poona, *Journal of the University of Poona*, 23-53-61.

Kapoor, Kapil, 2005, *Text and Interpretation: The Indian Tradition*, New Delhi: D.K. Printworld (P) Ltd.

Sastri, V.A. Ramaswami, 1955-56, "Bhartr̥hari's Interpretation of '*graham saṁmārṣṭi*' and '*pasunā yajeta*,'" Madras: *Journal of Oriental Research*, 25: 74-78.

Schauer, Ellen and Ellen Spolsky, 1986, *The Bounds of Interpretation, Linguistic Theory and Literary Text*, California: Stanford University Press.

Shastri, Charudeva, 1988, *Pāṇini Reinterpreted*, Delhi: Motilal Banarsidass.

Varma, Siddheshwara, 1950-51, "The Vedic Accent and the Interpreters of Pāṇini," *Journal of the Bombay Branch of Royal Asiatic Society*, New Series, 26 : 1-9.

C. Philosophy

Bhaṭṭa, Kumārila, *Tantra-Vārttika*, (ed./tr.) Sir Ganganath Jha (1903-24), Delhi: Sri Satguru Publications (1983).

———, *Ślokavārttika*, (ed., tr.) Sir Ganganath Jha (1900-1908), Delhi: Sri Satguru Publications (1983).

Chakravarti, P.C., 1930, *The Philosophy of Sanskrit Grammar*, Calcutta: University of Calcutta.

Dasgupta, Surendranath, 1922, *A History of Indian Philosophy*, vols. 1-5, 1st edn., Cambridge.

Datta, Dhirendra Mohan, 1932, *The Six Ways of Knowing*, London: George Allen and Unwin.

———, 1937, "Indian Epistemology," in *Cultural Heritage of India*, vol. III, Calcutta, 2nd rev. edn, 1953 (rpt. 1969), pp. 548-61.

Jawalaprasad, 1939, *Indian Epistemology*, Lahore: Motilal Banarsidass.

Kosambi, D.D., *The Culture and Civilisation of Ancient India*, Vikas, Delhi, 1970.

Matilal, B.K., 1971, *Epistemology, Logic and Grammar in Indian Philosophical Analysis*, The Hague, Paris.

———, 1985, *Logic, Language and Reality*, Delhi: Motilal Banarsidass.

———, 1990, *The Word and the World: India's Contribution to the Study of Language*, London: Oxford University Press.

Mukerji, Radha Kumud, *Hindu Civilization*, Bharatiya Vidya Bhavan, Bombay, 1957, Rpt. 1977.

Nāgārujuna, *Suhṛllekha*, Wenzel (tr.), P.T.S., 1886.

Quine, W.V.O., 1964, *From a Logical Point of View: Logico Philosophical Essays*, Cambridge, Mass.: Harvard University Press.

Radhakrishnan, S., 1923, *Indian Philosophy*, vols. 1 and 2., London: The Macmillan.

Ṣaḍadarśana-Sūtra Saṁgraha, Swami Dwarikadas Shastri (ed.), 1984, Varanasi: Sudhi Prakashnam, (Sanskrit Text, Introduction in Hindi).

Staal, Julian Frederick, 1962, "Negation and the Law of Contradiction in Indian Thought : A Comparative Study," London: *Bulletin of the School of Oriental and African Studies*, 25 : 52-71.

———, 1973, "The Concept of Pakṣa in Indian Logic," Dordrecht: *Journal of India Philosophy*, August.

Subramania Iyer, K.A., 1965, "Bhartṛhari on Dhvani," *Annals of Baroda Oriental Research Institute*, 46: 49-65.

———, 1977, *The Vākyapadīyā of Bhartṛhari*, Kāṇḍa II, Delhi: Motilal Banarsidass.

Umāswāti (also Umāswāmi), *Tattvārthasūtra* (Text in Sanskrit and Hindi commentary), Pt. Phulchand Shashtri (ed., exegete), 1991, Varanasi: Sri Ganesh Varni Digambar Jain (Shodha) Sansthan, Nariya.

Upadhyaya, Baldev, 1984, *Bhāratīya Darśana*, Varanasi: Chaukhamba Orientalia.

Varma, Siddeshwara, 1968, "Plurality — Philosophical and Grammatical — In Sanskrit Tradition," *Sri Venkateshwara University Oriental Journal*, 11: 1-4.

———, 1969, "Object — philosophical and Grammatical — In Sanskrit," Tirupati: *Sri Venkateswara University Oriental Journal*, 12: 39-44.

D. Poetics

Bhamaha, (sixth-seventh century AD) *Kāvyālaṁkāra*, with English Translation and notes, P.U. Naganatha Sastry (ed. & tr.), 1927, Tanjore: Wallace Printing House.

Bhandarkar, R.G., 1879, "Ācarya, the Friend of the Student, and the Relation between the Three Ācaryas," *Indian Antiquary*, 5. 345-50.

———, 1883, "Development of Language and of Sanskrit," First Wilson Lecture, *Journal of the Bombay Branch of the Royal Asiatic Society*, 16, 1883-1885, 245-74.

Chakrabarti, Tarapada, 1971, *Indian Aesthetics and the Science of Language*, Calcutta: Sanskrit Pustak House.

Chatterjee, Heramba Nath, 1960, *Comparative Studies in Pali and Sanskrit Alaṁkāras*, Calcutta: Sanskrit Pustak Bhandar.

Chatterji, Kshitish Chandra, 1933, "Pāṇini as a Poet," *Calcutta Oriental Journal*, 1 : 47-56.

Daṇḍin (seventh century AD) 1924, *Kāvyādarśa*, Sanskrit Text and English Translation, S.K. Belvalkar (tr.), Poona: The Oriental Book Agency.

Jagannātha, Pt. (seventeenth century AD), *Rasagaṅgādhara*, Pt. Madan Mohan Jha (ed.), 1969, Varanasi: The Chaukhamba Vidya Bhawan.

Kulkarni, V.M., 1955, "The Theory of Suggestion in Indian Semantics," Madras: *Brahmavidya: The Adyar Library Bulletin*, 19: 20-26.

Kunjunni Raja, K., 1961, "Tātparya as a Separate Vṛtti," *Proceedings of the All India Oriental Conference* 20, Bhubaneshwar (1959), 319-32.

Mookerji, Radha Kumud, 1923, "History of Sanskrit Literature from the Works of Pāṇini, Kātyāyana and Patañjali," *Indian Antiquary*, 52 : 21-24.

Shastri, Kapil Deva, 1964, "Bhartṛhari's Discussion on the Relation Between Upamāna and Upameya in his Vākyapadīya," *Festschrift Baburam Saksena*, pp. 229-33.

———, 1965, "Upamāna, Upameya and Sāmānya-vacana According to the Vākyapadīya of Bhartṛhari," *Vishveshvarananda Ontological Journal*, 3, Hoshiarpur, 19-28.

Shastri, Satyavrat, 1964, *The Rāmāyaṇa — A Linguistic Study*, Delhi: Munshiram Manoharlal.

Todorov, Tzvetan, 1973, 1982 (Eng. tr.) *Symbolism and Interpretation*, Catherine Porter (tr.), London: Routlege and Kegan Paul.

Yudhisthira, Mimamsaka, *Ācarya Pāṇini Ke Samaya Vidyamāna Sanskrit Vāṅmaya*, Ajmer: Bharatiya Pracya Vidya Pratishthana.

Index